Long Journey Home

To Lois

In friendship.

With love from the author.

Barbara Foxe.

Barbara Foxe

Long Journey Home

A Biography of Margaret Noble (Nivedita)

Rider and Company London

RIDER AND COMPANY
3 Fitzroy Square, London W1

An imprint of the Hutchinson Publishing Group

London Melbourne Sydney Auckland
Wellington Johannesburg and agencies
throughout the world

First published 1975

Set in Monotype Fournier
Printed in Great Britain by The Anchor Press Ltd
and bound by Wm Brendon & Son Ltd
both of Tiptree, Essex

ISBN 0 09 124040 9 (cased)
0 09 124041 7 (paper)

To Hallam Tennyson

Illustrations

Preface

In writing this book I was concerned to approach the life and world of Margaret Noble (Nivedita) and her friends and associates as closely as I could. I explored their own writings as well as the contemporary records, for these were people who knew how to use words to convey not only the great issues but the small difficulties, delights and frustrations of everyday living. Margaret Noble in the midst of a very active life was a writer of books and articles, and always an inveterate letter-writer.

I have quoted the original words whenever possible, as they have a vivid immediacy of their own, but I avoided the use of footnotes as I felt that these would prove an irritant to the reader. The ideas, emotions and reactions of the people in the book (not least, their sense of humour), as well as the facts and events, are, however, based on documented accounts or on their own writings, and where inverted commas have been used to indicate spoken words, this is because they were so used in the original extract, whether quoted or paraphrased.

For the framework of the facts of Margaret Noble's life I have relied upon the careful and accurate account written by Pravrajika Atmaprana, and from this I moved out further into the writings and letters of Margaret Noble herself and her friends and contemporaries; details of her girlhood given me by her relatives; the letters, books and writings of Swami Vivekananda and some of those people associated with him; other letters and books relevant to the social and political life of the period; contemporary newspaper accounts in which letters by or about her were published; photographs of the people and places involved, in England, America and India; and for the colour and texture of life as she experienced and observed it, I found that her own writings were the best illustration of all.

Details of some of the books which I have found most helpful are given in the Bibliography. My full acknowledgements are recorded separately, but there are also several people, not named personally, for whose interest and encouragement I am sincerely grateful.

Barbara Foxe

I

A postage stamp was issued in India in 1967 to celebrate the centenary of the birth of Margaret Noble. It is a fair reproduction of a photograph, showing a slim woman in her thirties gazing at us with that remote and non-committal expression so typical of the portraits of the loved and respected dead, but lacking the fire which was the quality always described first by those who knew her; there was nothing remote or non-committal about Margaret Noble.

A picture on a postage stamp is intended to honour its subject, but it has limitations. It cannot be expected to illustrate the contrasts and contradictions of a life which was both hidden and extremely public. It can suggest gentleness or calm, but not the enthusiasm of the girl who could never steer her bicycle straight, and who shouted anxious warnings to a tinker working at the side of the road because, as her brother observed, she knew from experience that if anything stood in her path 'she made a bee-line for it and ran it straight down'.

There were contrasts even in the places in which she lived: the England of gas-lamps and hansom cabs, and the small house in a back street in the Hindu quarter of Calcutta, with the rain pouring into the courtyard ('It is a little strange, during the rains, to have to take an umbrella to go upstairs'). When she left a late-Victorian drawing-room, and her meetings with Shaw, Yeats and Huxley, to live in Calcutta as a Hindu amongst Hindus, and eventually entered the lists as a champion against her own country, some people regarded her as an alarming piece of machinery liable to explode in entirely the wrong directions, and stood well back. Others gave her a devoted admiration and respect amounting almost to veneration, as she dealt with plague, rowed out to famine victims in the floods, addressed packed halls in a time of national ferment, or meditated in the Himalayas with Vivekananda; for in an age when he was acclaimed in India as national leader and saint, and well known in the West, she was one of his few Western disciples. The Viceroy and the British police regarded her with extremely mixed feelings, while most of the British in India were not aware of her existence. One or two close friends knew and loved her exactly as she was, and she repaid them with a loyalty that ran like an undeviating line through the often difficult and complex pattern of her life. Certainly nobody ever accused her of being dull.

The vivid and colourful picture of her life is as true to the facts as the serenity shown in the portrait, and both truths need the addition of others in helping us to know the real woman. She was essentially practical. When she walked eleven miles at night to Lucknow along an unfrequented railway-track through jungle and tiger-country because this was the only way to get there, she was not making a dramatic gesture, and nobody wrote about it in the newspapers. She simply did not want to keep the audience for her lecture waiting. When she wrote about meditation, she was referring to an exact experience; she did not confuse it with her feelings about the peace of the night sky in the mountains. She was very human indeed, especially in the emotions of a many-sided nature, but she always looked life straight in the face and was never willing to back away from what she saw there. She was, above all, the eventual disciple of a man who believed that what the world most needs is people of character, who took every nature exactly as he found it and encouraged it to develop in its own natural pattern.

Vivekananda's sense of humour always slightly side-stepped adulation and struggled to avoid the role of national hero and spiritual giant which was thrust at him on many continents. When they remarked on his great dignity of manner, using the word 'princely', he replied, 'That's not me – it's my walk.'

It is possible that Margaret Noble's reaction to the postage stamp, if she could have seen it, might have been very much the same. One thing is certain: the tribute from the India she so much loved would have made her very happy. She was a deeply loving woman as well as a blazing and controversial fighter. That was only one of the contradictions in her nature.

The first of the apparent contradictions began very early. Although Margaret Noble lived for most of her childhood, girlhood and throughout her twenties, in England, and always referred to herself as an Englishwoman, she was in fact Irish. Margaret was born at Dungannon, County Tyrone, on 28 October 1867, in an ivy-covered house in a square. Her grandparents were enthusiastic supporters of the agitation for Home Rule, and their heroes were the men they believed to be martyrs of the fight for Irish independence. The complications, violence and counter-violence and intercrossing of loyalties which later racked the unhappy country were far ahead in time; to the Nobles, the issue was clear, and both Samuel Noble, Margaret's father, and his wife Mary Hamilton were reared on stories of the heroism of Irish patriots fighting for Home Rule.

While Margaret was still a child, her parents left Ireland to live in Manchester, where Samuel became a student of theology in the Congregational Church. It was not until he had been ordained and worked for a time in Oldham that he settled in Great Torrington in Devonshire, and sent for Margaret; in the meantime she had been living with her grandparents in Ireland, and the fiery Irish nature which she had inherited was already well nourished by their stories of the fight for nationalism.

When Margaret at last rejoined her parents, she found that she now had a younger sister called May; the two girls became so close in companionship that Margaret was able to compensate at last for the loneliness of a childhood spent with grandparents. The two girls were Min and Peg to each other all their lives. Between 1870 and 1874 three more children were born, and died, two as babies and one at the age of four. Margaret and May learned from their earliest years to work rather than to be waited upon; the woman who later was to seize a broom and sweep the Calcutta streets in a plague epidemic began her training early, and she was not unfamiliar with death. She was completely devoted to her father, who took her with him when he conducted services or visited the poor, whose abject poverty probably began the first blaze of anger which later adversaries would come to recognize. When he died, tragically young, at the age of thirty-four, Margaret was ten; she had to face death, not for the first time, while she was helping her mother care for the new baby brother, Richmond, then three months old.

Like many daughters of the clergy at that time, she was accustomed to a high standard of education combined with a genteel poverty which trained her to inquire cautiously of her Irish grandmother, before a meal, whether anything was in short supply, so that she could refuse it politely at the right moment. She was as far removed from the dinner parties of the well-to-do, who expected to be offered eight very hearty courses as a normal average, as she was from the illiterate, grinding poverty of the truly poor. She accepted the fact that life was difficult, just as she accepted the street noises of that day – the organ-grinder, the muffin-man's bell, the clatter of horses and wooden wheels.

Life fascinated her, but she had never been too much shielded from it.

The lives of the two Noble sisters had been, from the beginning, unusually independent on all practical levels. After their father's death, their mother faced the fact that, while she might just manage to educate her two girls, a small and robust boy was more than she could manage. Richmond, at the age of three, was sent to live, as Margaret had been, with his Irish grandparents. However, it was not his mother, but Margaret, then aged under thirteen, who took him to Belfast from the south of England. His earliest memory was of the two of them, alone, facing the problems of transport in 1880, and Margaret made the return journey safely. In an age when it was the custom in England to regard women (unless they were poor) as objects to be protected, neither May nor Margot, as the family called her, saw female independence, even in a twelve-year-old, as anything unusual. It was later, when Margaret began to realize slowly how few paths were open for women, and how little real independence they could ever hope to achieve, that she sharpened the first of her swords, as a journalist, and her articles in furious defence of the poor, of women, and of Irish Home Rule, began to appear in the national Press.

The death of her father was a heavy blow. She had been very close to him, and had perhaps inherited his strong sense of independence of thought and integrity. There was much in his nature, especially in his care for the poor, that drew Margaret to him; it was the beginning of a pattern that constantly recurred in her life. First she drew close to him, and then he was wrenched away.

One apparent contradiction in her nature was already clearly marked. Many people who knew her spoke of her sweetness, but side by side with this, and sometimes almost acting against it, was the Irish fighting spirit which grew stronger with the passing years. Another contradiction was almost inevitable. She had a passionately emotional and affectionate nature, but she learned not to cling. People went away, death struck frequently, life was only too obviously insecure. She loved, but she learned independence, even in affection. Whether she was reconciled to the lesson is another matter. The child's grief at death is not recorded, but she wrote later of the intensity of her longing for religion, and her slow disillusion. Like her father she remained independent in thought as well as action, even as a child.

The religious influences in her life were enormous; but the orthodoxy of her widowed mother was so rigid that it must seem inevitable to us today that a brilliant girl with a mind of her own would begin to feel doubts. When young Richmond was at home for the school holidays, Mrs Noble allowed him to read only the Bible. When he reached the end of it, he was encouraged to return to the book of Genesis and start again. Margaret, however, saw things rather differently. She always had a strong streak of drama in her nature, which was to prove very useful in later years. Richmond was probably the first to appreciate it. She took him to see Shakespeare's plays at the London theatres, and she declaimed Mark Antony's speech from *Julius Caesar* to him. To a boy fed by his mother solely on a stark literary diet of the Authorized Version of the Bible, it was a revelation. In his middle age it led him to take a keen practical interest in the Irish theatre, and to write a book about Shakespeare. In one memory of Margaret, told by Richmond to his daughter long after, is the recognizable quality of the woman she later became: 'She couldn't steer a bicycle. When she saw something in the road, she made a bee-line for it. I remember her calling out, "Mr Tinker, Mr Tinker, get out of my way!" There was enough room, but she rode straight into him.'

In time, both girls were sent to the Congregationalist College at Halifax, and by 1886 Margaret was teaching in the mining town of Wrexham. Here the condition of the poor, and especially of pregnant women, appalled her. She began to write articles for the national newspapers, to attend meetings and to form groups; anything to make matters move a little, to whip up public interest beyond the point of a little kindly self-indulgent charity.

It was then, in her early twenties, that she fell in love. She met a young engineer from Wales who shared her ideals and her enthusiasm. They began to look forward to marriage.

Before the engagement could be announced, he fell ill, and the terrible pattern of bereavement, so common in the 1880s, shaped her life again. Like her young father, he died. She was accustomed to the death of the young. It was the bitterness of being forced to watch poverty and suffering, impotent to help, which, added to the burden of her own personal grief, began to shape her thinking. Life was cruel enough as it was. To add to this the unfeeling condescension of the rich towards the poor, and so pile suffering on suffering, struck her as being such a peak of insanity that only some sort of practical action on her part to help any suffering which could at least be eased a little, could make life tolerable to her at all.

As for the point and purpose of existence, the rigid and narrow orthodoxy against which she was already rebelling, offered no answers.

Her nature was of a kind which needed religion or philosophy, not as an escape but as the only possible air to breathe without choking.

She moved, in politics, towards the new Socialist ideals which were growing up. In religion the doubts set moving by Darwin tormented her and she found nobody who could speak with the certainty of experience. Everybody told her what humanity should do, but nobody demonstrated in his own life what humanity might become. They could draw conventional maps for her, but it was only too clear that they did not inhabit the country they were describing, and she turned from one branch of orthodox Christianity to another, desperately seeking, but unable to force her mind, in any honesty, to accept dogma.

At last she began to move away from orthodox Christianity altogether. She studied Buddhism for three years, and wrote: 'I became more and more convinced that the salvation preached was decidedly more consistent with the Truth than the preachings of the Christian religion.' This made her more unhappy still. She had always been devoted to the personality of Christ and in particular to his self-sacrifice. 'But after the age of eighteen I began to harbour doubts as to the truth of the Christian doctrines. Many of them began to seem to me false and incompatible with Truth. . . . For seven years I was in this wavering state of mind, very unhappy and yet very, very eager to seek the truth.' Seven years of unhappiness and truth-seeking is a long time when one is not yet thirty. But at least she could give practical help on some levels, and she threw herself into journalism, as a fighter for freedom in various directions, and into the world of education as a defender of very young children against what she regarded as the stifling idiocy of formal Victorian education. She saw the need for educating young children to learn by observing, playing, and constructing.

Her unusual childhood had given her certain advantages. She had never been oppressed and shaped, as so many brilliant figures of her generation were, by growing up in a great house with the rigidity of unmoving family life or a hierarchy. She did not need to fight free of this sort of background. On the contrary, even though she was unmarried, there was building up in her a longing for a settled place of her own. She had known more freedom, activity and responsibility than many women of her generation, but it had been at the price of much loss, and a constant moving to live in different places: Ireland, Devon, Halifax, Keswick, Wrexham, Chester, Liverpool.

In 1892 she opened her own school in London, at Wimbledon,

where she lived with her mother. She was able at last to use the modern 'free' methods of education, then being pioneered by Froebel and Pestalozzi, to 'liberate the children'.

She became a member, at that time, of Lady Ripon's Sesame Club. Here she met Shaw, Huxley and Yeats; she heard their lectures and gave one herself, on education. Her enthusiasm for the Socialist point of view grew stronger, though whether the recorded decision of the club members to employ a French chef met with her whole-hearted approval remains in some doubt. She was never entirely happy in the company of the excessively well fed.

At twenty-seven she must have appeared to those who knew her to be a woman already well established in a brilliant career as journalist, educationalist, lecturer and fighter for every kind of emancipation.

They were mistaken. Her career had not even started.

In 1895 she first met Vivekananda in London. She was not particularly impressed. 'When he said, "The universe is like a cobweb and minds are the spiders; for mind is one, as well as many", he was simply talking beyond my comprehension. . . . His system [of thought] as a whole, I for one viewed with suspicion, as forming only another of those theologies which, if a man should begin by accepting, he would surely end by rejecting . . .'

But revolutions often start quietly; their beginnings may not be recognized.

2

It is inevitable that today, knowing all we do of the impact which Vivekananda had already made on the American continent, and the impact he was beginning to make on Western religion and on the political aspirations of his own country, we may wonder whether there would have been any difference in Margaret Noble's reaction to him if she had known anything about him at all when she found him sitting by the fire in a London drawing-room on that cold Sunday afternoon in November 1895. Indian monks in ochre robes were not, in England at that time, a common sight. She thought he looked exotic. She found his ideas interesting. She was moved, interested, but not deeply impressed.

She did not know that life-size pictures of him had been posted up in the streets of Chicago. The *New York Herald* called him 'Undoubtedly the greatest figure in the Parliament of Religions' and the *Boston Evening Transcript* went so far as to claim:

> At the Parliament of Religions, they used to keep Vivekananda till the end of the programme to make people stay till the end of the session. On a warm day, when a prosy speaker talked too long and people began going home by hundreds, the chairman would get up and announce that Swami Vivekananda would give a short address before the benediction. Then he would have the peaceable hundreds perfectly in tether. The four thousand fanning people in the Hall of Columbus would sit smiling and expectant, waiting for an hour or two of other men's speeches, to listen to Vivekananda for fifteen minutes.

He detested this fame; indeed, on the night of his first great triumph he wept like a child afterwards, for he saw that he could be an obscure monk no longer and duty was going to force him into the limelight, whether he liked it or not. He saw his immense power with audiences as a very dangerous thing; on one occasion, when he held the huge audience in his hand, he suddenly stopped his lecture and walked away. Asked afterwards if he had felt ill, he simply replied that he had known, in that moment, that he could have told them anything and they would have accepted it; he could have led them where he wished; they were his. 'Which would have been bad for them – and very bad for me,' he said.

He had endeared himself to cowboys in the American West by continuing placidly with his lecture, standing on an upturned tub in the street, while they fired gunshots around his head to see if his teachings about calmness and self-control were rooted in experience. Finding them, on another occasion, practising their aim by trying to hit a nutshell floating down the river, he borrowed a gun and hit the shell with the first shot, explaining that he had never handled a gun before, but he had learned to concentrate, and that this was the secret of success in any project: to learn true concentration, and then apply the concentration to whatever action was needed. His own concentration, in meditation, was so deep that, as Margaret later recorded, it was often an embarrassment to him.

When he first went to America, it was extremely difficult for him to control the momentum that carried him into meditation. 'When he sits down to meditate,' said one whose guest he was in India, 'in two minutes he feels nothing, though his body be black with mosquitoes.' With this habit thus deeply ingrained, he landed in America, that land of railroads and tramways, and complicated engagement lists; and at first it was no uncommon thing for him to be carried two or three times round a tram-circuit, only disturbed periodically by the conductor asking for the fare. He was very much ashamed of such occurrences, however, and worked hard to overcome them.

The man who stood on the tub while the shots whistled round his head was also invited to address the graduate students of the philosophical department of Harvard, and made such an impression that he was offered a chair of Eastern Philosophy in the university, which he could not accept, as he was a monk.

That was the Vivekananda of America. In India his love for his own country was expressed in his passionate concern for its poverty and its oppressed classes, as well as its religion. He insisted that India should sit at the feet of the West as regards efficiency, organization and humanitarian work. But the West, he believed, must sit at the feet of India to learn spirituality. He wished each to bring to the other what it most lacked.

Margaret knew nothing then – or, indeed, until she finally reached India – of his own life, or what it would eventually mean to her. In her book *The Master As I Saw Him* she takes us with her into that first meeting in a London drawing-room with the sincere, doubting but wary interest of a woman who is anxiously seeking, but who has every intention of being extremely hard to convince.

The time was a cold Sunday afternoon in November and the place, it is true, a West End drawing-room. But he was seated, facing a half-circle of listeners, with the hearth behind him and as he answered question after question, breaking now and then into the chanting of some Sanskrit in illustration of his reply, the scene must have appeared to him, while twilight passed into darkness, only as a curious variant upon the Indian garden, or on the group of hearers gathered at sundown round the Sadhu who sits beside the well, or under the tree outside the village bounds. Never again in England did I see the Swami as a teacher in such a simple fashion. Later, he was always lecturing, or the questions he answered were put with formality by members of large audiences. Only this first time we were but fifteen or sixteen guests, intimate friends, many of us, and he sat amongst us in his crimson robe and girdle. . . .

She listened, politely, and as she said of herself afterwards, 'with coldness and pride'.

The audience – small as it was – had been hand-picked. Sceptics and doubters, to a man. 'Most of us had, I incline to think, been singled out for the afternoon's hospitality on the very score of our unwillingness to believe, for the difficulty of convincing us of the credibility of religious propaganda in general.'

He talked to them quietly, explaining that he was concerned to show the way to an experience, rather than to dogmatize or offer theories. There must be no 'dogma to end all dogmas'. As she had expected, he was telling them of the basis of Vedanta, which meant 'the end of the Vedas', or Hindu scriptures, and this was the part of the scriptures dealing with yoga, which, as she knew, regarded all life, including the soul of man, as manifestations of a great Absolute, and the whole purpose of life on this planet as being the full 'realization' or experience of this identity. It struck an echo. In life's worst moments, she had longed for a certainty: for experience, not theory. But as she sat with the others, watching the firelight, she was still dubious. She was more impressed by the personality of the man than by what he said. And clearly he refused to concede one inch to egotism or weakness, and spoke directly to the best in his listeners, giving them his great respect, which interested her.

As she had expected, he explained that the word 'Yoga' meant 'Yoke' or 'Union', and that what was to be yoked or united was the soul of man (which even in this life could experience its unity with the Absolute) with the whole universe: 'god within' united with 'god outside'; the ugly duckling not turning into a swan but discovering that he had always been one.

'The soul of Man is part of the cosmic energy which exists, which we call God.' Clearly he was describing a state of consciousness which was universal, whereas the West was restlessly seeking an individual and separate consciousness, very much identified with the body and the ego. But he also made it clear that he recognized many different paths, suitable for different natures, including devotion to Christ, Buddha, Ramakrishna or any great soul who had himself experienced this universal consciousness; this he called Bhakti Yoga, and the more abstract approach was Jnana Yoga; Karma Yoga was the Yoga of selfless work, and Raja Yoga was meditative; but all were aimed, without compromise, at eventually *becoming* that true identity, not theorizing about it.

She noted, writing ten years later, the points that he made and stressed that afternoon, and it is clear that, in them, he was giving almost a 'condensed essence of Hinduism' which was not intellectually new to her but which, as she went away and spent the winter in thought, began to mean more and more to her, if only, as yet, as an intellectual exercise holding the possibility of something more. Certain thoughts in particular stayed with her, and she returned to them again and again, in her mind, in the months that followed.

He dwelt for a while on the infinite power of man. . . .

He touched on the question of his own position as a wandering teacher and expressed the Indian diffidence with regard to religious organization . . . 'We believe,' he said, 'that organization always breeds new evils.'

The master-thought which he continually approached from different points of view, the equal truth of all religions, and the impossibility for us of criticizing any of the divine incarnations, since all were equally forth-shinings of the One.

She went away interested, but because of 'the habit [of doubt] born of the constant need of protecting the judgement against ill-considered enthusiasm' gave as her verdict, 'it was not new'. All these things had been said before.

In the week that followed, however, the personality of the speaker and the fact that he gave in one hour all that she had in general regarded before as highest and best, with the assurance of experience rather than theory, drew her to his public lectures.

'The feeling that great music wakes in us, grows and deepens with its repetition.' She was more and more strongly moved by his reiteration of certain points; her doubts about the existence of a personal God were given ideas rather than answers, but her mind fed upon the ideas. 'God is really Impersonal, but seen through the mists of the senses, becomes Personal.' 'The spirit behind an act is more powerful than the act itself.' 'All is That.' 'The saint described the bite of a cobra, when at nightfall he recovered, by saying, "A messenger came to me from the Beloved".'

In particular, her own worry over her loss of faith in the symbolism of God seen as Father, was assuaged by his teaching that in Hinduism the approach to deity in the form of a relationship was fully recognized as a necessity for some types of character, and indeed five such relationships, leading to five systems of worship, were accepted and encouraged, including the worship of the deity as Friend. 'He preached a religion which *began* with the classification of religious ideas.'

Still she determinedly fought off any total capitulation, with an honesty which he himself heartily approved, since his own reaction, in his early years, had been the same; he was a fighter and he approved of fighters; a facile acceptance was something he always regarded with contempt. Long afterwards when she was teased by a fellow-disciple for her early scepticism towards his teachings, he replied, 'Let none regret that they were difficult to convince! I fought my Master for six long years, with the result that I know every inch of the way!'

Continually she was drawn back to his character, to the fact that he spoke with the authority of one who has experienced, and always spoke straight to the highest in his listeners, without any pandering to timidities or weakness.

> It was by no means his intention to set forth dainty dishes of poetry and intellectuality for the enjoyment of the rich and idle classes . . . and yet he took his stand on what was noblest and best in us. . . . The thing that I found astonishing was a certain illustration urged by him. His audience was composed for the most part of fashionable young mothers, and he spoke of their terror and their flight, if a tiger should suddenly appear before them in the street. 'But suppose,' he said with a sudden change of tone, 'suppose there were a baby in the path of the tiger! Where would your place be then? At his mouth – any one of you – I am sure of it.' . . . His call was sounded in the name of that which was strongest and finest, and was not in any way dependent on the meaner elements in man.

By the time he left England, she had become more and more drawn towards his character, and to his complete and uncompromising honesty. She saw that, although 'as a religious teacher he had a system of thought to offer, nothing in that system would claim him for a moment, if he found that truth led elsewhere'.

She was drawn, but not yet committed. Next year, he was going to return to England, after a further tour of America.

Throughout the months ahead, while he was away, she thought about his ideas. Her own fierce championing of the cause of women and the poor had more in common with his life's work than she yet knew; and of the lighter side of his character, and of his own impressions of his visit to England, she knew nothing as yet. He was a great letter-writer, as she discovered later. Before he had left America, he had written a teasing letter to the young daughter of a friend. This daughter, Alberta Sturges, later entered Nivedita's life and concern; in this letter to her, Vivekananda, who notes that she is practising her scales, adds that he has been on the lake. 'The flies and mosquitoes rather gave me a wide berth, I think, because they were very orthodox sabbatarian flies and would not touch a heathen.'

He refers, in other letters written about his English visit, to his own changed attitude towards the English. His experience of them had previously been based on the English sahibs he had met in India, governing the Indians; he was amazed to find how utterly different were the people he met in England, and how different their attitude towards Indians.

You will find that I have changed a good deal of my opinion about England, and I am glad to confess it.

The Englishmen here are very friendly. Except for a few Anglo-Indians, they do not hate black men at all. Not even do they hoot at me in the streets. Sometimes I wonder whether my face has turned white, but the mirror tells the truth. Yet they are all so friendly here.

When he returned to England in 1896 Margaret had become eager to attend his lectures again; to her he was still simply a great monk, who had come to share what India had to give, in meditation and philosophy, with the West, and to take from the West to the poor, starving and uneducated in India whatever the West could give in the way of efficiency, workers, concern, or money. He gave some of the greatest lectures of his career at the premises of the Royal Institute of Water Colour Painters in Piccadilly, and this time Margaret, already eager, was enthusiastic. But she still had not fully realized the scope of his work or the many sides of his nature; he believed in 'speaking to each man in his own language', and his relationship with his workers, friends or disciples was different in each case. At this time, while he was staying in London, he wrote to the Hale sisters in America – very young daughters of Mrs Hale (whom he always referred to as 'Mother Church') a series of teasing letters, often addressed to 'Dear Babies', in which he refers to them as old maids (but determined old maids, evidently, for they were known to hurl back arguments at him in nonsense poetry, to which he replied with more nonsense):

. . . wrote a letter to Mother Church, weeks ago, but have not been able to get a line from her yet. I am afraid the whole party have taken orders and entered a convent – four old maids are enough to drive any mother into a convent. . . . What about *The Brahmavadin* journal? Are you pushing it? If four pushful old maids cannot push a journal, I am blowed. You will hear from me now and then. I am not a pin to be lost under a bushel. . . . I begin Sunday lectures from next week. The classes are very big and are in the house. We have rented it for the season. Last night I made a dish. It was such a delicious mixture of saffron, lavender, mace, nutmeg, cubebs, cinnamon, cloves, cardamom, cream, lime juice, onions, raisins, almonds, pepper, and rice, that I myself could not eat it. There was no asafoetida, though that would have made it easier to swallow . . .

On the same visit he was writing to a brother monk in India, stirring up his beloved country as he always did with a mixture of love and a continual pricking into action.

This City of London is a sea of human heads – ten or fifteen Calcuttas put together. One is apt to be lost in the mazes unless he arranges for somebody to meet him on arrival. . . . However, let Kali start at once. If he be late in arriving like Sharat, better let no one come. It won't do, to loiter and procrastinate like that. It is a task that requires the height of Rajas [activity]. Our whole country is steeped in Tamas [inertia] . . .

He was also writing to Professor John Henry Wright, a friend whose sixteen-year-old daughter had just died.

The forms are evanescent; but the spirit, being in the Lord and of the Lord, is immortal and omnipresent. All that we ever had are round us this minute, for the spirit can neither come nor go, it only changes its plane of manifestation.

It did not occur to Margaret that all she was seeing so far was one side of a many-sided personality, one small piece of work in England that had to be fitted into a whole complexity of other duties and the building of entirely new work in general which he was creating alone. She knew the monk, but she did not know the energetic organizer. Where he went on holiday in Europe, and what he did there, she did not know. Rest? Lecture? In fact, he climbed to the Swiss glaciers during his holiday in 1896, breathing again the air familiar to him in the Himalayas. It would not have surprised anyone who knew him well to hear that he made an ascent in a balloon, with some friends and other members of the public, at a national exhibition of Swiss handicrafts and industrial products in Geneva. If there was a balloon going up, he wanted to experience the ascent; no matter what anyone said, it would have been impossible to hold him back. He also wanted to ascend Mont Blanc on foot, though even he had to admit reluctantly in the end that this might be unwise. In later years, Margaret climbed the Himalayas with him, but she had never yet seen his abundant energy. She did not know his anger; he admitted frankly that he had a temper, rarely shown, and indeed claimed that a temper was a useful article to possess, since it gave one something to control. She saw him as 'the sage' and did not know that he admitted to making mistakes. 'When I make mistakes, I make big ones.' She had not seen his illness, or his worries.

She was already beginning to see his loathing of snobbery, and this especially attracted her. In America he had protested furiously against being introduced to 'the right sort of people', who could help him socially. 'The only "right sort of people" are those whom the Lord sends – that is what I understand in my life's experience. They alone can and will help me. As for the rest – Lord bless them in a mass, and save me from them!'

He did not make any particular gesture towards her own life or beliefs. It always surprised those who met him that there was a great difference between his attitude to 'friends' and 'disciples'. One Western disciple wrote of him:

> Unless the desire for discipleship was definitely expressed, and unless he was convinced that the aspirant was ready for the step, he left the personal life of those around him untouched.
>
> Friends might have a narrow outlook, might be quite conventional, but it was not for him to interfere. It seemed as if even an opinion, where it touched the lives of others, was an unpardonable intrusion upon their privacy. But once having accepted him as their guru, all that was changed. He felt responsible. . . . He refused to solve our problems for us. Principles he laid down but we ourselves must find the application. He encouraged no spineless

dependence upon him in any form, no bid for sympathy. 'Stand upon your own feet. You have the power within you,' he thundered. His whole purpose was – not to make things easy for us, but to teach us how to develop our innate strength. 'Strength! Strength!' he cried. 'I preach nothing but strength. That is why I preach the Upanishads' . . . This attitude had the effect of a tonic. Something long dormant was aroused, and with it came strength and freedom.

His method was different with each disciple . . .

Margaret was, so far, an inquirer; a friend. He did not interfere.

But now she began to attend every lecture he gave. She was coming nearer; she asked questions. And the basic question upon which her life depended, had to be asked. What was he doing? What, in essence, was he *after*? To what, in fact, was his life dedicated – What was his ideal? She had never been one to beat about the bush. She wrote and asked him.

And so, from St George's Road, London, on 7 June, a letter was written to this young woman who had been attending his public lectures, coming to his classes, and entering into discussion with him.

Dear Miss Noble,

My ideal can be put into a few words, and that is: to preach unto mankind their divinity, and how to make it manifest in every movement of life.

The world is in chains of superstition. I pity the oppressed, whether man or woman, and I pity more, the oppressors.

One idea that I see clear as daylight is that misery is caused by (spiritual) *ignorance*, and nothing else. Who will give the world light? Sacrifice in the past has been the Law – it will be, alas, for ages to come. The earth's bravest and best will have to sacrifice themselves for the good of many, for the welfare of all. Buddhas by the hundred are necessary, with eternal love and pity.

Religions of the world have become lifeless mockeries. What the world wants is character. The world is in need of those whose life is one burning love, selfless. That love will make every word tell like a thunderbolt.

It is no superstition with you, I am sure – you have the making in you of a world-mover, and others will also come . . . Let us call and call till the sleeping gods awake, till the god within answers to the call . . .

In each of his letters, he spoke in the language of the recipient; and at last Margaret was being addressed in her own language. This was the language she needed, and it was the call for which she had been waiting; in others he called out gentleness, patience, perseverance or humour; he called 'the sleeping god within man' to wake, in a hundred different ways, and in her time she was to see them all; but this language was for her, and she answered it with all the enthusiasm of a very enthusiastic nature: eagerly, and – as she often did – at first just a little too soon.

She was becoming restless in her London life. In one sense, it was home, and India was unknown and totally alien; but the rooms overcrowded with heavy furniture, the thick curtains, the endless clatter of horses' hooves drawing buses and cabs across uneven stones on wooden wheels; noise and fog; the lip-service she must for ever pay to so much that she could not believe; it was all familiar, but it chafed her. The battles that were being fought out within her, showed themselves in an aggressiveness that was often directed against men, for the bitterness of a brilliant woman trying to fight her way through a masculine-dominated society tended to make her champion the rights (and break her heart over the wrongs) of women, almost to excess; to Margaret, all her life, black was jet black and white was unblemished. Some comments written about her at this period, by her friend Eric Hammond, are illuminating.

> At this juncture we are confronted by a remarkable factor. Margaret Noble was essentially a woman's woman. Her temperament, her sympathies, her personality, all tended to attract persons of her own sex. These, from all ages, from children to adults, and to elders, admired her, reflected her. Men, on the contrary, seldom, if ever, experienced this attraction. Some subtle wizardry of souls held men-folk aloof from her . . .

Eric Hammond's gentle reference to this 'subtle wizardry of souls' suggests that he did not know of her previous engagement to be married, or of a second engagement that materialized shortly afterwards but came to nothing, nor of course could he see the many friendships with men – some of them great scientists, philosophers, poets and politicians – that she was to form in later years. In this period of her life in London, what Eric Hammond was witnessing was the growing militancy of a woman who must have felt a little like Gulliver tied down by a thousand ropes; always an extremist, she assumed that *all* her adversaries were Lilliputians.

> . . . She appeared, indeed, to enjoy this attribute of hers; to find joy in stinging them with a lash of caustic criticism; in making them comprehend that, in her consciousness, women occupied a loftier level on the mental sphere than man was destined to attain. Thus it was, happily, plainly palpable that her allegiance to the Swami was not in any wise coerced by his masculinity. It was, rather, the spirit within him . . .

The spirit within Vivekananda caught Eric Hammond, too. As he truly remarks, 'London is a very volcano of eruptions, sometimes pious, sometimes philosophical, sometimes pretentious, but mainly eager and earnest . . .' He is struck by the very point which so caught Margaret Noble, and the audiences of that day.

> The bedrock principle on which Sri Ramakrishna stood, and which Swami Vivekananda expounded, is stated by the letter in these few words: 'Do not care for doctrines, do not care for dogmas, or sects, or churches, or temples: they count for little compared with the essence in each man which is spirituality; and the more this is developed in each man, the more powerful is he for good. Earn that first, acquire that, and criticize no one, for all doctrines and creeds have some good in them. Show by your lives that religion does not mean words, or names, or sects, but that it means spiritual realization [experience].'

Eric Hammond, urged on by Margaret, journeyed 'from an outlying district, to his lodging' on 'a very uncomfortable evening, cheerless and dismal'. Vivekananda was not at home, but had left a message inviting them to follow him to the Sesame Club where he had gone, at brief notice, to speak in place of a lecturer who could not appear.

> They went to the Sesame Club [wrote Hammond] . . . we found ourselves in a big drawing room or hall, filled almost to overflowing by smart people in evening dress. Some courteous and obliging person ushered us close to a platform where one or two chairs were vacant. The position was conspicuous and so, alas! were we. Our overcoats were dripping with rain, nor were we otherwise clothed in fine raiment: not anticipating a summons to so distinguished a gathering. Most of those present were, we discovered, schoolmasters and schoolmistresses, tutors and the like . . .

There was something very characteristic of Margaret Noble, both in her natural acceptance of her own place as headmistress, journalist and writer, among the 'smart people in evening dress' in the 'big drawing-room', and at the same time her friendship with Eric Hammond seated so unhappily in his conspicuous position close to the platform, so very much not 'clothed in fine raiment', as he sat gently dripping rain on to the floor in this distinguished gathering.

After that evening Margaret began to follow every word that Vivekananda spoke, to go wherever he lectured, to attend discussions at the house where he stayed in St George's Road. She heard him give some of his greatest lectures.

He whom the sages have been seeking in all these places is in our own hearts, the voice that you heard was right, says the Vedanta, but the direction you gave to the voice was wrong. That ideal of freedom that you perceived was correct, but you projected it outside yourself, and that was your mistake. Bring it nearer and nearer, until you find that it was all the time within you, it was the Self of your own self. That freedom was your own nature . . . not only to see it intellectually, but to perceive it, actualize it, much more definitely than we perceive this world. Then we shall know that we are free.

Vivekananda's ideas she assimilated very slowly; his desire to help the women and the poor of his own country was easier to grasp. She learned for the first time that he was the St Paul of his master, Sri Ramakrishna, who had died ten years previously, but 'he never in public mentioned his own Master, nor spoke in specific terms of any part of Hindu mythology . . . neither then or at any after time, did I ever hear him advocate to his audience any specialized form of religion.' She did not yet realize that this was a part of 'speaking to each man in his own language' – that he was struggling to express for a doubting and cynical West, turning towards rationalism and science, the same truth that he also encouraged the believers of a simple faith to find in their own religion, in the worship of their own great prophet or Incarnation; that all these were paths equally to be respected. Instinctively she was expecting him to evangelize for some specific creed, to tear people out of one path and put them on another. 'But he never preached anything but that philosophy which, to Indian thinking, underlies all creeds.'

He was deeply convinced of the need for Indian thought, in order to enable the religious consciousness of the West to welcome and assimilate the discoveries of modern science and to enable it also to survive the destruction of local mythologies which is an inevitable result of all world-consolidations . . .

She was becoming more and more enthusiastic to help, at least with the work for the education of women, in his country, and one evening a friend told him of Margaret's willingness to join him in India for his work. 'He was evidently surprised, but said quietly, "For my own part I will be incarnated two hundred times, if that is necessary, to do this work amongst my own people, that I have undertaken".'

He did not refuse or accept her offer, and Margaret went on with her work as headmistress of the Wimbledon school as before. But she was becoming interested in another aspect of Vivekananda's work, and that interest bore much fruit later. She had always been fascinated by the expression of ideas. She had a quick mind, and she was already an efficient journalist. As a journalist she knew the difficulty of conveying a thought in words which the readers could grasp, where the concept was an abstract one. She watched his struggle to render into modern English an idea which he apprehended clearly, but which he was obviously trying to express in a language which contained no equivalent concept and no word to express it, and which was not really a suitable vehicle for it at all. She did not attempt to act as interpreter, either then or later, but very tentatively she found that she was grasping his ideas and beginning to act almost as a bridge across which some essentially Indian ideas could reach Western minds. For instance, the word 'maya', meaning 'cosmic illusion', was almost impossible for him to explain, and indeed she did not yet realize that he was thinking his way through into a new expression of Hinduism for Indians as well. He explained that the word did not really mean 'delusion' or 'magic', as most Westerners supposed. 'The maya of the Vedanta in its latest development,' he said, 'is a simple statement of facts – what we are and what we see around us.'

But, as she shrewdly pointed out, this was not the whole of the definition of what we are doing on this planet, what life in fact is. To the Western mind, either what we see around us is a fact or it is an illusion and a dream; it cannot be both. It seemed to her that he was explaining that the Universe, 'a Tantalus Hell' as he described it, in which 'we walk in the midst of a dream, half-sleeping, half-waking', was nevertheless an expression of the Ultimate, a dream which could be *used*, a dream which must be taken seriously in order that we find reality through it and become free. She tried to come closer to his own interpretation, and she wrote:

> By maya is thus meant that shimmering, elusive, half-real, half-unreal complexity, in which there is no rest, no satisfaction, no ultimate certainty, of which we become aware through the senses and through the mind as dependent on the senses. At the same time, 'And *That*, by which all this is pervaded, know *That* to be the Lord Himself.' In these two conceptions, placed side-by-side, we have the whole theology of Hinduism, as presented by the Swami Vivekananda in the West.

She was beginning to see him as a man who had experienced a reality which he was struggling to explain to those who could only grope for it dimly and that he was addressing audiences who were accustomed to think of good and evil, reality and unreality, as totally different and always opposed to each other. He was rigid in his adherence to good, but his acceptance of the necessary existence of evil was as surprising to some of his listeners as his assertion that this 'shimmering, elusive, half-real, half-unreal complexity' in which we are all caught, nevertheless is pervaded by, or is an expression of, 'That', 'the Absolute', 'Brahman', 'God'. He used many words, including 'the Lord' – but each of them implied 'the Ultimate Reality, call it what you will'.

His method of attaining freedom was always 'renunciation'. The battlefield, not the ballroom. But even the word 'renunciation' held a different meaning in the West, and it also contained a different meaning for orthodox Hinduism. This unorthodox Hindu (or unorthodox in his thinking on this matter, at least, it seemed to her) did not mean by 'renunciation' that a man should leave his duties and go out into the desert with a begging bowl. By 'renounce' he meant 'conquer'. Refuse to be ruled by desires, by the ego, by the body, by the emotions. He evidently believed that there were many forms of intense effort and self-discipline, including the work of a wife, mother, friend, servant, scientist – anything on earth to which one was called and which was one's own true path. The renunciation lay in a total abnegation of self. Even the smallest true self-discipline was worth more to him than all the abstracts of philosophy. To say 'I will meditate daily' and to do so only occasionally, without concentration; to say 'I will be selfless' and then to continue exactly as before, struck him as a sentimental folly for which he had no time at all. He gave the cosmic view and the theology on which his thinking rested, and he struggled to be specific in his terms because Western audiences were becoming increasingly sceptical of all religious theory. But he saw the life that would lead to ultimate freedom from maya as consisting of a long, tough path, and this life as being only one of many through which each soul must pass.

In December he returned to India, and Margaret did not know that he was given a hero's welcome with triumphal greetings, flowers and marches of thousands of people in the streets, because a nation ruled by a Western power had brought Hinduism to the West through Vivekananda's teachings. He was worn out in health and tired to death. After all the clamour, he now had to convince his fellow-monks, those few who had been boys with him as disciples of Sri Ramakrishna, that it was not enough to become monks, living austere meditative lives, along their own lines, keeping apart from the world; they must serve and worship the god in man by social service, famine relief and education; and this would mean the creation of a large relief organization, with lay helpers, and an organized monastery of the kind common in the West, rather than a life spent wandering with a begging bowl, and teaching a few disciples. This was not the Hindu concept of a monk's duty. This was revolutionary. In the end their faith in him, and the fact that Sri Ramakrishna had established him as 'elder brother' in their duty and affection (and in Hindu households, the elder brother rules, after the death of the father) won them to his side; but Margaret, at home in England, knew nothing yet either of the triumphs or the problems, until he began to write to tell her about them.

Back in England, the work proceeded. Margaret was enthusiastic; she was helping a fellow-monk of Vivekananda's to establish Vedanta work in Wimbledon, but she was more and more drawn to the work in India, as she received Vivekananda's letters. 'A number of boys are already in training, but the recent earthquake has destroyed the poor shelter we had to work in, which was only rented, anyway. Never mind. The work must be done without shelter, and under difficulties.'

A description like that was sheer torment for her to resist, it made Wimbledon and its pleasant, comfortable houses less and less attractive.

Then, in July 1897, he wrote to her and asked her to stay in London and work for him, instead of coming to India. 'You can do more work for us from England, than by coming here. Lord bless you for your great self-sacrifice for the poor Indians.'

It was a blow that she could not take. It might be too soon, she would wait – she would do anything – but it was India or nothing.

Vivekananda had doubts. He had travelled extensively in the West and he knew how very different the conditions were in India, and he knew far better than she what her difficulties would be. Also, he had seen something of Westerners working in India, with the kindest and best of intentions, and it had made him wary. He did not want a benevolent patronage given to the Hindus, and any work done for them by Europeans must, in his view, be done in the Hindu way, by Europeans living as and with Hindus. It seemed to him altogether too much to ask of an Englishwoman.

Margaret persisted, however, and his friends in England wrote to him on her behalf, supporting her appeals to be allowed to come to India to help, in whatever way he chose to train her. He was convinced at last, and wrote to her. 'Let me tell you frankly that I am now convinced that you have a great future in the work for India. What was wanted was not a man but a woman; a real lioness, to work for the

Indians, women especially. India cannot yet produce great women, she must borrow them from other nations . . .'

She began to wind up her work in London; there was a great deal to be done. She hoped to leave by the winter. She still believed, in all sincerity, that the attitude of Indians and English to each other in India was entirely happy, she still, as she put it, 'worshipped the flag'; some of Vivekananda's remarks still puzzled her. When he said, of London, 'And you have *blasted* other cities, to make this city of yours beautiful', she discovered, to her surprise, that there were other points of view.

> 'The English are born on an island, and they are always trying to live on it,' said the Master once to me, and certainly the remark seems true of myself, as I look back on this period of my life and see how determinately insular my ideals had hitherto been. I learnt no more of the Indian point of view during my life in England.

It was simpler now, however; whatever happened, she was going. She had always been a fighter, she had always sought a purpose in existence, and now she had found one. And she trusted Vivekananda implicitly. He had written to her:

> You must think well before you plunge in, and after work, if you fail in this or get disgusted, on my part I promise you I will stand by you unto death, whether you work for India or not, whether you give up Vedanta or remain in it. The tusks of an elephant come out but never go back – so are the words of a man never retracted. I promise you that.

On that promise, and in the certainty that at last she had found a life that would be entirely worth living, she prepared to go.

It is at this point that difficulties within the family circle might have been expected. The step she was preparing to take would be a controversial one even today. In 1897 it was unthinkable. To leave a Victorian drawing-room and a widowed mother of the most orthodox and even narrow religious beliefs, to go half across the world to – what? Discussions, worries and many anxieties there certainly were. But her small and closely-knit family supported her in her decision, and later, when they met Vivekananda, they became even more convinced that she was taking a course that was right for her. May took over the school at Wimbledon and remained at home to help care for their mother if necessary.

Mary Noble herself was perhaps the most remarkable of all. If ever a Victorian mother might have been expected to raise the very strong-

B

est objections to the decision of a daughter who was apparently determined to fling her life away after many struggles which had brought her into a respectable and settled career as headmistress and journalist, Mary Noble of all people might have been forgiven for fury, protest, or even icy disapproval. But she avoided the maternal trap of giving endless criticism where she could not always give understanding. Margaret wrote of her, later, 'That indiscriminating love that my mother gave me! I cannot tell you what a force it is in me yet! That all-giving love.' Certainly the family had seen Margaret's previous frustrations, restlessness and disillusionment. They had watched that pent-up vigour, pity, and wasted sense of dedication.

Years later, she wrote to a friend:

> Suppose Swami had not come to London that time! Life would have been like a headless torso. For I always knew that I was waiting for something, I always said that a call would come, and it did . . . How often and often I have sat down, pen in hand, to speak, and there was no speech, and now there is no end to it! As surely as I am fitted for my world, so surely is my world in need of me, waiting, ready.

Her life fell, in fact, into three distinct stages. The first might be described as one of seeking, and that was how she saw it herself. The second, on which she was now entering at the age of thirty, was spent in the shadow of Vivekananda. Whether climbing the Himalayas with him, or struggling on her own in India or America, her life was basically linked with his. When she moved into the third and most public section of her life, she entered the arena in a way which had certainly never occurred to her when she left England. If she could have seen the future then, she would have been not only disbelieving, but probably deeply shocked.

It was an eager, impulsive, half-afraid woman of considerable courage who left England simply because she felt that in Vivekananda she had found what she was seeking. She hoped to help him in his work and with any luck to open a small school in Calcutta. Nothing more spectacular than that.

3

England in the darkness of a cold January morning in 1898 was made darker still by fog drifting around the gas-lamps and muffling the sound of the cab horses. Margaret boarded the *Mombasa* at Tilbury dock. The final farewells to her mother, Richmond and May were almost unbearable. Mary Noble and May were in tears. They had supported her in her decision, but they had no idea where she was going to live in India, what her future would be, or when they would see her again.

Once on board, she looked back towards London; her home was there, her school, and the Sesame Club where Shaw, Yeats and others would continue to lecture and argue; all would go on as before. Her tendency to look life almost too squarely in the face, and rage against what she saw there, was subdued for the moment in a deepening anxiety about her family and her future. She had already discussed her worries with her friend Eric Hammond.

> She frequently referred to reasons for and against the proposal. She must trust others to cherish her aged mother, she must relinquish all those interests for which London claimed her and for which she was endowed with peculiar fitness. Above all, she must endure harsh mis-representation of her motive, and suspicion and disapproval on the part of her Christian 'connections'. She was assured that, whatever might occur, she could never return to her old home, the old familiar ways, the old friends, except perhaps for a brief vacation from work.

But Eric Hammond also wrote of her: 'Alive from head to foot, vibrant with intellectual energy, endowed with a personality which attracted and dominated, she revelled in argument and disputation. She would stimulate the combatants, and the fiercer the fight, the happier she grew.' As she left England, she was staking her future on her fighting qualities, and on Vivekananda, and she knew it.

The *Mombasa* passed Port Said on 5 January, Sinai on the 7th, and Aden on the 12th. Margaret was surrounded by passengers eager to reach India to meet a husband or wife, to take a holiday, or to begin a career. Some of them carried letters of introduction. She carried letters of warning – from Vivekananda.

You will be in the midst of half-naked men and women with quaint ideas of caste and isolation, shunning the white skin through fear or hatred, and hated by them intensely. On the other hand, you will be looked upon by the whites as a crank, and every one of your moves will be watched with suspicion.

She accepted this as a fair warning, perhaps just a little overstated. Her veneration for the British flag (except when it waved over Ireland) was, as she often said, very near to worship; in India the British rule was surely an entirely altruistic and benevolent one, accepted by the Indians with appreciation and gratitude?

His second warning was even stronger. She must accept once and for all that she was not coming to India to shelter under the protecting wing of a gentle father-figure.

I see persons giving me almost the whole of their love. But I must not give anyone the whole of mine in return, for that day the work would be ruined. A leader must be impersonal. I am sure you understand this. I do not mean that one should be a brute, making use of the devotion of others for his own ends, and laughing in his sleeves meanwhile. What I mean is what I am, intensely personal in my love, but having the power to pluck out my heart with my own hand if it becomes necessary, for the good of many, for the welfare of many, as Buddha said.

Now that the cold fog of an English January had been left behind and the ship sailed under a hot sun, Margaret was between two worlds, belonging to neither. Calcutta was a vague picture in her mind. Even the Ramakrishna monastery was not a place she could visualize. The first few monks of the Order were temporarily housed, she knew, in a garden-house lent by a devotee, after years in a derelict house. The voyage seemed never-ending. All this was for Vivekananda, and his certainties. Her own certainties were still in question.

'However we may argue, only one thing will satisfy us, and that is our own experience,' he had said. Margaret was not accustomed to wearing blinkers and plodding patiently where she was directed. A meek and unquestioning obedience had never been a part of Vivekananda's nature, and it was no part of her nature either. 'But it was his *character* to which I had thus done obeisance . . . For the rest, I studied his teaching sufficiently to become convinced of its coherence, but never, till I had had experiences that authenticated them, did I inwardly cast in my lot with the final justification of the things he came to say.'

On the morning of 24 January she reached Madras. But there was no immediate welcome, no joyful hastening on to Indian soil. The ship lay in harbour all day, and all the following night. What her thoughts were, as she waited, and continued to wait, we can only guess. She wrote in her diary, 'In spite of infinite kindness – very, very lonely. What Calcutta will be like, I tremble to think.'

At last an American disciple of Vivekananda arrived, and next day at ten o'clock in the morning she left Madras for Calcutta, where Vivekananda was waiting to meet her.

Her feelings when at last she met him are not recorded. What is recorded – it pours through her writings, explicit and beyond doubt – is that when, by his side, she saw Calcutta for the first time – the teeming life of the city, the noise, the colour and the peaceful movement of the brown waters of the Ganges – she fell utterly and irrevocably in love – not with Calcutta, but with India. It was a love affair that hit her with immense force because it was so unexpected. She had wanted to help with the work, she had been eager to come, but she had not expected anything like this. She often used the metaphor of one who falls in love, in talking of India. 'What a little thing it would be to any of us to die for one whom we really loved! . . . It is such a falling-in-love that India demands of English men and women who go to her to work.' The general view in England of 'life among the heathen' overseas had a deeper subconscious influence on her than she realized.

> How unlike the terrible pictures of the Hindu routine which, together with the Pharisees in the New Testament, had embittered my English childhood! Constant ablutions, endless prostrations, un-meaning caste restrictions, what a torture the dreary tale had been! And the reality was so different! Here, a brown baby, with black lines under his eyes, and a gold chain round his waist, carred in triumph by his mother or nurse . . . again, a quiet man with intellectual face and Oriental leisure; and, above it all, the palm trees, with little brown villages and fresh-water tanks nestling at their feet, while all kinds of birds flew about fearlessly just outside my window, and threw their shadows across my paper as I wrote. The golden glow of one's first sensation suffuses it all. It was like a birth into a new world.

In an age of television and jet travel, it is difficult to recapture the amazed disbelief and joy of her reaction. She never did – or felt – anything by halves. Years later, the *Church Times*, commenting on her book *The Web of Indian Life*, in which this enchanted passage occurs, commented dryly, 'The golden glow suffuses a little too much, and obscures.' But, as yet, the British in India were not aware of her, and she was totally unaware that their view of India might be a little different from her own. She did not even pause to notice that other English women, their skirts, like hers, stiffly sweeping the dusty streets, their dresses tightly fastened to the neck unlike the Indian saris worn by the Hindu women, walked the streets or drove in their carriages watching the Indian life around them as spectators watch through an invisible glass partition. She did not even realize that a glass partition was there.

The enchantment and the speed of life kept her busy for the next three months. She could not grieve for Wimbledon; there was no time. She visited schools, attended lectures, and began to take lessons in Bengali. She moved for a while into a cottage by the Ganges on the site of what was eventually to be the great monastery (or Math) of the Order of Ramakrishna, and two of Vivekananda's disciples, Josephine MacLeod, an American, and Mrs Ole Bull, the widow of the Norwegian violinist, the employer and friend of Ibsen, shared the cottage with her.

It was a significant beginning. The close friendship she formed with the two women lasted for the rest of her life. Josephine MacLeod, called 'Joe', 'Yum-Yum', 'Yum' and other teasing pet-names, was in her late years 'Tantine' to the monks and eventually practically honorary aunt to the entire Order and its associates, in her old age. She was the trusted friend of Vivekananda, and her understanding commonsense and loyalty kept letters flowing between herself and Margaret from all over the world in the years to come. On these letters much that we know of Margaret Noble is based. Mrs Ole Bull was a quietly faithful mother figure to Margaret and practically everybody else, and Vivekananda regarded her with respect as a 'mother' to whom he often wrote like a son. The tumbledown old cottage had already been made into a happy temporary home for the three of them by Joe MacLeod and Mrs Ole Bull, who were both relatively well-to-do and thoroughly enjoyed the chance of making a small home by the Ganges. Margaret could not have arrived at a better time.

With Vivekananda's permission, they had just had it whitewashed. Then the two women bought old mahogany furniture from the bazaars and made a drawing-room, half of which was furnished in the Eastern style, and half in the Western. What could be fairer? No favouritism was permitted. Vivekananda was much amused, and highly delighted to see the home they had made of a ramshackle house which many had thought was uninhabitable. He was always delighted by the initiative and practicality of Westerners, whom he regarded as 'being living Vedantins' in this respect, because, when something needed to be done, they did not dream about it. 'You *do* it,' he said. 'That is your power.' He brought all his visitors to see the transformed cottage. Home-making or monasticism, love or philosophy, whatever good it was that he saw done to its utmost, he saw it as a 'path out of maya' and encouraged it. He told Margaret, 'You will find that little house of Dhira Mata like heaven, for it is all love, from beginning to end.' 'Dhira Mata', meaning 'the steady mother', was his name for Mrs Ole Bull.

Margaret moved straight into the cottage, and was at once at home. In the afternoons they gave tea parties in front of the house, in full view of the river, where they were seen by all the boats going upriver, as they received their guests as if they were in their own drawing-room in some Western city. Margaret wrote of the cottage:

> Our cottage stood on a low terrace built on the Western bank of the river, a few miles above Belur. At flood-tide, the little gondola-like boat which to those who live beside the Ganges serves the purpose of a carriage, could come up to the very foot of the steps, and the river between us and the opposite village was from half to three quarters of a mile broad. Between us and the monastery were several other garden houses and at least one ravine crossed by a doubtful-looking plank made out of half of the stem of a palm-tree.

Here Vivekananda came daily at sunrise from the monastery, sometimes alone, sometimes with his brother monks, wearing the ochre robe of the Hindu monk which had looked so exotic when he lectured in Piccadilly, and here became simply a part of the whole colour and background of India. Sitting under the trees, or on the verandah above, he talked to them of Vedanta, of India, of Margaret's future work for the women of India. 'Never forget – in India, the word is, "Women and the People".' The other two women would return home, but Margaret would stay to become a nun of an Order which had no convent for women, no other nuns, and no tradition of Western women living, as she must do, as a Hindu among Hindus. He was anxious that she should not patronize the Hindus as though she had come amongst them as a benevolent outsider, and for her own sake she must learn to stand alone eventually.

Swami regarded no detail as too trivial to be important. To eat only of approved foods, to do this with the fingers, to sit and sleep on the floor, to bind myself strictly by the observances and feelings of Hindu etiquette – to this day, I shudder at the roughness and impurity of *blowing* out a light. In my teaching work, the essential qualification should be to look at the world, even if only for a moment, through the eyes of the taught.

In March she gave her first public lecture at the inaugural meeting of the Ramakrishna Mission. Vivekananda was delighted that she had made it publicly clear that she had come to serve India, not to patronize. On the outbreak of a plague in Calcutta she gave what help she could. It was a very small cloud, which, she guessed, might later loom very much larger. The extreme of humility and self-discipline which Vivekananda expected she was glad to give; but here, too, a small cloud began to move across the horizon and there was a rumbling of distant thunder. The expression on her guru's face as she spoke with delight of the British flag and of the altruism of British imperialism in India, and when she generalized in sweeping terms about Oriental nations ('The Chinese are an untruthful race') might have warned her. He had always insisted that total obedience on the part of the disciple must be combined with the granting of freedom of thought and experience by the guru, and he did not impose his own views on her. She had not yet discovered that, by living as she did, away from all contact with Westerners in India who were not Vivekananda's disciples, and without meeting Hindus who frankly regarded all Westerners as unclean, she was screened and protected from the realities of the situation. When he insisted that some of his Hindu Brahmin disciples must accept food from her hands, and drink water which she had poured, she had no idea of what a revulsion he was forcing them to overcome, and from how much he was shielding her.

Her early fears of caste-difference, customs, and the intricate rituals and taboos of an Indian household had been almost too thoroughly overcome; her ignorance of the Hindu background and point of view was still considerable. She had discovered, in the courteous gentle bustle of the Indian women at home, a sense of humour and a delighted relish of the absurd.

On another occasion I came in one evening at the moment of a distinguished friend's arrival. Such was the *empressement* of her reception, the warmth of the inquiries after her health and so on, that I felt myself to be certainly an intrusion. But a quiet hand detained me when I would have slipped away.

'Wait', said the mother, 'till I have finished – for I haven't the least idea who she is!'

Vivekananda watched the growing enchantment without comment. She had very little idea that the Indian households to which he introduced her were not open, as a rule, to Westerners, who would not in general wish to enter them. Her worship of the British flag had not extended to any study of politics; her passion for India did not yet reveal to her the life-experience of the average outcaste. She saw India and Britain as one happy family, and in this discovering of India the language of love wells out of every word she wrote.

What a beautiful old world it was in which I spent those months! It moved slowly, to a different rhythm from anything which I had known. It was a world in which a great thought or intense emotion was held as the true achievement, distinguishing the day as no deed could. . . . From all around the neighbourhood at sunset would come the sound of gongs and bells, the family chapel of each house, announcing Evensong . . . more and more, as the spirit of Hindu culture became the music of life, did that hour and that of sunrise grow to be the event of my day. . . . The change itself from daylight to darkness is incredibly swift. The sun descends, and at once we are alone in the deep purple and the tremulous stars of an Indian night. Far away in the North, hour after hour, outlines go on cutting themselves clearer against the green and opal sky, and long low cliffs grow slowly dim with shadows on the sea. The North has Evening; the South – Night.

She had no idea that the famine now raging was the worst in Indian history, that it would continue for three years and devastate the entire country, while the British continued to export grain from the starving country. Vivekananda said nothing, as yet.

For the first time, she began to see clearly the divergent aims and the inevitable cleft between the different types of work that Vivekananda was inaugurating, and the impression this made on her began to change the whole course of her thinking, and, later, of her life. In London she had seen the man of serenity and meditation who had come to bring some glimpse into Hinduism to the West.

'Oh, how calm,' he exclaimed, 'would be the work of one, who really understood the divinity of man! For such there is nothing to do, save to open men's eyes. All the rest does itself' . . . From the moment of my landing in India, however, I found something quite unexpected underlying all this. . . . It was the personality of my Master himself, in all the fruitless torture and struggle of a lion caught in a net.

Margaret Noble's own words set out his inner torment, as she and her friends observed it, very clearly indeed. As well as the serenity she had found in him in London:

I found in his own country another point of view, from which he was very, very human. And here, though the results of his efforts may have been choicer, or more enduring than those of most of us, yet they were wrought at the selfsame cost of having to toil on in darkness and uncertainty and only now and then emerging into light. Often dogged by the sense of failure, often overtaken by a loathing of the limitations imposed alike by the instrument and the material, he dared less and less, to dogmatize about the unknown.

This mixture of 'acceptance of what happens', and vigorous determination to begin a great project that he could never see fully developed, tore at him constantly.

In those last five and a half years particularly which were his crowning gift to his own people, he stood for work without attachment or work for impersonal ends, as one of the highest expressions of the religious life. And for the first time in the history of India an order of monks found themselves banded together with their faces set primarily towards the evolution of new forms of civic duty. In Europe, where the attainment of the direct religious sense is so much rarer and so much less understood than in the East, such labour ranks as devotional in the common acceptance. But in India, the head and front of the demand made on a monastic order is that it produces saints. And the value of the monk who, instead of devoting himself to maintaining the great tradition of the super-conscious life, turns back to help society upwards, has not in the past been clearly understood.

Once his mind was given to it, he plunged in fully, and it is difficult, as she says, to understand from a Western viewpoint how often this went deeply against the grain for him.

Men would be sent out from the Monastery to give relief in famine-stricken areas, to direct the sanitation of a town, or to nurse the sick and dying at a pilgrim-centre. One man started an orphanage and industrial school at Murshidabad. Another established a teaching nucleus in the South. These were, said the Swami, the 'sappers and miners' of the army of religion. His schemes however, sent much further. He was consumed with a desire for the education of Indian women and for the scientific and technical education of the country. How the impersonal motive multiplies the power to suffer, only those who have seen can judge. Was his life indeed a failure, as he was sometimes tempted to feel it, since there never came to his hands that 'twenty million pounds' with which, as he used to say, he could have set India on her feet?

For one individual to serve another, selflessly, as serving 'That', or 'God' in him, was an essential part of his belief; but there was every danger that an organization on this scale (and it could not be big *enough* to do all that was needed) would tear away the simplicity and detachment which he also taught. Even in the monastery he encouraged among the young novices (to the horror of the devout and orthodox) digging, gardening, rowing, gymnastic exercises, the keeping of animals, sinking a well, making bread. He earned much disapproval by encouraging his novices of high caste to heal (and therefore to touch) lepers, and to feed the outcaste. 'To a Western mind, it might well seem that nothing in the Swami's life had been more admirable than this.'

She was rarely alone with him, not often able to talk about herself. At this stage, like the friends with whom she was staying, she listened to him; she watched, sympathized, observed. And she began to understand a little more.

But it was inevitable that he himself should from time to time go through the anguish of revolt. The Hindu ideal of the religious life, as a reflection on earth of that of the Great God in the Divine Empyrean – the Unmoving, the Untouched, 'pure, free, ever the Witness' – is so clear and so deeply established that only at great cost to himself could a man carry it into a fresh channel. Has anyone realized the pain endured by the sculptor of a new ideal?

She herself realized it. Watching him, she saw the pain endured. And she presents his difficulty exactly as she saw it. 'It took the form of a play upon two different ideals, of which either was highest in its own world, and yet each, to those who believed in its fellow, almost a crime.'

But this was not his only difficulty. As a monk, he was dedicated to a life detached from politics; he asserted this again and again, and in his letters we find constant warnings that if India, herself, ever puts politics above religion, she will fall from the greatness of her own nature, and lose her greatest gift to mankind.

There was one thing, however, deep in the Master's nature, that he himself never knew how to adjust. This was his love of his country and his resentment of her suffering. Throughout those years in which I saw him almost daily, the thought of India was to him the air he breathed. True, he was a worker at foundations. He neither used the word 'nationality' nor proclaimed an era of 'nation-making'. 'Man-making' he said was his own task.

As she listened and sympathized, the seeds of her own future were being given their first light, though she did not know it. But she had fallen in love with India, and here was the man who above all could have helped India, torn because of the limitations imposed by his own breadth of range; what was needed, as he once said, was a score of Vivekanandas. She saw that, for him, politics would have been a step in the wrong direction, a path that could only lead to a watering-down of his ideals. But, loving India as she did, and homesick as she must sometimes have been for England (just as on her visits to England she yearned for India) she listened to him. And then she wrote down what she heard.

He told us how he had longed, when in the West, to stand once more at dusk some little way outside an Indian village and hear again the evening calls – the noise of children growing sleepy at their play, the evensong bells, the cries of the herdsmen and the half-veiled sound of voices through the quickly-passing twilight. How homesick he had been for the sound of the July rains, as he had known them in his childhood in Bengal! . . . The most beautiful sight he could remember was a mother whom he had seen, passing from stepping-stone to stepping-stone across a mountain brook and turning as she went, to play with and caress the baby on her back. The ideal death would be to lie on a ledge of rock in the midst of Himalayan forests and hear the torrent beneath, as one passed out of the body, chanting eternally, 'Hara! Hara! The Free! The Free!'

And so she listened, and saw, as she said, 'the armour of the warrior under the habit of the monk'. But she also saw that this battle must be fought by different warriors. She agreed totally with his concept of India – not old and effete as some critics thought, but standing on the threshold of the twentieth century. And she never forgot, in spite of the years of struggles of different kinds that lay ahead of her, one remark of his. 'I feel myself to be the man born after many centuries – *I see that India is young*.'

4

Argument had not yet begun; Margaret still listened. In those early morning sessions when Vivekananda came each day at sunrise and talked to the women disciples in the little cottage – sometimes accompanied by his brother monks – they sat and listened, rarely breaking into his talk with questions. In the cool of the early morning, before the heat became intolerable for Westerners, he was giving them, slowly and with time for assimilation, much that was going to be needed in their work for India.

The ideals which they must accept as the backbone of Hindu religious thinking were not as easy to understand as might be supposed. The vital importance of concentration of mind, deliberately cultivated, was placed far above the instinct of benevolence. Without it, benevolence could not go far enough to be of much use. Impulsive charity could be simply a gratification of the desire to be kind, a convenient easing of one's own pity, or even a form of self-admiration. The highest benevolence came from a nature used to the deep concentration of meditation, which acted quietly and very surely, in the right way and at the right time, by an inner spiritual instinct. In personal matters, a detached, impersonal standpoint, 'Be the Witness!', rather than involvement, was as far from Margaret's own impulsive nature as any ideal could well have been, but it was reiterated again and again, and she listened, sitting with her friends under the trees by the Ganges. 'Praying for our enemies' was regarded as inconsistent, because recognizing someone as an enemy would have seemed a proof of hatred. This alone must have gone against the tide of her militant Irish nature. Purity and renunciation as the absolute basis for the good life – this was emphasized again and again, unsparingly and in a hundred different ways, with a total absence of compromise to the drawing-room sophistication of the Western world. The sense of ultimate oneness – the story of the saint who fainted when bullocks were beaten in his presence, whilst on his own back were found the weals made by the lash – all this they absorbed, and accepted slowly.

One point that was hard to accept, though in time it was to stand her in good stead, was that just as important as concentration of the mind was the freedom of the individual soul, including all the minor rights of thought, opinion, and action. The 'approach to religion' of each individual must be regarded as sacred; the object of worship, whether Buddha, Jesus, Ramakrishna, or the Absolute was referred to as 'the chosen ideal' – and it was chosen, not imposed.

She was startled to find that in the monastery he was establishing were some men who did not in fact approve of Vivekananda's talking to women at all, for some of the monks held to the old orthodoxies.

> The religion of one might be described as atheism tempered by hero-worship; that of another led him to a round of practices which to most of us would constitute an intolerable burden; some lived in a world of saints, visions and miracles; others again could not be away with such nonsense, but must needs guide themselves by the coldest logic. The fact that all these could be bound together in a close confraternity bore silent witness to their conception of the right of the soul to choose its own path.

In spite of this, the monks accepted the four women with the greatest kindness, and when Vivekananda had to be away, they were never neglected or forgotten.

> They milked the cow that gave us our supply, and when the servant whose duty it was at nightfall to carry the milk was frightened by the sight of a cobra in the path and refused to go again, it was one of the monks themselves who took his place in this humble office. Some novice would be deputed daily to deal with the strange problems of our Indian housekeeping. Another was appointed to give Bengali lessons. Visits of ceremony and of kindness were frequently paid to us by the older members of the community. And finally, when the Swami Vivekananda himself was absent for some weeks on a journey, his place was always duly taken at the morning tea-table by some one or another who felt responsible for the happiness and entertainment of his guests.

It was an almost idyllic period. The teaching was given slowly, and gently; members of the Order understood how difficult it must all be, at first, for these Westerners who stood alone on the Hindu side of the fence in a British-occupied country; the monks were touched, and as can be seen from some of their own recorded comments, regarded with considerable respect, the courage, integrity, and the willingness to learn, of those who had come so far from the comforts of the West.

One very basic point, which Margaret records, in Vivekananda's teaching at that time, contained a note of warning to her as an Englishwoman (and an Englishwoman of her temperament in particular) coupled with high praise for a basic English characteristic which might, in itself, have been a caution.

> . . . he gravely warned us, again and again, as the great fault of the Western character, against making any attempt to force upon others that which we had merely found to be good for ourselves. And yet at the same time, when asked by some of his own people what he considered – after seeing them in their own country – to be the greatest achievement of the English, he answered, 'that they had known how to combine obedience with self-respect'.

During this period, her own great day, her initiation as a Brahmacharini (novice) came and went as quietly, as privately and with as little fuss, as all the greatest moments of her life.

On 25 March, the Christian Feast of the Annunciation, Vivekananda came to the cottage as usual in the morning, and with him they went to the Math (or monastery) which was still temporarily housed in the garden-house of a devotee. Vivekananda took Margaret to the chapel, taught her the worship of Shiva, and she was then initiated as a novice of the Order of Ramakrishna and given the new name, 'Nivedita'.

'Nivedita' means 'the dedicated', and it is by this name that she was ever afterwards known in India; by this name she appears on the postage stamp; this marks the end of the first stage in her life, when she was Margaret Noble, and it is as Nivedita that we should, in future, refer to her, for her approach to her life's work was at an end. She was now embarking fully upon it.

It was now that the difficulties began, now that the relationship between herself and her guru began its first crossing of swords; now that she was through the kindergarten stage, she must learn in a tougher school. And this schooling started when she least expected it.

After the first minor outbreak of plague had been brought under control, Swami Vivekananda left, with a large group, for Almora in the Himalayas, followed by a tour of Kashmir; the Westerners were going to see a little of India at first-hand; they were still learning. The party included several of Vivekananda's fellow-monks, Mrs Ole Bull and Miss MacLeod, Mrs Patterson (the wife of the American Consul General) and Nivedita, now officially known as 'Sister Nivedita'.

The clash was inevitably coming; and yet the beauty of those days lit the rest of her life. 'The summer of 1898 stands out in my memory as a series of pictures, painted like old altar-pieces, against a golden background of religious ardour and simplicity and all alike glorified by the presence of one who, to us in his immediate circle, formed their central point.'

Both the beauty of those wanderings, before the toughest and hardest part of her life began, and also the difficulties to come in her clashes with her guru, she has recorded with total frankness. He had suggested that she should join the travelling party for the purpose of receiving his personal training for the work she was to do in India. She did not anticipate that the words 'personal training' meant any close relationship of spiritual question and answer. She already knew him better than that.

'The Swami himself was, on personal subjects, intensely reserved . . . no one ever lived who more anxiously sought to escape the office of spiritual director.' He answered questions, but the impact was more often from his direct personality than from theorizing; he would describe his own experiences on occasion, but there was always a withdrawal 'from such merely theoretical questions as appeared to him too intimate a revelation of the personal experience. I have sometimes heard inquiries forced upon him in his London classes . . . when it was clear to all listeners that he would rather have endured a careless touch upon an exposed nerve.'

But to those whom he trusted, he gave constantly: teaching, explanation, and a little of his own experience. It was all very general, however, none of it personal to Nivedita.

We would sit in garden or verandah and listen, all together, to the discourse of the hour, each appropriating as much as she chose and studying afterwards as she liked. In that year of 1898 I can remember only one occasion when the Swami invited me to walk alone with him for half an hour – and then our conversation was rather of the policy and aims of the future than of anything more subjective.

But matters were to become a little more personalized than she realized. She had perhaps forgotten that after her initiation, he had asked her to what nation she belonged then, and to his surprise she had replied, 'To the English nation', and had spoken of her passion of loyalty and veneration for the British flag. He had made no comment.

However, at the beginning of this new journey, she was completely happy, passing Banaras and Lucknow, learning from him their history and watching their people; but more especially did he love the villages and farms of the Plains, and he would explain their agriculture, and the hospitality of the poorest of peasants, always offered gladly to a wandering monk, and though the bed offered might be only straw in an outhouse . . . 'the mother steals in at the last moment, before she goes to rest herself amongst her sleeping household, to place a tooth-brush twig and a bowl of milk where the guest will find them, on waking in the morning . . .' As they crossed the heat of the Terai, he told them that this was the very earth on which Buddha had spent his youth, the wild peacocks were used as illustrations of Rajputana, and elephants became the text for tales of ancient battles. The travellers were enchanted by India, soaking in it, drenched by it.

Although he knew only too well all that was wrong with British rule, and Nivedita herself was soon to begin to see a little of it for herself, still as they crossed the boundary from Bengal into the North West Provinces, he told them of

> the wisdom and methods of the great and merciful English ruler who was at that time at the head of their administration.
>
> Unlike others, he understands the need of personal government in Oriental countries, where a strong public opinion is not yet developed, so no hospital, no college, no office knows the day when he will pay it a visit of inspection. And even the poorest believes that if only he can reach him personally, he will receive justice at his hands. [Vivekananda regarded the importance of personality in Eastern governments as vital.]
>
> We realized sometimes, as we listened to him, how hard it had been for the Indian poor, to understand the transition from the personal rule of sovereigns, always accessible to appeal, always open to the impulse of mercy and able to exercise a supreme discretion, to the cold bureaucratic methods of a series of departments.

He told them of how some simple folk in the early years of British rule had spent all they had, 'trying to reach Queen Victoria and speak to her personally, at Windsor, and had usually died of want and disillusionment, far from their villages and even further from Windsor'. Of individual Englishmen in scattered outposts, who had done their utmost for the villagers in their care, he always spoke highly. Nivedita probably accepted this, so far, as being no more than a generalization about the excellence of British rule.

They passed through mountain forests of the Himalayas on the way to Almora, travelling first on tongas and then on horseback, and were guests at the house of Vivekananda's disciple, the Maharaja of Khetri.

As they began to climb higher, they passed rose forests, wild pomegranates and honeysuckle. During the night they passed through the forest with torches and lanterns. Next day the route was more bleak and bare as they climbed higher.

When they reached Almora, Vivekananda and his party stayed with Captain and Mrs Sevier (two of his disciples from England), in their house, and Nivedita and the other women stayed in a bungalow some distance away. At Almora, the early-morning and breakfast-time talks continued; different races and countries, and their respective ideals, philosophies and creeds were all discussed. As usual, in London and elsewhere, Nivedita argued and fought for her own point of view; and her point of view, as regards England and British imperialism in India, was totally prejudiced. She did not weigh up 'for and against', as he was prepared to do; it was 'my country right or wrong' – an oddly inconsistent point of view in a woman who fought like a tigress against any compromise with British rule in Ireland. He had to prove to her, as she later said, 'how determinately insular my ideals had hitherto been'.

She battled with him, too, on the question of the current European estimate of women. She would not listen quietly, think over what he said, and reach conclusions later. She knew that he worshipped womanhood as a manifestation of 'Mother', and he gave a frankness and equality to his women disciples and friends which was almost unique in Hinduism. But this was not enough for her, at this stage, and she records the fact, against herself, with disarming honesty. Women and the British flag were not subjects that she was prepared to discuss calmly.

They were many conflicts; they were both strong-willed, neither could compromise. In a culminating outburst of anger he said to her, 'Really – patriotism like yours is sin! All that I want you to see is that most people's actions are the expression of self-interest, and you constantly oppose to this the idea that a certain race is all of angels. Ignorance so determined is wickedness.'

It nearly broke her, but still she fought back. In a more cynical age, it is not easy to understand her 'idea that a certain race is all of angels' (except in its treatment of the Irish). But this was at once her great weakness and her great strength; her total loyalty and dedication, wherever she was committed (and he had aptly named her 'Nivedita', 'the dedicated'), always cast its own shadow of prejudice against the other side, of what she calls 'the blindness of a half-view'. This could make or break her life in India; it could, when she was left alone, leave her vulnerable and totally exposed. For her own sake, he gave no quarter, and attacked mercilessly. He had always encouraged the fighter in her, however, and still she fought back.

During this period of bewilderment and depression, unexpected help came to her. It came in the person of Swami Swarupananda, a young monk who had been received at the monastery within a few days of her own admission to the vows of a novice. He was her daily teacher in Bengali and in Hindu religious literature, and from their totally different backgrounds both he and Nivedita had reached the same point in their lives by a great similarity of outlook in some respects.

The story of his mental development was of extraordinary interest to me. For this man had been brought up in his childhood in the Vaishnava faith, that is to say, in an idea of God as the kind and loving Lord and preserver of men, which is practically tantamount to the Christianity of the West. The usual revulsion, familiar to all of us, had been encountered. . . . Passing through a crowded street one day, he found a poor woman kneeling and crying softly, as grain by grain she picked up from the dust a handful of rice that had been jostled out of the bowl in her hand by a passer-by. And then the man found himself, in his passionate pity, crying indignantly, 'What the devil would God be doing, if He existed, to let such things happen?'

Two or three such experiences precipitated him upon a year of mental suffering so keen that he never again knew perfect health. But he emerged from it in the peace that comes of a settled attitude towards life. *He would break the dream.* He saw in the ignorance and selfishness of the mind itself the source of such things, and he determined to reach the point of utmost insight and certainty. Under his influence I began seriously the attempt at meditation.

He understood her own attitude to life; but he was very much more closely on the wavelength of Vivekananda. He stood almost as interpreter between them.

For I have always thought that it was due to the fact that I found myself on the line of communication between his mind and that of our Master – as on the pathway of interaction between some major and minor heliograph – that I owed my ability thereafter to read and understand a little of those feelings and ideals with which the air about us was charged.

There, among the Himalayas, she was finding both difficulties and help. Problems were by no means healed as yet. She found that a 'strange new element' had crept into the morning talks. 'On one side, a curious bitterness and distrust, and, on the other, irritation and defiance.'

But all this went much deeper than the matter of her own unquestioning devotion to the British Raj. There was, behind it all, a strong emotional streak in her attitude towards Vivekananda on her part, and a clear determination to end it on his. The emotion was, as Eric Hammond rightly pointed out, not in any way that of a woman 'coerced by his masculinity', but very much the almost adoring devotion of a daughter to a beloved father. She had been devoted to her own father; he had died only too soon after her reunion with him as a little girl who had been left so long with grandparents in Ireland. It was Vivekananda's custom, whilst retaining his own dignity and sense of slight distance, to accept whatever relationship with friends, disciples or colleagues that they themselves found most natural, according to their varying natures – and their natures certainly varied considerably. On his first arrival in America, he wrote with amusement to a brother monk in India that the young girls who became his friends and disciples and with whose families he stayed, tended to regard him as an elder brother, and teased him, looked after him, respected him, and since he was a monk and therefore 'of another world' accepted him with complete frankness and naturalness. But he did not stay in any place long, so the relationship was a loving, friendly, but detached one; he moved constantly about America and back to India. In the same way, older men and women came to regard him almost as a favourite son, others as friend, and some simply as a great guru. In many cases, Westerners twenty years older than he – for he was then in his mid-thirties – regarded him as their spiritual father, for he seemed older psychologically and spiritually than they were themselves.

In none of this was there any bondage, or any strong overemotionalism; it was indeed a part of the science of religion in India, and, as she says, 'It is there understood and accepted that without some such dramatization of their own relation to it, ordinary minds cannot be made susceptible of a great religious impulse.'

To her dismay, there at Almora the relationship began to change. She described it, now, as 'one of clash and conflict'. And, in spite of his warning letter to her ('I see persons giving me almost the whole of their love. But I must not give anyone the whole of mine in return, for that day the work would be ruined . . . A leader must be impersonal. I am sure you understand this') she was totally unprepared.

But I had been little prepared for that constant rebuke and attack upon all my most cherished prepossessions which was now my lot. Suffering is often illogical, and I cannot attempt to justify by reason the degree of unhappiness which I experienced at this time as I saw the dream of a friendly and beloved leader falling away from me, and the picture of one who would be at least indifferent and possibly, silently hostile, substituting itself instead.

It would be easy enough to dismiss all this as the inevitable friction between two strong natures, or simply as a study of a devoted, honest, but emotional and sometimes naive woman confronting a man vastly more experienced, more spiritually advanced, who was carrying intolerable and complex burdens, and knew that his own death was only a few years away. But it is always too facile to speak from hindsight, or to judge lightly by some similar circumstance in the West. There is no similar circumstance in the West. And in the East, at that time, with no convent for women, and the nun in question a determined British woman, the circumstance was unique.

The relationship between guru and disciple, she found, is not simply that of teacher and taught: Sri Ramakrishna had emphasized that the guru is regarded as the manifestation on earth of the 'chosen ideal' who is worshipped by the disciple; he initiates the disciple with the mantra, the name of God, the 'seedword' which is the vital essence of the disciple's future spiritual life, whether the guru lives or dies. Ultimately, the chosen ideal, the guru, and the disciple are one. The attitude of disciple to guru is based upon a total acceptance and passive humility, and the bond is voluntarily entered into, not imposed; the guru encourages the inner nature of the disciple to develop to its own highest point. Obviously, when the disciple's own nature, at its highest, is a strong and militant one, and where passive humility is combined with too much emotion, the guru has to take strong action, the medicine may be disagreeable. It is probable, too, that Nivedita did not realize how severely, in the training of monks, the ego was crushed while the spirit and intellect were encouraged in liberty; she had no opportunity of seeing others go through the same treatment.

It is impossible even to guess how Vivekananda saw the situation. Certainly it is clear that he would go no further until the relationship was established on a less personal footing. The relationship of disciple to guru is expected to be the closest relationship on earth – but it is not basically an emotional one. For Nivedita, all relationships, at some stage, tended to be emotional. And all causes must be hotly defended.

On a human level he was fully aware of his own difficulties, and hers. In a letter written to her much later, in America, he warned her, 'Steady, child!' and pointed out that his nerves and her emotions could 'make a mess of everything' if they were not careful; each of them had difficulties to fight, and his difficulty was the overstrained nervous system of a dying man on whom everybody leaned for help. But he did not say that yet; first she had to conquer her own ego, as he had long ago learned to conquer his.

When Vivekananda felt his own inner need for greater strength, he had learned how to find it: he went away, into solitude; he became again the wandering monk. Time and again, in some letter from a crowded city, he spoke of his yearning to have done with all the responsibilities, to leave it all and become again the solitary, the scholar, the meditator. And he was now in his beloved Himalayas; on many occasions throughout this tour he simply walked away, alone, sometimes for long periods, and when he returned those who greeted him always recorded the impression he gave of having brought back an inner radiance, a simplicity and serenity, that suggests the reverse of what Nivedita had previously recorded. In this case, the monk's robe was the true one; he no longer wore the armour of the warrior.

She noted her own impression. There is, of course, no record of his.

> Fortunately it never occurred to me to retract my own proffered service, but I was made to realize, as the days went by, that in this there would be no personal sweetness. And then a time came when one of the older ladies of our party, thinking perhaps that such intensity of pain inflicted might easily go too far, interceded kindly and gravely with the Swami. He listened silently and went away. At evening, however, he returned and finding us together in the verandah, he turned to her and said with the simplicity of a child, 'You were right. There must be a change. I am going away into the forests to be alone and when I come back I shall bring peace.' Then he turned and saw that above us the moon was new and a sudden exaltation came into his voice as he said 'See! the Mohammedans think much of the new moon. Let us also with a new moon begin a new life!'

He blessed Nivedita, before he left. She added that, 'It was assuredly a moment of wonderful sweetness and reconciliation. But such a moment may heal a wound. It cannot restore an illusion that has been broken into fragments.'

The 'illusion' was that of a personal and emotional relationship and she explained that she only spoke of it in order to add the sequel. For in meditation, alone, that evening, she found an Impersonal experience.

> . . . the everyday reality of the experience related in the Hindu books on religious psychology. I found myself gazing deep into an Infinite Good, to the recognition of which no egoistic reasoning had led me. And I understood

for the first time that the greatest teachers may destroy in us a personal relationship only in order to bestow the Impersonal Vision in its place.

She felt that she had achieved a vital stage on the path of deep meditation.

Vivekananda then went away alone, for a few days. He said nothing to members of the party about his health, but letters written by him at that time speak of his illness, his choking breathing, and heart trouble; his need of peace and retirement, from every point of view, was obvious; later, in Kashmir, numbers of Hindu admirers who had heard of his great fame, would enter his boat and sit watching him, leaving him no privacy. 'The life of the hidden hermit,' as Nivedita remarked, 'he thought of as the lover might think of the beloved.'

Meanwhile, Nivedita herself, with the storms at last subsided, stayed quietly at Almora. She wrote to a friend in London, 'I cannot tell you how real this idea of meditation has grown to me now. One can't talk about it, I suppose, but one can see and feel it here, and the very air of these mountains, especially in the starlight, is heavy with the mystery of peace that I describe to you.'

She was training herself, too, to use and experience solitude, having been taught by Vivekananda that the European idea that a man could not live alone for twenty years and remain quite sane, was the exact opposite of the Indian belief that until a man had been alone for twenty years, he could not be regarded as perfectly himself.

On 11 June they all left Almora for Kashmir. The road was lined with ferns, primroses and violets. They passed forests and troops of monkeys. Then began the long trek to Kashmir, where in houseboats they spent a month centred in Srinagar whilst they explored Kashmir. This time, as they journeyed, it took a whole afternoon to cross the Terai by rail. It was malarial country, and as they came down the mountain roads, they met parties of the local people escaping to the upper hills, with their families and all their belongings, to avoid the malaria which would follow the rains.

There are two centres of pilgrimage in Kashmir, both regarded as extremely sacred. One is Kshir-Bhowani, a spring at which the Divine Motherhood (of God) is worshipped, and the other is Amarnath, a mountain cave in which there is an ice emblem of Shiva. Vivekananda announced that she could join his pilgrimage to Amarnath.

Kashmir seemed in those weeks to be full of pilgrims . . . everywhere we saw the march of the gathering hosts. It was all very quiet and orderly and picturesque. Two or three thousand people would encamp in a field and leave it before dawn with no trace of their occupation, save the ashes of their cooking-fires. They carried a bazaar with them and at each halting place, the pitching of tents and opening of shops took place with incredible rapidity. . . . There were hundreds of monks of all the orders with their 'orange-coloured' tents, and amongst these Swami Vivekananda's influence appeared to be magnetic.

At first they objected strongly to the admission of 'foreign ladies'; but he persuaded them to change their minds. Nivedita was seeing an India no other Englishwoman could have seen. Vivekananda 'speaking to each man in his own language' observed every rule of conduct and custom of the other pilgrims of all faiths, eating one meal a day, telling his beads when other pilgrims did so, and worshipping where others worshipped.

The party saw very little of Vivekananda from now on; he lived on his one meal a day and did not seek company, except for that of other monks. At the next halt, Chandanwara, they camped on the edge of a ravine. It poured with rain all afternoon. Vivekananda visited Nivedita and chatted for five minutes, surrounded by servants and the other pilgrims, but she was happy enough, sitting quietly under a dripping fir-tree, continuing her botanizing for a while in the intervals between showers. It was a happy journey in every way.

The path became more and more difficult as they went on; they passed the snow-line and pitched their tents beside a frozen river; Vivekananda insisted that Nivedita did her first glacier on foot. Then followed a climb of many thousand feet. Then they followed a path that twisted along the mountains, and climbed again. The first mountain was carpeted with edelweiss. At last they camped at 18 000 feet, far above the fir-trees overlooking the glacier. Next day, a shorter march took them to Panchatarani – the place of the five streams. At Panchatarani, Vivekananda and other pilgrims entered the ice-cold waters of each of five holy streams.

Nivedita was particularly concerned with botanizing; she was quite willing to risk her life for edelweiss, myosotis or gentian, and she found a new kind of forget-me-not with 'little hairy silver leaves', columbines, Michaelmas daisies and wild roses. On 2 August, on the great day of Amarnath, the pilgrims left by moonlight, along a narrow and dangerous ledge; then followed a walk of miles along the glacier. About nine miles before the cave, ice ceased and the pilgrims bathed in the river. Vivekananda told Nivedita to go on to the cave, while he bathed with other pilgrims. Later he entered the cave and prostrated before the great ice-Shiva. His spiritual elation, and his physical exhaustion, were both so great that doctors afterwards said that his heart ought to have stopped beating, and had undergone a permanent enlargement instead.

The cave was enormous. In a niche to which sunlight never penetrated stood the great ice-lingam, worshipped by the pilgrims. The crowd swarmed around, pigeons fluttered overhead. Vivekananda prostrated himself two or three times, and then quietly left the place. He told them afterwards that he saw Shiva Himself in the ice-lingam. Nivedita experienced nothing. He told her that she did not understand yet, but she had made the pilgrimage, and she would understand better, later. Causes must bring their effects, and the effects would come.

How beautiful was the road by which we returned next morning to Pahlgam. We struck tents that night immediately on our return to them, and camped later for the night in a snowy pass a whole stage further on. We paid a coolie a few annas here to push on with a letter, but when we actually arrived next afternoon we found that this had been quite unnecessary, for all morning long, relays of pilgrims had been passing the tents, and dropping in, in the most friendly manner, to give the others news of our impending arrival. In the morning, we were up and on the way long before dawn. As the sun rose before us, while the moon went down behind, we passed above the Lake of Death, into which about forty pilgrims had been buried one year, by an avalanche which their hymns had started. After this we came to the tiny goat path down the face of a steep cliff, by which we were able to shorten the return journey so much. This was little better than a scramble, and everyone had perforce to do it on foot. At the bottom, the villagers had something like breakfast ready. Fires were burning, Chapatties baking, and tea ready to be served out!

And so, by slow degrees, they returned to Srinagar.

This was all, indeed, a great way from Wimbledon. Nivedita watched everything, recorded much in her diary, and wrote to a friend:

I am learning a great deal . . . That there is a certain definite quality that may be called spirituality, that it is worth having . . . that nothing I have ever called nobility and unselfishness was anything but the most feeble and most sordid of qualities compared to the fierce white light of real selflessness . . . I cannot yet throw any of my past experience of human life and human relationships overboard . . . At present, I am just groping in the dark, asking an opinion here and there and sifting evidence. Someday I hope to have first-hand knowledge.

With equal honesty she admitted a little disillusionment about the British rulers of India.

> You cannot imagine what race hatred means, living in England . . . One of the monks has had a warning this morning that the police are watching the Swami through spies. The Swami laughs at it, though I cannot help attaching some importance to it. The Government would be mad to interfere with him, for it would rouse the country, and I, the most loyal Englishwoman who ever breathed in this country (I would not have suspected the depth of my own loyalty till I got here), would be the first to rise up. But let us hope we shall change all this suspicion.

In a letter written a few days later, she says wistfully, 'It is the dream of my life to make England and India love each other.'

But her hopes were smashed. In Kashmir, the Maharaja had offered land to Vivekananda for the establishment of a monastery and college. A site was selected. But the choice was then twice vetoed by the then acting Resident, Sir Adelbert Talbot, when it was on the agenda for the Council. Everybody concerned interceded and Mrs Patterson, wife of the American Consul in Calcutta, did all she could, but the Resident was adamant. Vivekananda, bitterly disappointed, nevertheless accepted the blow quietly. He had told his followers again and again that in the childlike mood of spiritual acceptance that had come to him on the pilgrimage, 'All my patriotism is gone . . . All men are good, only we cannot reach all. Who am I that I should teach anyone?'

It is perhaps significant that at this time, while she watched his quiet acceptance, Nivedita herself wrote furiously in a letter, 'As for the attitude of the English to the native – oh! you would blush as I do if you could see it all.'

Whatever changes were taking place in her attitude, she was eager at last to return to Calcutta; she still had to find a permanent home in which to live during her future life; and she had come to India to start a school for women. She had no idea that life was likely to take her any further than that; but those two objectives lay immediately ahead.

Vivekananda asked her what her plans were for the school. He explained to her that he had not forgotten it, it was simply that his mind had been full of the work he had established in Madras, in America, in England, Ceylon and Calcutta.

Tentatively, she explained her ideas, and as she set them out, they seemed impossible. She asked him to criticize her plans, and he refused to do so.

That I cannot do. For I regard you as inspired, quite as much inspired as I am. You know, that's the difference between other religions and us. Other people believe that their founder was inspired, and so do we. But so am I, also, just as much so as he, and you as I, and after you, your girls and their disciples will be. So I shall help you to do what you think best.

He encouraged her to carry on with her own plans. But 'Yes, you have faith, but have not that burning enthusiasm you need. You want to be consumed with energy.'

So she was to return to Calcutta, to find a house and start a school, both of which projects, in her circumstances, were – at the most optimistic estimate – a little difficult.

Meanwhile, at Baramulla, in Kashmir, the party took four of the local houseboats, called dungas, which were each about seventy feet long and broad enough for two single beds and a corridor between, covered with matting. The roof could be lifted in the daytime, so that they lived in the open. Mrs Ole Bull and Josephine MacLeod shared one dunga, Mrs Patterson and Nivedita had another, Vivekananda and one of his monks a third, and the fourth was kept for meals, where they all met. They stayed for three months in the boats, but in September it became cold, so the Westerners took an ordinary houseboat, with real fireplaces, for one month. On most days, Vivekananda rose at five in the morning, and when the women heard him talking to the boatman, they rose too, and the whole party walked in the cool morning mist while Vivekananda taught them about the history of India, its architecture, its people, and its religions.

Many of the streets in Baramulla, as in Venice, were canals. So the party had its own small boat, in which they could go to and fro from the mainland, but since the merchants came out in small craft to sell, haggle and bargain directly to the boats, the women did most of their shopping leaning over the rails of the houseboat.

Each of the boats cost thirty rupees a month, and this included the boatmen, who fed themselves. The 'boatmen' consisted of father, mother, son, daughter, and tiny children. Often the smell of the family's own cooking was so delicious that the Westerners begged for a taste. The boat itself was moved either by being punted upriver, or dragged by the boatmen walking along the shore, or by rowing. When they wished to visit a lake, they could be moved there in the night, and wake to find the boat quietly moving, while the servant who had walked ahead had a hot meal ready cooked for them, which he made over a small trough long and narrow enough to hold three pans, one for soup, one for meat, and one for rice; the dexterity needed for this was something which enthralled the Western women, and which they never became accustomed to.

Sometimes there were visitors. Respectable Hindu pandits visited Vivekananda, and told him that it was terrible that he should have anything to do with these ladies. 'They are Mlechchhas' (untouchable, unclean). Westerners who visited the ladies in question pointed out angrily to them that Vivekananda was not treating them with proper respect. 'He meets you without his turban!'

'So we had great fun,' Josephine MacLeod commented with considerable relish, 'laughing at the idiosyncrasies of each other's civilization.'

Vivekananda was not always laughing, however. They watched him anxiously. He did not speak of his health, but they knew that he was often ill. Walking quietly with them among the wild flowers in the early mornings, he seemed as strong as the Himalayan air had made him, but sometimes his boat disappeared from sight, and they knew that he had been rowed away to visit a young Brahmo doctor who was staying in Kashmir that summer, and who treated him with the greatest kindness and care. Without a doctor somewhere in the background they would not have felt that it was safe to continue at all, but even as things were, his bouts of ill-health increased.

He seemed to be almost possessed by his own mind, as though it were being used whether he wished it or not, like an instrument with only a limited time left to play a tune which must be played to the last note. He told Nivedita that his brain was teeming with thoughts. He complained bitterly of the necessity for thought, as though thinking were an illness which 'would consume a man, leaving him no time for sleep or rest, and would often become as insistent as a human voice'.

He was oppressed not only by his illness and by all that he still had to do, and to think out, added to his deep disappointment at the vetoing by the British Resident of the land offered for building a monastery and college, but she knew that he was also still suffering from the after-effects of human grief.

While they had been staying at Almora, news had been brought to him of the unexpected death of J. J. Goodwin. This English disciple had given his life up to him in complete devotion; in particular he had taken on the work of noting down all his lectures in shorthand, typing them the same day to hand over to the newspapers, and creating the various books which were in fact Vivekananda's lectures taken down and published, since he spoke extemporaneously and rarely had time for writing.

The blow of his death had been a very heavy one. He wrote to Goodwin's mother, 'In him I have lost a friend true as steel, a disciple of never-failing devotion, a worker who knew not what tiring was, and the world is less rich by one of those who are born, as it were, to live only for others.'

He also received the shock of the death of the great Hindu saint, Pavhari Baba, whom he loved, as he once said, 'second only to Ramakrishna'.

She had been with him at Almora and had watched him struggling, like a man swimming against a heavy tide, with the grief of human loss.

> Standing there for an hour or more, he talked of the awful self-discipline that one must impose on oneself, if one would indeed be unattached. As time passed he complained of the weakness that brought the image of his most faithful disciple constantly to his mind. It was no more manly, he protested, to be thus ridden by a memory, than to retain the characteristics of the fish or the dog. Man must conquer this illusion, and know that the dead are here beside us and with us, as much as ever. It is their absence and our separation that are a myth. And then he would break out with some bitter utterance against the folly of imagining Personal Will to guide the universe.

Watching him, they began to see that his love of people, and his tenderheartedness, sometimes pulled hard against the detachment and serenity which were also so deeply ingrained in him that people who met him for the first time often described the chief impression he gave them as one of 'bliss'. In terms of the Yogas, Bhakti Yoga pulled against Jnana Yoga; though 'love' and 'renunciation' were usually accepted in Hinduism as two quite different religious paths. Like his love for religion, which he would never allow to capitulate to his love for his country by entering politics, like his vocation for the life of the wandering monk which inevitably warred against the greater need he saw for practical humanitarian work, the strain was heavy in human terms, and only those closest to him saw any glimpse of it. 'If only,' they said to each other, 'if only he had good health, more help, a long time to live', but he had trained them fully in an acceptance of things as they are. He had no patience whatever with 'if only'. There was no choice but to watch patiently and see what he would do, and take from it whatever each of them could use in their own lives later.

They noticed that he reacted now, especially when things were worst, in two ways. He withdrew continually into solitude and meditation. But also he shed the fire of the great teacher, for the simplicity of the child. The parent god he worshipped was Mother Kali, and she was no mere symbol to him. Like his master Ramakrishna, he saw in the terrible figure of Kali, bearing blessings in one pair of hands and in the other pair a dripping sword and severed head, not the four-armed horror which so distressed Westerners, but the truth of life, a reality that was personal, a presence he continually felt. If the good was to be worshipped, so was the terrible: the 'pairs of opposites', pain and pleasure, good and evil, joy and sorrow; both must be fully accepted in order to reach the state which was beyond both. Kali was 'maya' – she was 'time', she was death; but as long as he was involved in life ('and I have become *involved*,' he said, with some sadness) then he would accept everything in full. 'She is the organ. She is the pain. And She is the giver of pain. Kali! Kali!'

On 30 September he went away, leaving word that he was not to be followed. He went to Kshir Bhowani, the coloured springs, and did not return until 6 October.

On the afternoon of 6 October they saw his dunga coming slowly back to them up the river. He was standing in the front of the dunga, holding the bamboo roof-pole with one hand. In the other hand he was holding some yellow flowers. As the boat came nearer, they saw that the flowers were marigolds.

He entered their houseboat and came to each of them in turn, blessing them and putting the marigolds on their heads.

'I offered them to Mother,' he said at last, and sat down, smiling at them. 'All my patriotism is gone. Everything is gone. Now it's only "Mother! Mother!"'

They sat silent, and at last he said, 'I have been very wrong. Mother said to me, "What, even if unbelievers should enter My temples and defile My images! What is that to you? Do you protect Me? or do I protect *you*?" So there is no more patriotism. I am only a little child!'

He told them a little of his physical break-down following his mental perplexities. 'I may not tell you more, it is not in order,' he told them gently, 'but spiritually, *spiritually* I was not bound down!'

For the last few days, they saw very little of him. He was nearing the end of their time in Kashmir, and going ahead of them to Lahore. He rarely spoke, and took long walks by the riverside entirely alone.

He did not speak to them of his health, though in a letter written on

16 October he said that his health had completely broken down. Early next year, when he wrote a letter to Mary Hale, one of the 'old maids', in his usual teasing style, referring to this period at Almora and Kashmir, he admitted, 'Well, I have been in a sort of merry-go-round with my body which has been trying to convince me for months that it too much exists. However, no fear, with four mental-healing sisters as I have, no sinking just now. Give me a strong pull and a long pull, will you, all together, and then I am up!' He added a sardonic post-script. 'Write when you find time between dances!'

But that teasing mood was many months later, and Mary Hale had not been with them on the Himalayan tour, and on that last day, when Nivedita wrote, 'We had that day lived through hours within whose radiance all our future would be passed.'

On the Wednesday morning he came to say good-bye before he left, as they finished breakfast, and he stayed awhile to talk to them. Always he spoke of Kali. Who was he that he should feel responsible for teaching the world? It was all fuss and vanity. 'There was no way but love. If people sinned against us, we must love them till it was impossible for them to resist it.'

She tried to write down all that they received of 'vastness' from him that morning, but found it impossible to express. At last, he left them. Everyone went to wave good-bye to him as he left by tonga, for he was returning by road. Disciples, friends, servants, and the boat-people, parents and children all gathered by the roadside.

'One sturdy little figure, the four-year-old daughter of his chief boatman, whose devotion to him we had long noted, trotted determinedly at his side with a tray of fruit for his journey on her black head and stood, smiling farewell as he drove away.'

5

When Nivedita returned to Calcutta, she had nowhere to live. She immediately, 'with insular rigidity, insisted on being made the guest of the women'. These are her own words. She was always frank in her self-criticism. The revolution that had to be carried out before this hospitality was made possible, she did not yet realize; she recorded it later.

The women to whom she refers were Hindu women. The head of the household in which she 'insisted' on staying as a guest was Sri Sarada Devi, the widow of Sri Ramakrishna himself, who was usually referred to as 'Mother', or 'the Holy Mother', and little did Nivedita realize what she was asking.

Sri Sarada Devi had been married, by the Hindu custom of that day, to Sri Ramakrishna, when she was a child of five, and he a young man; but she had not left her village to join her husband, until she was eighteen. She grew up working in her peasant village, carrying all the responsibilities of a woman who worked with her hands, and trained in a very self-effacing modesty. When she was eighteen, she joined Sri Ramakrishna and found him living in his one room in the Temple gardens at Dakshineswar, near Calcutta. He was dedicated to living the celibate life of a solitary monk, but to him came disciples, devotees, and the young men who later became the first monks of the Order founded by the 'elder brother' of them all, Swami Vivekananda. Sri Ramakrishna told her that, though it was her right to demand a married life with children, he himself would prefer to continue his celibate life; she accepted his ideals fully, and became wife, nun and disciple to him.

Close to his room, in the Temple gardens, was a Nahabat, a small stone building where music was once played. In the top room lived, until her death, Sri Ramakrishna's old mother, and in the tiny room below lived Sarada, surrounded by cooking pots and utensils; here she cooked for her husband and lived, ate and slept, caring for her old mother-in-law. A screen was erected outside the Nahabat to give her seclusion and privacy. Often she saw her husband only once a day, when she took in his food, and sometimes she would return to her native village to help her widowed mother, and husk paddy. It was a situation less remarkable than it appears, for in Western Bengal, married Hindu women were veiled and lived secluded lives, seldom appearing on the street; custom in this respect varied enormously in different parts of India. She found Sri Ramakrishna to be, as well as a man of iron character and renunciation, also a man of great sweetness, gaiety, and possessed of a strong sense of humour. He was venerated as one who had realized God, and was later worshipped as an Incarnation of God. She outlived him by many years, as he died at the age of fifty in 1886, when she was still young; she lived until 1920. He had predicted that, although she had no children, after his death so many people would call her 'Mother' that she would almost tire of the name; and indeed, she became 'Mother' to thousands. Her extreme gentleness and motherliness were combined with enormous strength of character and an endless capacity for hard work and endurance, all of which she needed. By many she was literally worshipped, both as the widow of Sri Ramakrishna and in her own right; in the Hindu worship of God as 'Mother'. No one would have presumed to sleep in the bunk above hers in a railway carriage, for instance. When Swami Vivekananda came to visit her, although he was the great national figure and 'holy man' of his day, he would purify himself with prayers and Ganges water for many miles before he reached her house, and prostrated himself at her feet when he arrived. To touch her, or her food – this, for an 'unclean foreigner' might not only bring public scandal upon Sri Sarada Devi herself, but upon everyone connected with her. She was in her silent way, a very famous figure indeed. And it was in this household that Nivedita intended to stay.

The reason that she did not fully understand all that she was asking, may lie partly in the fact that she had already met Sri Sarada Devi once, and there is a record of this in Nivedita's own words:

> She is the very soul of sweetness, so gentle and loving, and as merry as a girl, and she had always been terribly orthodox, but all this melted away the instant she saw the first two Westerners. Fruit is always presented to visitors immediately, and this was naturally offered to her, and she, to the surprise of everyone – *accepted!* This gave us all a dignity, and made my future work possible, in a way nothing else could have done.

Vivekananda also wrote to a brother monk, 'Sri Mother is here and the European and American ladies went the other day to see her and what do you think, *Mother ate with them even there!* Is not that grand?'

The implication of this acceptance of food taken from the hands of 'unclean foreigners', against every orthodox religious taboo, was understood and appreciated by Nivedita; it therefore seemed perfectly natural to her that she should now ask if she could stay in the house, if only for a few weeks until she found a house for herself.

Swami Vivekananda made the request himself on her behalf, and Nivedita was granted permission to use an empty room in the house.

> This was one of the occasions [Nivedita wrote] on which people look back, feeling that their courage was providentially determined by their ignorance. It is difficult to see how else a necessary solution could have been found. Yet had I deeply understood at the time the degree of social embarrassment which my rashness might have brought not only upon my innocent hostess but also on her kindred in their distant village, I could not have acted as I did . . . As it was, however, I imagined caste to be only a foolish personal prejudice – which must yield to knowledge – against some supposed uncleanness of foreign habits – and, thus cheerfully assuming all the ignorance to be on her side, confidently forced myself upon this Indian lady's hospitality.

The honest self-mockery of that last sentence comes across the years to us almost as strongly as Nivedita's later work in plague and famine, or her fight for Indian independence.

She was accepted totally into the household; even when she had her own house, she came back to visit in the afternoons. 'And when the hot weather came, it was by her express command that I returned to her better-arranged house for sleeping quarters. And then I occupied no room apart, but shared the cool and simple dormitory of the others, with its row of mats, pillows and nets against the polished red earthenware of the floor.'

Nivedita, having left her own mother and family in England, had now found a mother living in India and tirelessly available to her children. The difference this made to her life was immeasurable. Nivedita was not only enchanted by Sarada Devi's gentleness, but startled by her nature as a whole, which she had not expected to find in this veiled seclusion.

> And yet, to myself, the stateliness of her courtesy and her great open mind are almost as wonderful as her sainthood. I have never known her hesitate in giving utterance to large and generous judgement, however new or complex might be the question put before her. Her life is one long stillness of prayer. Her whole experience is of theocratic civilization. Yet she rises to the

height of every situation. . . . Does one carry to her some perplexity or mortification born of social developments beyond her ken? With unerring intuition she goes straight to the heart of the matter, and sets the questioner in the true attitude to the difficulty.

Nivedita found that Sri Sarada Devi was no sentimentalist; her life was hardworking, and she was not above housework.

The Mother can read, and much of her time is spent in reading her Ramayana. But she does not write. Yet it is not to be supposed that she is an uneducated woman. Not only has she had long and arduous experience in administration, secular and religious, but she has also travelled over a great part of India . . .

At that time, Sri Sarada Devi was at home, staying there with the ladies of her household, two of them child widows (that is, women who had been married in childhood to boys who had died, and who were not allowed to marry again, so lived like nuns).

'Long before dawn, one and another rose quietly and sat on the sleeping-mat – from which sheets and pillows were now removed – rosary-beads in hand, and face turned to the wall. Then came the cleansing of the rooms and personal bathing . . .' The days were spent in prayer, meditation, housework, and continual helpfulness given where it was needed; apart from laughter and singing there seems to have been no room in this life for 'consideration of one's own pleasure' at all, and yet Nivedita records that she had never felt such peace and joyfulness. It seemed at first an odd life, to a Westerner '. . . for the simple reason that no one can place himself sufficiently outside his own consciousness to find out that others were born, not only with a different equipment of associations, but also with a different instinct as to their value.'

These values, in this gentle household, she absorbed to the full. In the evening, the servant came with a lighted lamp. Each woman prostrated before a picture or image and touched the feet of the 'Mother' and of old Gopaler-Ma, as a sign of respect. It was a great honour that Nivedita was sometimes allowed to sit by the 'Mother' at the evening meditation, to learn the salutations to the guru which, to Sarada Devi, formed the beginning and end of all worship.

One of the household – the oldest – came, later on in Nivedita's life, to mean much to her. She was a very old woman, called Gopaler-Ma or 'Gopal's mother'. All the women had been direct disciples of Sri Ramakrishna; she, a child widow, had been old when she came to him, and her 'attitude to God' had been that of a mother towards the child-God, 'Gopala' (the child Krishna) whom she worshipped. She had recognized Gopala in Sri Ramakrishna himself. He had unhesitatingly accepted this role towards her, and her attitude towards him had been that of a mother towards a son: she thus always referred to Sarada Devi as 'daughter-in-law'. She lived alone – and had lived so, in austerity, telling her beads and meditating – in a room by the Ganges, and stayed with Sri Sarada Devi when she came to Calcutta. Sometimes, during this visit of Nivedita's, the old lady would return for weeks to Kamarhaty, and some of the others would visit her. Nivedita became fond of her, and sometimes anxious.

There a few of us went, one full-moon night, to visit her. How beautiful was the Ganges, as the little boat crept on and on! And how beautiful seemed the long flight of steps rising out of the water, and leading up past the terraced lawn, to the cloister-like verandah on the right, where in a little room – built probably for some servant of the great house at its sides – Gopaler-Ma had lived and told her beads, for many a year. The great house was empty now. And her own little room was absolutely without comforts. Her bed was of stone, and her floor of stone, and the piece of matting she offered her guests to sit on, had to be taken down from a shelf and unrolled. The handful of parched rice and sugar-candy that formed her only store, and were all that she could give in hospitality, were taken from an earthen pot that hung from the roof by a few cords. But the place was spotlessly clean, washed constantly by Ganges-water of her own sturdy carrying. And in a niche near her hand lay an old copy of the Ramayana, and her great horn spectacles, and the little white bag containing her [rosary] beads . . .

The radiant white moonlight made the trees and flowers outside seem like black shadows, moving and whispering in a dream-world of white marble. But nothing could seem so dream-like, as, in the midst of our busy hurrying world, the thought of spots like this little cell of Gopaler-Ma, enshrining her silent intensity of peace . . .

She, of all of them, had perhaps gone through the greatest struggle to accept Nivedita.

'In Calcutta, Gopaler-Ma felt, perhaps a little more than others, the natural shock to habits of eighty years standing at having a European in the house. But once overruled, she was generosity itself. Conservative she always was: stubbornly prejudiced, never.'

At last Nivedita acquired a house of her own in the Baghbazar, near the house of Sarada Devi, in the northern part of Calcutta. It might be described – and frequently was – as a back lane in a Calcutta slum; few

Europeans ventured there. To live alone, among Indians, in Bosepara Lane (today named 'Nivedita Lane') would have struck them as insanity. To Nivedita, it was the lane made holy by the feet of Sri Ramakrishna himself, it was inhabited by his devotees, and full of high-caste Brahmin neighbours of immense respectability and often of great poverty. 'To live and move about those streets was like walking in some twilight of gods, where the forms of men and women loomed larger than their wont', she wrote later. She had no criticisms or complaints; she could not have been better pleased.

My home is, in my eyes, charming. With its two courtyards, its limited second storey, and its quaintly-terraced roofs, built at five different levels, it is a rambling specimen of the true old Hindu style of building. In the whole place there is not an inch of glass; the lower casements are protected by iron, and the upper by wooden bars, and so, while the sunlight outside my little study is softened by mats made of dark green splints, my bedroom is always open to the stars.

The requirements of a nun who slept on bare boards and lived mainly on raw fruits, and milk or tea, were not large; but the cleaning and care of the premises had to be undertaken by someone who was always available. Lecturing, teaching, travelling, and organizing plague and famine relief would not leave time for housewifery. A servant had to be found, and the mistrust of British intruders in Bosepara Lane was considerable. As a woman, and a nun, she was safe from abuse or attack, but as an Englishwoman she was unclean; she would probably begin to convert their children to Christianity, she would despise their customs, she might report them to the authorities, why couldn't she stay where she belonged? In any case, in India nuns are nuns, they wander alone with begging bowl and shaven head, or live in a convent, they have their own obligations and duties, and the duties and daily rituals of householders are equally binding; the two do not mix. The whole situation was impossible. They did not yet know what happened when Nivedita encountered the word 'impossible'.

There were, however, certain practical difficulties in life. It had taken some time, in the first place, to discover a house that could be let to an Englishwoman, and when this was done it was still a few weeks before a Hindu caste-woman could be found who would be my servant. She turned up at last, however, in the person of an old, old woman who called me 'Mother', and whom I, at half her age, had to address as 'Daughter' or 'Jhee'. This aged servitor was capable enough of the wholesale floodings of the rooms which constituted house-cleaning, as well as of producing boiling water at stated times for the table and bath. For some reason or other she had determined in my case to perform these acts on condition that I never entered her kitchen or touched her fire or water supply. Yet hot water was not immediately procurable. And the reason? We possessed no cooking stove. I asked the price of this necessary article, and was told six farthings. Armed with which sum, sure enough, my trusty retainer brought home a tile, a lump of clay, and a few thin iron bars, and constructed from these, with the greatest skill, the stove we needed.

It took some days to set and harden, but at last the work was complete. Afternoon tea, prepared under my own roof, was set triumphantly before me, and my ancient 'daughter' squatted on the verandah facing me, with the hot kettle on the stone floor beside her, to see what strange thing might come to pass. I poured out a cup of tea and held out the pot to Jhee for more hot water. To my amazement she only gave a sort of grunt and disappeared into the inner courtyard. When she came back, a second later, she was dripping with cold water from head to foot. Before touching what I was about to drink, she had considered a complete immersion necessary.

With afternoon tea, prepared under her own roof, the new resident of Bosepara Lane was entirely content. She had come home. And not only home to her house, but to the entire lane, and her neighbours in it.

They felt a curious sense of responsibility, as if I were the guest of the whole of our lane. They were constantly sending me food . . . If I expected guests, they would provide the repast, and I rarely knew even the name of the giver.

This sense of responsibility may have been not unconnected with the warmth and sympathy they found in their new neighbour. When preparing supper, one evening, she heard wailing from the courtyards of some servants' mud huts opposite. She went to them immediately, and, finding a girl dying, stayed until she died, then stayed for hours more with the weeping women while the men prepared the funeral pyre on the burning ghat. She took the mother of the dead girl in her arms, soothing her and telling her that her child was with Kali, the mother-god. Nivedita and Bosepara Lane became very much at home with each other, one way and another.

6

If her first arrival in India may be seen as the opening stages of a love affair with a whole country and way of life, the lover herself leaped with joy into even the toughest difficulties of what might be called 'the early days of marriage'. To a woman of colossal vigour and determination, with a strongly emotional strain of motherliness in her nature, difficulties were matters to be swept aside with something very like contempt for even the suggestion that they might exist; the first horrors of a plague epidemic were met almost with the exultation of a mother who at last has a chance to fight for her young.

When I first discovered that my work would mean living in the Hindu quarter of Calcutta, the usual protests were forthcoming on all sides. One would have supposed that the chances of immediate death from cholera or typhoid were to chances of safety as fifty to one. I have not seen this alarm justified, however. I have been here now for some months without finding any reasons for a day's illness.

She opened a room of her house as a school for one or two young girls of the neighbourhood, teaching them not only reading and writing but a little painting and clay modelling. The opening of the school was performed by Sri Sarada Devi, the 'Holy Mother'. Vivekananda and some of his fellow-monks were present, and at the end of the ceremony Sarada Devi gave a whispered blessing. The school itself opened on the next day, and a maidservant was appointed to bring the girls to school each day, as it was impossible that they should be allowed out alone. Vivekananda and his brother monks visited the school on its first working day. It was now formally and officially open. After some hesitation, the mothers became friendly and brought gifts of fruit and milk, and, very gradually, doors were opened to her. She herself continued to record, with utter delight, the impact of this new home called India. There is not a trace of the later tensions and fury: all is contentment.

A house of my own, in which to eat, sleep and conduct a girls' school, and full welcome accorded at any hour of day or night that I might choose to invade the privacy of a group of women friends hard by; these were the conditions under which I made my entrance into Hindu life in the city of Calcutta. I came when the great autumn feast of the Mother was past; I was there at the ending of the winter when plague broke out in our midst, and the streets at night were thronged with seething multitudes, who sang strange litanies and went half-mad with religious excitement; I remained through the terrific heat, when activity became a burden, and only one's Hindu friends understood how to live; I left my home for a time when the tropical rains had begun, and in the adjoining roads the cab-horses were up to their girths in water hour after hour.

There were now two things to be coped with: the rains and the plague. The rain did not worry her in the slightest; on the contrary, she revelled.

It is a little strange, during the rains, to have to take an umbrella to go upstairs, but without my two courtyards in the middle of the house the hot weather would have been insupportable in Calcutta. These make the Eastern home, by day, a cave of all winds that blow, and at night a tent roofed in by the starry universe itself. No one who has not experienced it can know quite what it means to return in the evening and open the door upon the sky and stars that one is leaving without. The Indian night is in itself something never to be forgotten. Vast and deep and black it seems, lighted by large soft stars that throb and gleam with an unknown brilliance, while the stillness is broken only by some night-beggar who chants the name of God in the distant streets, or the long-drawn howl of the jackals crying the quarters of the night across the open plain . . .

Meanwhile, Vivekananda had inaugurated and established what was to be the final monastery at Belur Math; a great step forward from the first old house, unwanted because it was believed to be haunted, where a handful of boys who had been disciples of Ramakrishna shared one respectable wearing-cloth between them – to be used by whoever needed to go out – and gave up their university careers to become monks of the future. 'A rickety little old house has been rented for six or seven shillings', Vivekananda said in a letter at that earlier time. The new Belur Math was only beginning, but it was a great step forward to Vivekananda's dream of an Order which would train both monks and a vast multitude of what the West calls 'the laity' in meditation and the discovery of 'the sleeping God' within them, while at the same time it developed a huge organization for feeding the poor, for famine and plague relief, for education, and the emancipation of women. Nivedita was overjoyed to discover, in talking to him, that there was going to be no watering down of his ideals, no concessions to timidity. He said to her, 'The history of the world is the history of a few earnest men, and when one man is earnest, the world must just come to his feet. I am *not* going to water down my ideals, I am going to dictate terms.'

The outbreak of plague brought the first testing time; and for Nivedita herself, under the shrewd eye of Vivekananda, it was a test as well. She was torn between a longing to nurse the dying plague victims, especially the children, and to comfort their mothers; and – since she could hardly halt single-handed the entire epidemic that swept through Calcutta – the obvious necessity of leaving some victims to die alone, in order that she might grapple with the root cause – dirt and sanitation – and so halt the spread of the disease before it claimed more victims.

Her first impulse, naturally, was to care for the sick; and here we have one of the most illuminating glimpses into that part of her nature which refused to see herself as heroic, but which reported, with sardonic amusement, her own mistakes.

She was the disciple of the man who had written from America to his young monks in India, 'Now remember, my boys – slow and steady work – no name-and-fame-making – no newspaper humbug!' and who, when asked by an inquirer in America if he had himself achieved the highest states of meditation which he was describing, sidestepped the question (to which he could only, in truth, have replied 'yes', and thus effectively have canonized himself) with a roar of laughter and the reply, 'Now, do I *look* as though I have? A big fat man like *me*?'

It is illuminating to compare two accounts of her nursing a dying child. First, her own account, which is vivid in its description of the scene, but in which her own part is played down, and she accuses herself of stupidity in trying, at first, to keep the mother away from her child for fear of infection. Whenever she refers to this incident, it is always this mistake which she emphasizes. But secondly we have the account of Dr Radha Govinda Kar in the local newspaper. It is from his account that we learn much that she never recorded of what she was doing for the household, and in the poorer homes of Calcutta.

Her own account is careful and straightforward; she must have written it in her study in the house at Bosepara Lane, with the shadows of the birds falling across the page as they darted past her window; there were too many cases, too much work, to be recorded in detail, but this first case of plague nursing she wrote down, and later published it in a book, *Studies from an Eastern Home*, which described what Indian life was like, viewed from the inside.

My first case of plague... It was an ordinary mud hut, with its tiny unlighted compartments opening on a central court. In one room lay a quantity of clean linen, for the people were Dhobies; in another division was the family cow; and at the moment of our entrance the matter in hand was the lifting of the invalid out of a confined room to a small wooden bed on the verandah. Utterly lethargic he lay there, poor child, a bright promising boy of twelve or fourteen . . . and with the gravest predictions and repeated instructions the doctor hurried off to attend just such another.

It was so little that could be done. Food, medicine and a bath – all these could be given. Yes, and the head could be shaved, ice applied and a fan kept going; but when all was said and done, one was sitting there to watch a human being die – to watch, without hope of saving . . . The evening would come, and he would die. So the doctor had said. Not that I realized this. If I had, I doubt whether I could have driven the mother off at once, as, to my bitter regret, I did, possessed by the notion that isolation and disinfection, the only services I could render, should be thoroughly performed. She was busy near her boy, fanning him perhaps, and constantly inhaling the air that he was breathing out. Did I know she was his mother? I should like to think not. I should like to make any excuse for the fact that I pointed out to her that it would be wise if she sat some distance away. She went at once, crushed and broken-spirited, without a word. But, quietly, the tears began to flow down her poor thin face, and she broke into stifled sobs. That was too much – I found something that she must do, and with careful advice brought her back to do it. And there she sat, thenceforward, curled up beside the pillow with the boy's head at her feet.

He was violent now, and the great effort was to keep him quiet, for one unlucky movement might be fatal. But even in his delirium I had this always before me – the sight of perfect love between a mother and her son. Once, indeed, mistaking me for her, he snatched at my hand, and carried his own to his lips, and often, not catching his mother's eyes, he would smile at me... I was reminded of that moment earlier in the morning, when he had caught the announcement that no barber could be got for him under two or three pice, and struggling to rise from his bed had cried that *he* would bring him for *one*.

He was evidently a good boy, in more senses than one – for every now and then, as a gleam of consciousness would displace the awful look of alienation in the great brown eyes – every now and then he would call loudly upon Shiva, Kali! or repeat words of worship; and nothing soothed and quieted him like the incessant repetition of 'Haribol', the holy name, or the hymn that was commonly sung about the streets at that time:

> Call on the Lord,
> Call on the Lord,
> Call on the Lord, my brother.
> Than this name of the Lord,
> For mortal man
> There is no other way.

'There is no other way,' the weak voice would murmur in snatches after me . . . And so the end came. All day long the family had watched in the courtyard, his mother and myself on the little verandah . . . At five in the afternoon the doctor returned. 'He is getting very low,' he said; 'another hour or two at most and the outburst will end in a collapse of the heart.'

How long the minutes seemed! For the last outburst of violence was very short-lived, and ended in a wild attempt to repeat the 'Haribol' for a length of time. I took up the words, and stood saying them over and over to the movements of the fan, while with a look of relief the lad's head sank back on the pillows. He lay quiet, the breath came in shorter and shorter gasps, and he died.

'Give me twelve instead of one,' said the doctor, 'and I can try steam baths.'

The account given by Dr Radha Govinda Kar is less understated; he was accustomed to dealing with bubonic plague; he was entirely unaccustomed to an English memsahib who not only walked into poor houses and helped with the dirty work, but who accepted with reverence the Hindu love of the mantra, the 'Holy Name of God', which flows unceasingly through the lives and minds of the people, and in speaking which, the devout die unafraid. The mantra is to the Hindu what the sacrament is to the Catholic. The doctor's amazement and enthusiasm were as strong as Nivedita's own enthusiasm for the Hindus, and as freely expressed.

During this calamity, the compassionate figure of Sister Nivedita was seen in every slum of the Baghbazar. She helped others with money without giving a thought to her own condition. At one time when her own diet consisted only of milk and fruits, she gave up milk to meet the medical expenses of a patient . . . That morning I had been to see a plague-stricken patient in a slum in Baghbazar. Sister Nivedita had come to enquire about the arrangements made for the patient and to take upon herself the task of nursing him.

When I went to visit the patient again in the afternoon I saw Sister Nivedita sitting with the child in her lap in the damp and weather-beaten hut in that unhealthy locality . . . She remained engaged in nursing the child in that hut, having abandoned her own house. When the hut was to be disinfected she took a small ladder and began whitewashing the walls herself. Her nursing never slackened even when death was a certainty. After two days, the child lay in eternal sleep in the affectionate lap of the merciful lady.

Vivekananda reacted rather differently. He took her away from plague-nursing and put her on to tackling sanitation.

Swami says my great fault is attempting too much, in which he is emphatically right! I am to give up all thought of plague-nursing and throw my heart and soul into the work of sanitation we now have on hand. This is an infinitely higher proof of self-sacrifice on my part than the delightful excitement of risking plague would be. To my great amusement, when I reported today, he just winked and said, 'Plague, Margot, plague!'

He was concerned to tackle the plague at its source; he may also have been concerned about her exhaustion.

It is so hot, and we have been rushing about so over plague that I feel tired out, body, soul and spirit, and scarcely know how to write, but I could not lie down for very shame, for the children have begun to troop into school.

One of the monks, Swami Sadananda, began to organize groups of boys to sweep the streets; on one occasion when none were forthcoming, Nivedita, who had been helping as well as lecturing and writing to give instructions, took a broom and began to sweep the streets herself, until the neighbourhood boys were shamed into coming to help her.

On 6 April 1899 a letter appeared in the *Statesman*, signed by 'Margaret E. Noble, (Sister) Nivedita', appealing for financial help for plague work from the European community, and making it clear from the opening sentence that the letter was not sent from some Lady Bountiful on a visit, but that the writer lived in the midst of the epidemic, and was already tackling it on a practical level.

Sir, – As one living in the native quarter, and doing what she can to grapple with sanitary necessities here, may I use your valuable paper to appeal for money from those who live in the better-served portions of Calcutta?

It is well known that the Town Conservancy has an insuperable difficulty to deal with in the first six wards – not in the bustees alone. But only those who have examined a bustee personally can have any idea of the number of huts and little bye-lanes or the length of drainage that the term includes. An irregular rambling village is our nearest equivalent . . . Either outside or within the outermost of these rows of cottages runs a narrow open stone channel that serves all the purposes of drainage, whatever its condition, its importance to the people is incalculable . . .

When the readers had recovered from the shock of learning that she *had* examined a bustee personally, they learned in extreme detail – and she spared them nothing, in a long letter – of what the sanitary conditions were, and what she was doing, of how the people,

once assured that we are private persons working from disinterested motives, begged our help in interior cleansing, and have listened gladly to our advice about sanitation and disinfectants. They have allowed and even invited us to enter their houses, and have not been afraid to show us their terrible poverty. There are something like a couple of miles of drain and lane, three days ago unutterably filthy, where today an English woman can walk without annoyance.

She finished the letter with an appeal for funds.

Next day, 7 April, a letter signed 'A Ratepayer' appeared in the *Statesman*, cheering her on, but asking – inevitably – what about the rates? A certain sardonic note in this letter probably speaks with the voice of experience and is directed, not at Nivedita, whom he praises, but at the Municipal Executive, whom he does not.

There can be no doubt that, if private individuals subscribe funds, and organise private conservancy parties, we shall at no distant date have the town so much cleaner than it is, that we may expect (even if we don't get it) an appreciable decline in the death-rate. But will the Municipality, in consideration of our taking matters into our own hands, and doing their work for them, remit any portion of our taxes? We cannot all pay both the taxes and the subscriptions which the scheme set forth in your correspondent's letter calls for . . .

On 1 May, a newspaper report described a lecture delivered by Nivedita, and introduced by Swami Vivekananda at the Classic Theatre in Beadon Street, to a large audience of college students, many professors from the various colleges, and some European men and women. Here she went into even further detail of the sanitary conditions of the street, and appalled her audience. She attributed the cause of throwing refuse on the roads to the Zenana system of female segregation which kept the women indoors and off the streets, which prevents women realizing the state of their surroundings, or the bearing of private cleanliness on the public weal – and also to ignorance of the first principles of health and comfort. We must remember that in cases like that of this large bustee, whatever effort a woman might make, she could never take the household refuse far enough from a remote house to be placed on the line of the conservancy cart.

She attacked with fury the suggestion that the responsibility of setting matters right lay with the owners of the huts.

Are men who owe two rents already – one to the landowners and one to the moneylenders – are these men, starved as they are out of poverty, to be made the trustees of the health of one of the greatest cities and most important ports of the world? And until they can afford to set things right are we to sit with folded hands and submit to the ravages of plague? . . . We want one thing, the education of the people by practical example. Let us with our own hands perform the necessary service. Let us glory in the shame of such service before the people. . . .

At the close of the meeting, the paper records, 'a large number of people came up and enrolled themselves as volunteers in the work proposed'.

She went on lecturing, writing letters to the papers, appealing for funds, rolling up her sleeves and supervising the worker boys, striding into houses where she was asked for help; there is a vigour and a delight in tackling difficulties where she could be of real, practical use, that sounds clearly in everything she wrote at that time.

One of the first and greatest services rendered by plague has lain in the humanizing of the lower castes. Their labour is at this moment in high demand. Bright little sweeper-boys command the wages of full-grown men, with short hours and plenty of encouragement and stimulus to work. How proud of themselves the conservancy gangs look, spades in their hands and buckets on their shoulders! . . . The real inferiority of the lower castes is that they require so much organization and superintendence from their more fortunate countrymen. In the case of the one gang in which I am interested, three people devote time and attention to overlooking the labour, and under these, again, there is the foreman of the gang, and every bit of this is absolutely necessary.

One of the most intolerable evils is the arrangement of bamboo 'sanitary structures' in large clusters in the very centre and in close contact with dwelling huts. These and the tanks which continually receive sewage and other contaminations from the Bustees, constitute the great permanent nuisances of the town. Nothing short of complete effacement could be efficient sanitation . . .

In the pursuit of difficulties there is, I find, a limit at which toil becomes more or less sullen and despairing . . . Anyway, whatever may be the future of our boys, for the present they are full of fun and enthusiasm. A really bad drain is quite a find to them all.

7

The plague epidemic broke out in March, but before that, Nivedita had been giving four public lectures. These were her first important introduction to Hindu audiences. Characteristically, she began her lecturing career by choosing a controversial subject which was causing enormous disagreement amongst Hindus themselves. She put a spark to highly inflammable tinder. She spoke about Kali-worship, and praised it highly, at the very moment when many Hindu religious leaders were claiming that the worship of Kali when indulged in by those who were not Yogis, mystics or seers, simply resulted in animal sacrifice, debauchery, and everything that appealed to the lowest instincts of the mob; however true, theologically speaking, might be the belief that God, worshipped as 'Mother', represents 'Maya', the illusion of life, and holds both blessings and horror in her hands for her children, so that the terrible as well as the good should be worshipped in order to transcend both.

On 13 February 1899 she lectured to a huge audience at the Albert Hall, Calcutta. She had previously discussed her lecture with Vivekananda, who approved it. The hall was packed. For an Englishwoman to speak there at all was startling enough. For her to speak on Kali-worship was unbelievable. Most of her audience probably agreed with her opening sentence, 'I am aware that I have little right to stand here, and offer myself as lecturer on Kali-worship.'

She opened the lecture with a gentle and reasonable account, to which no exception could be taken, of the 'Motherhood' of God, using all religions as illustrations, including the Catholic veneration of the Virgin Mary, the tenderness of Jesus Christ towards little children, the Semitic teaching, 'Like as a *father* pitieth his children', and the Aryan, 'Like as a mother pitieth her children', and culminating in the three Hindu concepts of motherhood as symbols of God: Durga, Jagaddhatri, and Kali.

So far, so good. Using Christianity as an illustration, she thanked God for 'certain elements of crudity and superstition that Christianity contains, that carry it to places that without these it could never reach', and then carried this plea for 'as many men, so many paths' into a much more controversial form, with the words, 'the man who derives brutal satisfaction from life, or who sees no further than the surface of things, this man has a right to find these satisfactions, and to make for himself a worship which shall express these instincts'.

She was moving on to difficult ground here. Her next statement was 'He who with precisely the same instincts as these, is full of the pity of life and of creation – pitiful and compassionate – will see in God, the Refuge of all – the Divine Mother – pitiful and compassionate.' This, as her audience knew, side-stepped the question of where the line was to be drawn, if indeed it could be drawn at all, and how much toleration was to be given to those whose idea of Kali-worship had become progressively debased. One British woman on a platform, arguing the extreme of one type of Hinduism, against a divided audience of Hindus. She was not prepared to tell them how to set their house in order. Her thesis was, 'reform, do not destroy or forbid'.

The audience was becoming both restive and excited. 'No betrayal of truth is so terrible as that of choosing what is beautiful and easy and soft, to be believed and worshipped. Let us face also, just as willingly, the terrible – the ugly – the hard.'

But it was the sacrificial goats who had to face it, in this instance, as the audience knew. As usual Nivedita was driving straight for the basic truth of a subject with arguments that were not always logical, and were sometimes more idealistic than exact, but which forced her audience to argue, to discuss and to think things out. She claimed that the sacrifice of animals to a god was no worse than man's constant killing of animals for his own use, which was hardly the point. But she slashed hard at the 'faction-squabbling' which was muddling the whole issue in the city at that time, and she also explained why she, as a Westerner, accepted the hideousness of the Kali-statue without the revulsion with which most Westerners regarded it. Kali danced on the inert form of her husband, wearing a garland of skulls around her neck, two hands holding a sword and a severed head, two hands outstretched in motherly blessing. Black as a raincloud, beautiful and hideous, the paradox of ultimates.

Is that the picture of a young Hindu woman? She that has no individual existence apart from her husband, she that is so graceful, unobtrusive, retiring, always covered from head to foot, always the gentle, the soft, the loving mother. If anything, Kali is the exact reverse of the Hindu woman.

And it is precisely this, Nivedita maintained, that contains the meaning of a very great symbol which must never be forgotten or lost.

> If Kali were painted as the ideal Hindu woman, she would have been real. To convey her unreality – as she shows herself, she is painted as the ideal *non*-woman . . . the universe of phenomena which frightens us with its innumerable terrible faces is in reality but a *show*, a false appearance, the one truth being the Sat-chit-ananda (ultimate bliss) which is back of it all . . . she has to be seen through, she has to be crossed over . . . The seer tells Kali that she is not what she seems, she is really Brahman (the Ultimate, beyond the illusion of Maya) and in no other light would he see her.

Already she was thinking in Hindu terms, and beginning to see the difference there must always be between her approach to Hindu audiences, and to Westerners. Vivekananda considered the 'Kali-issue' as entirely a Hindu one. 'The worship of the terrible,' he had told her, 'was a truth for heroes.' The bulk of mankind would always think of God as a Divine Providence, a tender preserver, and the great difficulty, especially for the West, was how to link this with the highest philosophy, and the highest experience in meditation, in which both good and evil were accepted in order that both might eventually be transcended, to reach the state which was beyond both; whilst at the same time the individual threw his own weight always on the side of the good. As he once wrote in a letter to Mary Hale, 'Kali-worship is *not* a necessary step in any religion, I only preach what is good for universal humanity.'

But today Nivedita was considering a local issue which concerned Hindus.

In her own mind, though, she did not say so, she had never been happy about the animal-sacrifices or the many abuses that had grown up around Kali-worship. But she never saw it as her duty to tell Indians what to do and how to do it. She made the principle clear, as she saw it, and left the application of the principle to them. In the course of it, as usual, she stirred up argument, irritated some and roused others to enthusiasm, raised several important issues which she did not fully answer, and then ended with a clear declaration of her own views.

> We are aware of the many beastly and corrupt rites which have come to be associated with Kali-worship. While our regret for them is boundless, we do not see the wisdom of inveighing against Kali-worship in the wholesale manner as is often done by some of our sisters and brothers. Destroy the weeds, but save the garden!

Dr Mahendralal Sarkar then spoke against her lecture, objecting that she was praising a superstition which they were trying to eradicate. This roused a member of the audience who was a fervent devotee of Kali, who shouted him down. Emotion in the audience came near to the point of riot, the chairman was unable to restore order, and at last Nivedita herself, who was used to difficult audiences and on the whole rather enjoyed them, calmed the situation.

Two days later she wrote:

> My lecture on Kali came off on Monday. The Albert Hall was crammed. The chairman spoke against Kali and me, and was very touching, when unfortunately a devotee got up and amidst tremendous excitement called him all sorts of names. I am sorry to tell you that I laugh whenever I think about it all. Swami was greatly pleased with the lecture, and I trust there is some reason, for I have several times since been inclined to think that I had done nothing but harm.

However, the Haldars of Kalighat invited her to speak again on Kali at the Kalighat Temple. She was a little dubious about the wisdom of this, but Vivekananda told her that she would be striking a blow against exclusiveness. She accepted.

This time, she prepared answers to the questions which had been raised at the Albert Hall, first consulting Vivekananda and his brother monks. Vivekananda had once condemned image-worship and symbolism of every kind, believing as he did in the heights of abstract-philosophy of Advaita Vedanta. This had been the main point of his six-year-long struggle with his own master, Sri Ramakrishna, who had taught that the Ultimate – inexpressible and beyond all that we now know – can indeed be experienced in this life, but it is Maya, this 'universe and state of things which we now see and experience', which is symbolized by Mother Kali; and ultimate Brahman and 'Shakti' are one, just as fire and its heat, milk and its whiteness, or the snake lying still and the snake moving, are one. 'How I used to hate Kali!' Vivekananda said. 'And all her ways! . . . But I had to accept her at last! Ramakrishna Paramahamsa dedicated me to her and now I believe that she guides me in every little thing I do, and does with me what She will.'

Nivedita knew of his experiences in the Himalayas, and the continual balance he kept between the religion of austerity and philosophy, and the childlike acceptance of God. He had returned from Kshir-Bhowani saying 'These gods are not merely symbols! They are the forms which the Bhaktas have seen!'

The issue was a crucial one at that time. Kali symbolized the acceptance of suffering and evil as being as much a part of the whole, and, ultimately, a good part, could we stand far enough back to see it, as the good, the love and the blessing. Christianity, through the missionaries, was teaching Hindus that evil was in some way separate from good; something that God, as it were, regretted. It seemed to Nivedita totally unacceptable to assume that God was *only* kind; it did not fit the observable facts; she did not believe that God could be all-benevolent *and* omnipotent. It was precisely this point which had wracked her for so long in England, before she met Vivekananda. In every way she was drawn to the Kali concept. As for image-worship in general, she had already accepted that some natures need a concrete form as a focus for devotion, and visions of the gods were as true an experience to some, as the highest reaches of philosophy were to others.

Perhaps there was something stormy in her own nature which responded to the symbolism of Kali; certainly she had no fear of the terrible, and she had seen enough suffering; while the finest side of her own nature was a gentle and motherly one. The two sides of her nature often clashed, and in Kali-worship the clash may have been echoed, and resolved for her.

Since this could to some extent be said of all human beings, it seemed to her that Kali-worship should be encouraged. The opposition claimed, roughly speaking (and there was plenty of rough speaking), that this was all very well, in theory, but could not be justified in fact.

She gave the lecture on Sunday, 28 May, at 5 p.m. before a crowd of nearly three thousand. Vivekananda, who was an increasingly sick man, was not able to come, but he asked her to insist that if any of her European friends attended, they should enter barefoot, as a mark of respect to the temple worship, and to the subject, as the Hindus did. Nivedita did so, and she herself walked to the temple in bare feet. Her lecture was an enormous success, and ended with the words:

> It was so easy to say that God is love, and to think our own private happiness proves it. God is love – but when do we learn that? How do we know it? Is it not in moments of anguish in our own lives, that the great reality is borne in upon us as all Love, all Beauty, all Bliss? This was the paradox so boldly stated in the image – this paradox of nature and of the universe and of the soul of man – that She who stands there surrounded by all that is terrible to humanity is nevertheless, the mother, and all we, her babes.

This symbolism of Kali grew more and more strongly into her thinking and meditation as her life proceeded; not Kali-worship in its crude and brutal deterioration from the original concept, which was so often, understandably, criticized, but Kali who was worshipped with total love by the gentle and compassionate Sri Ramakrishna, whose own nature was, Vivekananda told her, 'as soft as flowers, as hard as adamant!'

Sometimes Vivekananda referred to Kali-worship as the worship of death. Once Nivedita dreamed that a short road led up to Kali, but the nearer she approached, the further back from her Kali went, till at last Kali became a lofty black door at the end of the path. Beyond that door lay the infinite ocean of Bliss which was Ultimate Brahman, and, she understood that Kali was death.

In March 1899 Nivedita was ordained a Naisthika Brahmacharini, which might be described as a second and more complete vow, 'for life', which left her still a novice; in India a notiviate is a long business, and monks of the Order might be required to serve a fifteen-year novitiate. In April she asked Vivekananda what more she must do to be worthy of becoming a full Sannyasini (or nun). He replied, 'You just keep as you are', and she decided that if this was his wish, she would remain in what might seem to Westerners to be a 'semi-fledged' state, for the rest of her life. Later events showed the wisdom and necessity of this: as a 'fully fledged nun' her future life would have been very different. The 'intermediate' state – roughly corresponding, perhaps, to the life of a lay-sister in a Catholic convent – permitted more active contact with the outside world, more mixing with people who were living a non-monastic life. As well as her public lectures, there was also her school to be considered. There were now thirty girls on the roll. But the school had been started with a small sum of money given to Vivekananda by the Raja of Kashmir, plus Nivedita's own savings. There was no permanent fund nor steady source of income, and he was not happy about the future she might have to face. There was very little hope of money from a country which could hardly feed its own inhabitants, and in which state funds were administered by a foreign power. He wanted her to take boarders, and to train child widows whose child husbands had died, and who therefore faced a life of virginity, since by Hindu custom remarriage was forbidden. The other girls were taken away from school for marriage long before their education was completed. He raged against the marriage of little girls, but he was a realist. The law could not be changed overnight. Child widows were regarded with respect, as little nuns, with shaven heads; they could be the educators of the immediate future.

The tiny school was still at a very experimental stage. Nivedita taught the children in relays; four classes of two hours each. Her knowledge of Bengali was limited, so craftwork and kindergarten techniques occupied most of the time. There was no doubt of the popularity of these classes amongst the children. They disapproved strongly of the Western habit of closing the school on Saturdays and Sundays.

I remember how the first Saturday morning a crowd of uproarious little people had gathered outside the door at six o'clock, evidently determined to gain admission. A workman who could speak a little English was inside and he came to me. 'The baby people, the baby people, Miss Sahib! Let me open!'

Vivekananda had decided to go back to America for another tour, and suggested that she should go with him. Arrangements could be made with some lecture bureau in America that would help her to earn money for the school; perhaps people would contribute a minimum of one penny, two cents, or one anna a year. She was delighted. 'I believe in tiny subscriptions to work done for the people, by the people, as a joy to the worker and the user.'

She was still thinking in small terms, still charmed by the concept of her own place in this microcosm of the emancipation of women. Memories of life in England made her think of the making of jam and chutney by the girls, for sale. It is startling, in her later years when she dominated a greater and more public stage, to read her rapture, in those early years, about the possibility of this small and humble project, in a letter to Josephine MacLeod.

You have no idea of the deliciousness of green mango jam. And of course, you know Bengali chutney. I am sure we can do this, and it would be widening the scope of our work educationally. To be managed entirely by women, think of that! Of course, we would make a very small beginning. Oh, I am dying to really *earn* what we want!

'To be managed entirely by women, think of that!' Eric Hammond who, in England, had written of her, 'the fiercer the fight, the happier she grew', had also noted her militant feminism. 'She appeared to find joy in stinging men with a lash of caustic criticism; in making them comprehend that, in her consciousness, women occupied a loftier level than Man was destined to attain.'

Vivekananda, who knew her fighting qualities, and encouraged them, knew also the emotional, excitable and motherly side of her nature which possibly Eric Hammond had not been shown. He was fully aware of her feminism and even of her passion for the manufacture of chutney and jam. He did not allow her to take herself too seriously in some matters. Later, in a letter to Mrs Frances Leggett, from Paris, when he had been attending a 'Congress of Religions', he commented:

We had a congress of cranks, here in this house.

We were having great difficulty in electing the president . . . I proposed Joe [Josephine MacLeod] but she refused on the ground of non-arrival of her new gown – and went to a corner to watch the scene, from a coign of vantage . . .

'Chutney is the thing,' said a voice near the door. We all looked back, and saw Margot. 'It is chutney,' she said, 'chutney and Kali, that will remove all difficulties of life, and make it easy for us to swallow all evils, and relish what is good.' But she stopped all of a sudden, and vehemently asserted that she was not going to speak any further, as she had been obstructed by a certain male animal in the audience. She was sure one man in the audience had his head turned towards the window and was not paying the attention proper to a lady, and though as to herself she believed in the equality of the sexes, yet she wanted to know the reason of that disgusting man's want of due respect for women. Then one and all declared that they had been giving her the most undivided attention, and all above the equal right, her due, but to no purpose. Margot would have nothing to do with that horrible crowd, and sat down.

Very little seems to have escaped Vivekananda. He had seen her passion for the British rule as the dangerous inconsistency it certainly was, for a woman who identified herself with the Hindus and had fought for Irish Home Rule; he saw that in driving herself too hard in the plague outbreak, she was endangering herself and the work; his enthusiasm for the emancipation of Hindu women, and his admiration of emancipated womanhood in the West, was balanced by a flat refusal on his part to offer the gallantries and excessive courtesies to women that were fashionable then: he regarded this as an insult. There is very much both of Nivedita and of his observation of her, in that dry comment, 'though as to herself she believed in the equality of the sexes, yet she wanted to know the reason of that disgusting man's want of due respect for women'.

Now he proposed that she should come with him to America, to lecture to American women about the life of women in India, and to collect a little money, if possible, for the school. She was going to see him in a very different background; she would be stepping on to a wider field herself and addressing audiences without him, audiences who would not necessarily be as enraptured as the Hindus had been.

It was arranged that in June, Vivekananda and a brother monk should sail to England. Nivedita would accompany them. She was to stay in England for a while to attend the wedding of her sister May and then she too would cross the Atlantic to America.

Before the little school closed for the summer holidays in mid-May (for it was now that the most intense heat of the year was beginning) she took the children to visit the museum, and arranged a little exhibition of their paper-work, sewing, and painting, in a room in Sarada Devi's house, which was visited by the women and children of the locality. This was, indeed, something very new for young girls. They were delighted about it, though not so happy to hear that Nivedita was leaving them. She promised that she would come back.

They were sailing on 20 June. Nivedita spent the morning of 18 June with Sarada Devi; she was going from one land to another, indeed from one mother to another, and she had moved a long way from the doubts and uncertainties of her arrival in India. In the evening she went to the monastery at Belur (the Belur Math) where a tea party was arranged in her honour, and flowers and a farewell address were given to her.

She went on to the Temple of Dakshineswar, which had been the home of Sri Ramakrishna, and stayed there in meditation until the late evening, when she returned home in pouring rain.

On the evening of 20 June 1899 monks and friends assembled at Prinseps dock to wave the party good-bye as they sailed on the *Golconda*. As usual, in the heat of the summer evening, all Calcutta seemed to be pouring out of the streets and the overcrowded city, down to the river, in search of air. The colours were bright, the evening air was unlike the air of an English summer. Once again, she was between two worlds.

8

The voyage of the *Golconda* was a rough one from the beginning. In the Bay of Bengal the ship was tossed on mounting waves; it was the time of the monsoon. The contrast with Nivedita's quieter passage to India from England was not a matter of regret, however. Then she had been deeply lonely, uncertain of herself and of the step she was taking. Now she was returning home to Wimbledon, travelling with Vivekananda and his brother monk Turiyananda. To be with Vivekananda all day, listening to him talk, putting questions; this was an opportunity that thousands in India and elsewhere, would have envied her. It was the last prolonged period of time that she was to have with him. She wrote afterwards, 'To this voyage of six weeks I look back as the greatest occasion of my life.'

On 24 June they reached Madras. The news of Vivekananda's arrival had been telegraphed ahead, and a great crowd was waiting to greet him. They were disappointed, however. Because of the outbreak of plague in Calcutta, passengers from the *Golconda* were not allowed to land in case they should bring infection to Madras.

Nivedita stood on deck all day, watching well-wishers come as close as they could, in small boats, to greet Vivekananda and his party, who stood at the rail to talk to them. Gifts of fruit and flowers were passed up from the little boats. Nothing more than this was allowed, to her great relief. He was completely exhausted, and a day of crowds, processions, and the giving of public talks would have been more than his health could stand. '. . . It was sufficiently tiring to have to look down and be polite to the constant succession of boat-loads who came to the ship's side with presents and addresses all day.'

Then they sailed on to Colombo, where again he received a great ovation. They landed here and Nivedita had a chance to visit some schools; one of her many ideas, which did not materialize, was to start a school at Colombo.

On 28 June they left Colombo, and the sea remained very rough all the way to Aden. The weather was at its fiercest at Socotra. The captain of the ship told Vivekananda that this was the very central point of the monsoon.

Vivekananda exulted in it. The sea-air, the leisure, the peace, were all improving his health. In particular his asthma improved, after the choking, humid heat of Calcutta. He walked round the deck with Turiyananda, taking daily exercise; as usual, his mind was working endlessly and he talked, discussed, and explained. He was also writing some Bengali articles for the journal published by his Order. They were later collected and made into a book, called *Parivraja* or *The Wandering Monk*. It was a humorous book, interspersed with serious thoughts, and is untranslatable in its own native Bengali spirit; it was almost a work by a potential 'Mark Twain' of Bengali literature.

Nivedita began to see that this voyage was an opportunity that must not be wasted. She spent every minute with him that she could, refusing all invitations from other passengers to talk or take up her time, and when she was not with him she spent her time in writing and needlework. She wanted to be ready constantly to take down and keep everything that he said. 'From the beginning of the voyage to the end, the flow of thought and story went on.' The man himself had always been too busy to write very much down. He wrote letters to friends and disciples, endlessly. They poured from him, and into those went some of his greatest sayings. At the end of her life, Nivedita collected his letters for publication. His lectures had been taken down for publication by his faithful English disciple Goodwin, now so recently dead. Some were lost for ever. He read, thought, formulated ideas and discussed; he slept very little; he seemed to pass across the world from country to country like a cyclone, leaving behind brother monks to start and maintain Vedanta groups. He had no time for writing. 'I have no time even to *die*,' as he said in more impatient moments.

Nivedita saw that his ideas, which were still being shaped and clarified, must be preserved. She listened to everything he said, and wrote it all down afterwards. 'I listened with an anxious mind, striving to treasure up each word that he let fall. For I knew that here I was but the transmitter, but the bridge, between him and that countless host of his own people, who would yet arise, and seek to make good his dreams.' He had a habit of leaping straight into discussions at almost any time, and she had to be ready.

One morning she met him walking on the deck with Turiyananda before breakfast, and with the words, 'I have just been talking to Turiyananda about conservative and liberal ideas', she realized that they were off on a discussion at full gallop, and breakfast could wait. This time it was the 'conservative' East as against the 'liberal' West, with submission shown as the ideal in the East, and struggle as being more admired in the West, a point to which he often returned on the voyage. He questioned Buddha's teaching of non-resistance or non-injury, which he admired, but saw behind it the danger of weakness. 'It is weakness that conceives the idea of resistance. I do not think of punishing or escaping from a drop of sea-spray. It is nothing to me. Yet to the mosquito it would be serious. Now, I would make all injury like that. Strength and fearlessness.' This seemed to him to be the same thing as non-injury, but a wiser way of regarding it. This morning, he finished, typically, 'It is selfishness that we must seek to eliminate! Whenever I have made a mistake in my life, it has always been because *self* entered into the calculation. Where self has not been involved, my judgement has gone straight to the mark.'

She had always been a woman who loved ideas. Practical as she was, and much as she enjoyed vigorous action, her energy poured into ideas as well. Throughout her life in England, discussion groups had sprung up wherever she went, and her friendships with men of ideas as well as men of action were already beginning to make her known in liberal, political, and philosophical circles. The cause of much of her championing of women and her bitterness against men in general, apart from a few brilliant men of broadminded views, was that she was unable in England to be accepted as an 'ideas woman', for this was unfashionable. She might have been acceptable as an 'unpractical intellectual', which she was not; or as a practical woman of simple faith who worked hard for humanity, but left the thinking to the men; which, also, she was not.

Now, more patient and receptive than she had been at Almora, she listened, she discussed, she treasured carefully everything that was said, and wrote it down afterwards. Writing and needlework. It is probable that, of the two, needlework took second place on that voyage.

Vivekananda enjoyed talking to her. He had instructed Turiyananda to remind him each day when the time for his walk on the deck, for exercise, arrived, but now he replied, when reminded, 'Not today. I am keeping quite well on board. And I am now talking to Nivedita. She is a foreigner and has left her country to learn about these things from me. She is very intelligent and I feel great pleasure in talking to her.'

Because she was 'a foreigner', though becoming rapidly less and less so, she asked him many things that were not always clear to her. For instance, 'What I want to understand, is this habit of always seeing people from their strongest aspect. Where did it come from?'

He thought about it, and answered at last that it was rooted in the training given by Sri Ramakrishna, who had come to it by the much more difficult path of eating, dressing, feeling, worshipping in the way of different faiths and types of people, and so proving to himself that he could reach the same high spiritual state by treading these different paths. He quoted Sri Ramakrishna's words, 'One must learn to put oneself into another man's very soul!'

So she came to see that to him, a nationality, a person, a religion, an individual, had all the sacredness of a church, 'a church whose inmost striving was to express its own conception of ideal manhood'.

In discussing the future of the women's work with her, he explained, 'You have to set yourself to Hinduize your thoughts, your needs, your conceptions and your habits. Your life, internal and external, has to become all that an orthodox Hindu Brahmin Brahmacharini's ought to be.' As she realized, 'in the case of a worker, he knew how to substitute for the walls of a convent, the Indian people and their life'.

But now that he had more time, on the voyage, he explained, carefully and exactly, the necessity of training herself in an Eastern calm which was not a superficial placidity, but was what the West might call 'recollectedness and peace', which he described to her as being not the mark of saintliness but the self-control of a truly adult character. The expression of emotionalism, and the constant display of one's own reactions, he regarded as simply childish.

> It was in this way that he laboured to overcome that restlessness and emphasis of Western manners, which appears to the Eastern-mind so crude. The constant expression of feeling, whether of pain, admiration, or surprise, was to him shocking. It was not necessary to stigmatize it as irreligious, for it was ill-bred.

Reading these words, it is possible to see how far she had come in her acceptance of his thinking. The extent to which she was ever able to put it into practice was a different matter, especially in her later career; but at least she accepted it, and she struggled to live up to it.

The Oriental expects of a man that he should feel, and keep his feeling to himself. Any constant pointing-out of the curious or the beautiful appears to him an unwarrantable intrusion on the privacy and self-directedness of thought.

The phrase 'struggle to realize yourself without a trace of emotion!' seems very far indeed from the emotional, excitable, and easily elated or depressed strand in Nivedita's character. And yet the other strand in her, so constantly noticed by those who knew her, and those who saw her by the bedside of the dying or waiting patiently outside temples where she was not permitted to enter, may have rejoiced in that instruction. Her self-abnegation was as strong as her gushing emotion; always an extremist, she was capable of that extreme too, and the sweetness in her nature was particularly strong during Vivekananda's lifetime. She accepted the instruction, and here in the peacefulness of the voyage, there were no problems about it. This was not a moment of what he sometimes called 'fuss and botheration'.

She was particularly eager to discover how he visualized the future of Indian women. He constantly emphasized that the best of the 'old way' must never be lost in the development of new lives for women, or India would be ruined. How to combine the two was the problem; he saw it as a long slow development and refused to be too definite about the future, for these problems must be solved by women themselves. 'Only let Women and the People achieve education': after that, they would be competent to settle their own future. He mistrusted theories that became too 'set'. 'Formed' and 'dead', with him, were synonymous. A social formation that was fixed, was like a tree that had ceased to grow.

But there were certain absolutes on which he was adamant. Chastity was the greatest. During the voyage, some missionaries travelling on the ship were displaying silver wedding bracelets which they had bought from Tamil women who had been forced to sell them, in famine, to buy food. Nothing but the threat of starvation for their families would have forced them to part with the wedding bracelets. The conversation turned to the superstitious dislike that wives, whether of East or West, have always felt, of taking off or giving up wedding rings and bracelets. ' "You call it a *superstition*?" exclaimed the Swami, in low pained tones of astonishment. "You cannot see the great ideal of chastity behind it?" '

The woman of the future, he told her, must be as faithful, chaste and devoted, as a wife, as the Hindu woman had always been, though probably with more freedom of choice and more encouragement of individuality than before. 'He could not foresee a Hindu woman of the future entirely without the old power of meditation. Modern science women must learn; but not at the cost of the ancient spirituality.'

He was fascinated to consider the possible ways of training little girls in Nivedita's school. He suggested that they might have a Vedic altar, so that the children themselves could share in the service of lighting the Vedic fire. Dogs, cats, and birds could be looked after and fed; he hoped for a renewal of the old arts and crafts, with painting, photography and embroidery added. And not only book-learning, but above all else, the children should learn the worship of humanity. 'Let your women develop it. Make poetry, make art of it.' This might include the feeding, nursing and care of real babies, not only dolls. It was all to be part of 'the worship of humanity'. He was never fond of the word 'compassion' or 'pity'; the worship of the god in man by serving one's fellow-man, was the great worship that he wanted the children to learn. It was to be a worship and a privilege, not a kindly charity. ('A God who could not in this life give a crust of bread, was not to be trusted in the next for the Kingdom of Heaven.')

She wrote down and remembered all that he said during the voyage about his hopes, his ideas, everything from modern politics to his views on Buddhism. But of greatest interest to her were the few glimpses of his own life that he gave. It had been very rare indeed for him to talk about himself.

She already knew a little more of his boyhood.

> Then he talked of the fever of longing to reach God, that had wakened in him as a boy, and of how he would begin repeating a text before sunrise, and remain all day repeating it, without stirring. He was trying here to explain the idea of Tapasya [a self-discipline of religious austerity].

Now he told her more about it.

> He drifted into a talk that I can never forget. First he explained how everything, short of the absolute control of mind, word and deed, was but 'the sowing of wild oats'. Then he told how the religious who failed would sometimes be born again to a throne, 'there to sow his wild oats' in gratifying that particular desire which had led to his downfall. 'A memory of the religious habit,' he said, 'often haunts the throne.' For one of the signs of greatness was held to be the persistence of a faint memory. . . . Carried away by the talk of memory, he lifted the visor for a moment, on his own soul. 'And whatever you may think,' he said, turning to me suddenly and addressing me by name, 'I have such a memory!'

He told her how, when he was two years old, he would play at 'being a holy man', and if a wandering monk came to the house to beg, his mother locked him away upstairs to prevent his giving too much away. He felt that he was a monk, too, at that age and that for some mischief he had been 'sent away from Shiva'. His family increased this feeling . . . 'When I was very rebellious, they would empty a can of water over me, saying "Shiva! Shiva!" And then I was all right, always. Even now, when I feel mischievous, that word keeps me straight. "No!" I say to myself, "not this time!" '

'Even now when I feel mischievous' was spoken by a man whose life seemed to her to have been in many ways one long tapasya. She knew that he had been destined by his family to be a lawyer, educated at Calcutta University. As a young man, difficult, brilliant, argumentative, cynical and full of Western doubts, refusing to accept anything that did not seem to him to be true, with a startling ability to concentrate and a total recall which enabled him to repeat whole chapters of a book long after he had read it, he came to Sri Ramakrishna, who was living in his one room in the Temple Gardens at Dakshineswar. He did not capitulate easily; indeed, at first he thought this holy man was mad. His change to the life of a monk was a very slow one, not completed until the death of Ramakrishna six years later. In the meantime, Vivekananda's father died, and as he became head of the household he had to support his mother and younger brothers and his sisters, in an abrupt descent into poverty. He was then so poor that often he stayed away from home, pretending that he had eaten, so that there was one less mouth to feed at the family table. He wandered from office to office, trying to find a job. When a friend sang a song about the overflowing grace of God, Vivekananda told him to shut up, as such songs were only for those born with a silver spoon in their mouths, and no starving relatives at home. He was discovering that in India people did, in fact, starve. As he said later, at that time his constant thought was 'Does God really exist? Then why is there so much woe in his kingdom? . . . *I was exceedingly cross with God!*'

When Ramakrishna died, he left his disciples (one of whom was Vivekananda), a wife, Sarada Devi, and nothing else. He had lived in one room, owning nothing. As he lay dying of cancer he never ceased to teach, to help, to give to all who came to him. Vivekananda became his for life. Everything that he later became, belonged to Ramakrishna 'who *was* that great life' as Vivekananda said; but his disciple had to give to the truths his guru had lived out, a form and an expression for the modern world. He travelled through India on foot, heartbroken by the poverty he saw. He became determined to feed the starving in their thousands and ten thousands, and to bring hope to the lives of Indian women. All this would mean money and an organized monastic Order, while his entire instinct and longing was for the life of the scholar and the wandering monk. He had no illusions about organizations, still less about money. And he regarded spiritual freedom as a greater gift to bring to the world, ultimately, than freedom from hunger. So began the long years of struggle, and the fame which he did not want. Though he expressed, especially in his book *Jnana Yoga*, all the greatest heights of philosophy for which the West was asking him, always he came back to the simplicities.

His voice sank into silence, and we sat looking out over the starlit sea. Then he took up the thread again. 'As I grow older I find that I look more and more for greatness in *little* things. I want to know what a great man eats and wears, and how he speaks to his servants. I want to find a Sir Philip Sidney – greatness! Few men would remember the thirst of others, even in the moment of death.

But anyone will be great in a great position! Even the coward will grow brave in the glare of the footlights . . .

More and more the true greatness seems to me that of the worm, doing its duty silently, steadily, from moment to moment, and hour to hour.'

Some moments remained in her mind, in the years ahead.

Some of the most beautiful scenes in the world have been made for me more beautiful by listening, in their midst, to these long soliloquies.

It was dark when we approached Sicily, and against the sunset sky, Etna was in slight eruption. As we entered the straits of Messina, the moon rose, and I walked up and down the deck beside the Swami, while he dwelt on the fact that beauty is not external, but already in the mind. On one side frowned the dark crags of the Italian coast, on the other, the island was touched with silver light. 'Messina must thank *me*!' he said. 'It is I who give her all her beauty!'

She had never been so happy in her life before. Perhaps she was never quite so happy again, in the simple sense of an American expression he had once used in a lecture:

'If a bad time comes, what of that? The pendulum must swing back to the other side. But that is no better. The thing to do is to stop it.' As American children used to say when swinging, when they let the swing slow down until it hung quite still, he added, 'Let the old cat die.'

Sister Nivedita

Sri Ramakrishna

Swami Vivekananda

Below, left to right: Miss Josephine MacLeod, Mrs Ole Bull, Swami Vivekananda and Sister Nivedita in Kashmir, 1898

All her life, she swung between emotion and calm, energy and quietness, militancy and motherliness, the extreme of hope, and sudden depression. On this voyage it all ceased; even work ceased for a while. The swing had slowed down. It became still. For six weeks, she lived in the moment, content.

She landed at Tilbury dock bringing a little of that peace with her. The family were waiting to meet her, with some friends and disciples of Vivekananda, including Christine Greenstidel who had come from Detroit simply to meet him. If Christine and Nivedita had never met, their lives would have been different. But for the moment, they met and parted.

Nivedita and her family went home to Wimbledon, and took Vivekananda with them.

The trees were green and shady on Wimbledon Common, and every house had its small neat garden, where late roses bloomed on the trellises in an English summer that was light and cool after the burden of heat in Calcutta, with a small breeze blowing across the privet hedges.

The swing had hung unmoving and at peace for six weeks, and now very slowly but gathering speed, she knew that it was beginning to swing again.

9

The first days of the homecoming to the house in Wimbledon High Street were happy ones. The preparations for 'Margot's' return, the excitement of May's forthcoming wedding, the meeting with Vivekananda, her obvious delight in her life in India; there was plenty of cause for happiness.

But the reunion took courage as well. Probably only Vivekananda realized to the full how much Nivedita was pulled in two directions, how difficult readjustment might be. England was still home, its roots reaching down to her childhood. But India was much more home to her now. She had been trained to the life of a Hindu nun, in the smallest particular; she had her own house in Bosepara Lane, and the school, the friends, and the audiences who waited for her on the other side of the world.

She was back now in the world of the hansom cab, the horse-drawn bus, the women in their long skirts and swept-up hair walking in Wimbledon High Street beside the men, not hidden at home in seclusion. Neat English houses, and no bubonic plague. Roast beef and Yorkshire pudding on Sunday. Caste-rules more subtle and less obvious than those in India, but still existing under the surface. The dichotomy was inevitable. She had not even the universality of the totally detached nun with a begging bowl who belongs nowhere and everywhere.

The difficulty was overcome at first in the pleasure of talk and gossip and exchange of news. 'Min' and 'Peg', always close, were doubly close now. Each was embarking fully on her own life. Richmond was excited by all her accounts of life in India, but probably not surprised. He had seen his sister declaiming Shakespeare's speeches, and after *Julius Caesar*, the addresses given to large audiences on Kali-worship, whipping them up into excitement and fierce argument, were only to be expected.

Vivekananda himself stayed with them for a few days. The impact he made on the household was recorded later by Richmond, who wrote: 'That my sister should have obeyed his call was nothing wonderful, for I myself saw Swamiji and I knew his power. Swamiji brought certainty with him, and he gave assurance and confidence to the inquirer. This I think was what he did for my sister, and it was the certainty which led her to obey the call fearlessly, and once having obeyed without hesitation, she never had cause to regret.'

Vivekananda's name itself indicated much in his character which Richmond noticed. Amongst monks, the ending 'ananda', meaning 'having the bliss of' was always preceded by the name of a quality or deity. 'Viveka' is the quality of spiritual discrimination; discrimination between the real and unreal, the eternal and the illusory. It also denoted a discrimination between the apparent personality, and the truly great elements in the characters of those he met. Nivedita noted and often recorded his refusal to invade the privacy of his friends, or to permit any attempted invasion of his own inner life, but he seemed to experience an empathy so deep that for a time he almost became the other person, seeing life through his eyes, standing to some extent where he stood, giving, as Richmond said, 'assurance and confidence'. Those who, like the Nobles, were attracted to him, were evidently very strongly attracted indeed.

Those who reacted against him were usually the rigidly orthodox of East or West, or those who had a preconceived idea of what a Hindu monk should be, and were annoyed because he refused to fit it. The extremely respectable sometimes objected to his habit of chatting freely with everyone, including prostitutes, though he had an excellent precedent for this, as he never failed to point out. Orthodox Hindus objected to his eating with Westerners, and Christian missionaries often objected to his preaching Hinduism in America and Europe.

'I am about to deluge America with idolatrous heathen missionaries', he wrote to Nivedita when he departed with a couple of his brother Swamis to give some lectures.

None of these objections arose in the Noble household.

He moved on to visit other friends after a few days, and left for America two weeks later, with Turiyananda and two American disciples, Christine Greenstidel and Mrs Funke. Nivedita stayed in England for May's wedding. She did not join him in America until late September.

During the remaining weeks in England, she met many old friends, especially those connected with the Vedanta group which had been started before she left England for India. There were some arguments. Difficulties arose. They frequently did, and she was not by nature a pourer of oil on troubled waters. Mr Sturdy and Mrs Johnson, she noticed with annoyance, seemed to keep away from Vivekananda whilst he was in England this time, and it was Mr Sturdy who had started the group and with whom Vivekananda had stayed on his earlier visits to London. In her view, he did not welcome the new Swamis who were to take over the work. He rashly criticized Vivekananda in a letter to her. She replied bitterly, and the friendship was broken off. The criticisms of Vivekananda were petty, and the small irritants which arise when a strong personality is removed from a group, had led to bickering. Mrs Johnson and Miss Muller, two of the original enthusiasts of the group, also left. The difficulty appeared to be that they both objected to Vivekananda's illnesses. Yogis, they said, should not be ill. This implied a lack of holiness. There was perhaps a vague feeling that the word yoga must imply Hatha yoga, which is the yoga of body-control and physical exercises. This in fact was a highly specialized form of yoga, not encouraged by Ramakrishna among his disciples, as he believed that it could lead to overmuch importance being given to the body and its functions. The popularity of Christian Science at the time increased this hopeful expectation in the West that holiness was automatically equated with good health, and so illness was sometimes suspect.

Nivedita, who had watched Vivekananda choking with asthma and coping with a plague epidemic at the same time, while his meditation and worship continued each day as always, could hardly have been expected to take this sort of criticism of her guru placidly, and she did not. Sparks flew from her, even before Vivekananda left England.

As usual, he seems to have been aware of her feelings. In a letter written to Josephine MacLeod, from Wimbledon, before he sailed for America, he wrote: 'Sturdy is away, Mrs Johnson and everybody. Margot is rather worried at that. She cannot come to US till next month.'

He reassured Josephine MacLeod about his health. He was always having to reassure people about that. In New York he was going to try osteopathy. 'Say, I look several years younger by this voyage. Only when my heart gives a lurch, I feel my age. What is this osteopathy, anyway? Will they cut off a rib or two to cure me? . . . Whatever it will be, it will be hard work for him to *find* my bones.'

When he arrived in America, he went from New York to stay at Ridgely Manor, on the Hudson, in the Catskill mountains. Here Nivedita was to join him later. It was a time of rest and refreshment for him (including treatment by the osteopath!) before any further travelling and lecturing. His two brother monks stayed in New York to establish a Vedanta group there, and came to see him and to report from time to time.

When Nivedita sailed for America, after seeing May married, her feelings about staying at Ridgely were mixed. It would be a welcome breathing-space before she plunged into her own lecture-tour of America, and she certainly wanted to see Vivekananda again; also, her closest friends amongst his Western disciples were there. But could she be an all-renouncing nun, sleeping on bare boards and meditating in silence and peace, which, after all the wedding excitement at Wimbledon, she so badly needed, in that beautiful American manor house where the hosts were wealthy and where the young people, naturally enough, swarmed everywhere with their friends, and teased and laughed and probably played guitars, and where eating and entertainment was luxurious? She had not acquired her guru's faculty of meditating wherever he was, of bringing his own atmosphere with him, and of being equally at home at an eight-course dinner, or sitting cross-legged on the floor in a Hindu peasant home, eating with his fingers. She needed austerity, and she did not think that Ridgely Manor was the place to find it.

Against that fact there were the people. Josephine MacLeod and the Leggetts: Mrs Leggett was Joe's sister, and her daughter Alberta, with her delicate face and muslin dresses, awoke all Nivedita's maternal instincts. But just at the moment, much as Nivedita loved her friends, she wanted to avoid involvement.

She need not have worried. Both Vivekananda and the practical Joe MacLeod, who had not forgotten staying in the cottage by the Ganges, knew what she needed, and her hospitable hosts, the Leggetts, were perfectly willing to see that she had it.

The matter was settled simply enough. After she had stayed in the house with the others for a while, she asked Vivekananda, who was staying with his brother monks in a cottage near Ridgely Manor, if she might have a few days' retreat, and if in the future she could adopt a plain, gown-like dress more suited to a nun. The Paris gowns and hour-glass figures of the other women were not for her; she wanted simplicity. He agreed to both requests, and she moved into a small outhouse cottage building on her own, where she completed the book she was writing, *Kali the Mother*, and dedicated it to Vireshwar, the lord of heroes.

It was not long before Vivekananda plunged into action again. She knew that from now on she would only meet him in snatches, and hear from him through his own letters, or in letters from Joe MacLeod or other friends. In November she left for Chicago, travelling with Mrs Ole Bull's daughter Olea. As a lecturer, she was now on her own.

In Chicago, she plunged straight in, lecturing or giving brief talks whenever she was asked to do so, without any definite plans. She began simply enough, by giving a talk on 'India' to some children at an elementary school, then next day she spoke before a Board of missionaries, and so it went on. In November she heard, with considerable relief, that Vivekananda was coming to Chicago. She had to lecture in December on 'The Ancient Arts of India' and wanted to consult him first.

Vivekananda stayed with the Hales. Nivedita had already met Mary Hale, and by a complicated process of reasoning, since Mary Hale regarded him as a brother, and he referred to the two young Hale sisters and their two cousins as his 'old-maid sisters', Nivedita called Mary Hale 'aunt Mary'. Her own status as his 'daughter', and her conviction that she herself could always speak for him and interpret his message, did not endear her to Mary Hale. They were good friends, but two women could not have been more temperamentally unalike.

Vivekananda helped her with the preparation of her lecture, and, when she finally gave it, she was delighted to be paid, for the first time. At last she had earned a little money for the school.

But by no means all interviews and lectures were happy. After one of the less happy occasions, Nivedita wrote:

> I feel as if I want impulse and inspiration and am probably tired out. I had a most exhausting evening yesterday. One of the ladies I met was like twenty storms in one teacup; she talked vividly and exhaustively about women and the spiritual forces of the day . . . with a mixture of the enthusiasm of a fine nature and the mystery of theosophy. It was tiring to be assured, every third sentence, that the American Woman was the only creature on earth who could claim direct descent from Olympian Zeus.

Vivekananda might possibly have regarded that last sentence as the perfect example of the 'biter bit', and as illustrating a certain poetic justice on the part of Fate. But she was often buoyant in her enthusiasms, or totally cast-down. Vivekananda had already said 'the confession of weakness makes weak', but she found relief in pouring out to Josephine MacLeod her own weariness and depression in what might be described as an occasional good grouse.

> It is so like climbing in gravel! Most people make me sit down for hours and tell them all about everything, and then they say they are so much interested and I have given them so much pleasure, but they never offer to give me anything, not even one dollar.

There is something that draws sympathy in seeing a friend whose entire life is dedicated to a cause, fighting against heavy odds for it, and in particular, fighting irritation and depression and lack of success. Joe MacLeod was sympathetic, and probably glad that Nivedita had 'someone to grouse to' occasionally.

Unfortunately, Nivedita still could not resist the temptation to pour a little of her depression or gloom on to her 'Father' and she was too often liable to see his serenity, his strength, his acceptance of life ('Nothing is more enticing than to put oneself into the attitude of generalissimo of the forces, and make splendid plans, compelling fortune; but Swami just waits, and drifts in on the wave . . .') and to forget the colossal cost, in nervous strain, of responsibility and anxiety. 'Drifting in on the wave' was not always possible, to a man whose health was crumbling, who was deluged by letters telling him that his monastery at Belur was desperately short of money, and not enough was coming in; that the New York Vedanta Centre was not doing well, that people were changing their ideas or going away in some places, in others there were arguments, funds were needed, and how about the famine in India? He also faced a lecture tour across America which ran eventually to over a hundred lectures, and letters from personal friends and disciples must not be left unanswered. And, on top of everything else, there was Mr Sturdy, in England. As Nivedita had recently discovered, the Vedanta Centre established there was not going well; and now Vivekananda heard from him that 'Mrs Johnson is of opinion that no spiritual person ought to be ill'. She objected to monks smoking, and Miss Muller had left the Centre because monks must not be ill, if they wanted her approval. At first, he replied equably, if drily.

> In India, the same defects plus eating with Europeans have been taken exception to by many. I was driven out of a private temple by the owners for eating with Europeans . . . I have had a good deal of love given to me by the world; I deserve a good deal of hatred therefore . . . As for me, I stick to my nature and principle – once a friend, always a friend – also the true Indian principle of looking subjectively for the cause of the objective.

I am sure that the fault is mine, and mine only, for every wave of dislike and hatred that I get. It could not be otherwise. Thanking you and Mrs Johnson for thus calling me once more to the internal.

I remain as ever with love and blessings,

Vivekananda

Mr Sturdy persisted. Obviously the work was crumbling; he continued to justify, to explain and to criticize. The next letter from Vivekananda was still mild.

It is quite probable that very much of your criticism is just and correct. It is also possible that someday you may find that all this springs from your dislike of certain persons, and I was the scapegoat.

A third letter from Sturdy, however, went beyond all limits; and the furious reply would have caused half India to shake if they could have read it; in particular Vivekananda defended his brother monks still in England.

They do nothing but what I insist on their doing . . . they are my brothers, my children.

It was not often that Vivekananda lost his temper, but this time several pages flew across the Atlantic which left the recipient in no doubt that he had gone too far; though even here, several pages of thunder and lightning drew to a quiet close.

And I, the least of India's children, love you, Sturdy, with *Indian* love, and would any day give up a thousand bodies to help you out of this delusion.

Later, Vivekananda's letters to him were quiet, peaceable and tranquil; his angers were brief.

Nivedita knew none of this. She wrote to her guru when she felt dejected; she complained of difficulties. He replied that he, too, had found no change in his fortunes, but he told her – not for the first time – that depression or cheerfulness were as catching as disease. It was a favourite comment of his, that if one could not shake off gloom, one should at least keep away from other people, and avoid infecting them with one's own depression.

If you are really ready to take the world's burden, take it by all means. But do not let us hear your groans and curses. Do not frighten us with your sufferings, so that we come to feel that we were better off with our own burdens. The man who really takes the burden blesses the world and goes his own way. . . .

But he knew her difficulties; he never forgot that she had left her own country and a successful career to struggle and endure for his own country, and for Vedanta. He ended his letter in the one way that she always longed for (and as he very rarely did): 'Ever with love, *your father*, Vivekananda.'

So she took fresh heart, and decided to tour other American states, continuing her twofold purpose of teaching the West a little about Indian women, so that the women of both countries should draw closer in understanding, and also hoping to collect money for her school, if only from the fees she was paid for her lectures; sometimes donations were forthcoming as well. Before she left Chicago, she tried to form a committee to carry on her work, which included the 'putting across' of Vivekananda's own teaching. As she herself wrote, 'Shall a child not rejoice in speaking its father's message?'

She asked Mary Hale if she would become secretary of the committee. It was a staggering blow to her when she received a total refusal. Mary Hale not only refused to act as secretary, but informed Nivedita that neither she nor her family wished to identify themselves with her work.

The Hales had been friends, followers and helpers of Vivekananda, for years; Mary Hale, as his 'sister', had been the recipient not only of his teasing and some of his funniest letters, but also of some of his greatest and most profund thinking. It was not on a public platform, but in a letter to Mary Hale, that he wrote those words which are among his most famous, and which are still constantly quoted in India and all over the world:

> May I be born again and again, and suffer thousands of miseries, so that I may worship the only God that exists, the only God I believe in, the sum total of all souls – and above all, my God the wicked, my God the miserable, my God the poor of all races, of all species, is the special object of my worship.

In her dejection, Nivedita wrote to Josephine MacLeod; she did not attempt to write to Vivekananda this time, which was perhaps just as well.

She was completely bewildered. Her thoughts were so expressive of his, that she sincerely felt that in her talks she was simply giving his message; being 'the bridge', 'the mouthpiece'. Indeed, any comment against him irritated her. So why should friends who accepted him so completely, and who were accepted by him so completely, back away from *her*?

There seems to have been a naiveté in her attitude towards people, especially people in the West, which was very different from the penetrating understanding and commonsense she so often showed in India. It may be reminiscent of a certain type of mother, whose self-sacrificing devotion to the family is occasionally flawed by a non-comprehending tactlessness that causes her to leap into situations which a less busy and single-minded woman might have avoided. She had a very real humility, but the faculty of laughing at herself was not often in evidence; she would have been temperamentally incapable of writing the teasing nonsense that Mary Hale wrote to Vivekananda or of understanding that he might have accepted and enjoyed it. The very real sympathy and understanding between her guru and the Hales was of a very different kind from her own.

She was cast down from the heights to the depths again, and wrote to Joe MacLeod:

> Yes! I know it is their right to disagree, they must be free! But oh! do give *me* a little comfort, for I feel utterly discouraged. If this is the attitude of Swami's people, how can I ever expect to do anything anywhere?

She received more than 'a little comfort'; she received commonsense which put its finger straight on the difficulty.

> You know, and Swami knows, that I have always felt you had a mission – your own message for this work – and you can do better work where he is not known. No one who has ever known and loved him can ever take anybody else's version of him – not even yours.

The truth of that last sentence is so obvious that it seems surprising that Nivedita herself had not seen it. Josephine MacLeod went on to point out that Nivedita must begin to see her own work as quite separate from Vivekananda's, that she must use this as a time of training in the West, to make her own audiences. She added, 'Your message of Kali is your own and Swami had nothing to do with it.' There were even people who had been indifferent to Vivekananda, to whom Nivedita could appeal.

> The Hales adore Swami in their own way and not ours. They give him all they can, but the perception that our Indian life gave us of him, they are incapable of understanding, and none of his friends will ever understand that. And so you must go into a fresh new element where he may never be known . . .

Nivedita could see the truth of that. The Hales had not been at

Almora; they were not there in the plague. In India, she had been accepted in many places *because* she was his disciple; here she must stand apart from him. The message was being spelled out, however kindly, however roughly, from all sides: 'Stand on your own feet.'

So she went on, and addressed the women of Ann Arbor and Jackson, and was well received. She asked them to contribute a dollar a year, and became hopeful of getting it.

In Detroit, however, where Vivekananda himself had been given a rough passage, she had to stand on her own feet in the worst gathering she had faced yet.

10

In Detroit, Nivedita had to face the 'Church Women' whom Vivekananda had described as '. . . awful fanatics. They are under the thumb of the priests there. Between them and the priests they make hell of earth and make a mess of religion.'

Thus prepared for the worst, she went to a Ladies' Club at which she was invited to speak, and kept an iron grip on her patience. She addressed a hall packed with women, and then, with steadily sinking spirits, waited for the questions.

As she had expected, questions came in floods, and nearly swept her off her feet. Child-marriage and polygamy were the first obvious difficulties; she had been expecting those, and wondered inwardly how long it would be before they came in to the attack, on the caste question. One woman struggled hard to drag her into a discussion which would put Nivedita in the position of attacking the Christian missionaries in India. Nivedita flatly refused to criticize the missionaries. The atmosphere became more and more stormy as she represented polygamy as the *only* substitute for divorce. The President of the Club said it was as bad 'as our Mormons'. Nivedita fought down an impulse to defend the Mormons. 'Not like Mormons, I think. Rather, not so bad as Christians.'

That reply can hardly be regarded as conciliatory, but nothing would have quietened the uproar now.

One woman insisted that Nivedita should remonstrate with husbands and wives in India for not eating together, and that she ought to 'put a higher way' before them. Nivedita replied that in her opinion married couples should be left to settle such things between themselves, as it was no one's business but their own.

'Ah, there you are mistaken,' said the questioner. 'So the world always says – but it's everyone's business, really!'

'Well it's not mine, anyway,' said Nivedita firmly. 'I refuse to be put in such a position.'

She asked what American couples would think if she offered them

English advice on their marriages, but this did not quell the audience.

The usual questions now poured in about Hindus feeding their babies to the crocodiles as a regular article of diet; the straightforward answer, 'No, they don't', was swept aside.

At last, one member of the audience with a loud voice, who was obviously beginning to sympathize with the unfortunate guest speaker, tried to change the subject to something less controversial.

The 'less controversial' topic she chose unfortunately proved to be the caste system. '. . . She insisted on caste being sympathetically explained, by way of turning attention to safer topics. I never was in a gathering so like a lunatic asylum. Oh! how I recognized the steps that Swami had trodden before me!'

If he could tackle tough audiences, so could she. She struggled on at other places. She learned not to jump to conclusions too hastily, and time and again she found that both the heights of her optimism and the depths of depression were mistaken, and, with her usual honesty, admitted it.

> I am finding daily that Kali's ways are not ours, if one may put it so. She puts one person out of the way, only to discover someone else standing ready when one had no more dreamt of help than of flying.
>
> Did I tell you at the last centre how my most blessed helper was the thorniest of all thorns at the beginning of the week? And here it is just the same; two or three of the strongest workers are the most unspeakably unexpected. . . . after all the love and warmth I had in one town, I reached another and found myself fuming and chafing against the artificiality of people about me . . . and it was these very people, from whom I would have escaped at once if I could, who proved Mother's appointed instruments.

She knew that Vivekananda, too, was finding things difficult, and this made her more determined than ever that she would not give in. In January, he wrote to her:

> I am afraid the rest and peace I seek for will never come. But Mother does good to others through me, at least some to my native land, and it is easier to be reconciled to one's fate as a sacrifice. We are all sacrifices – each in his own way. The great worship is going on – no one can see its meaning except that it is a great sacrifice.

After her birthday, Vivekananda sent her a poem of benediction. In her reply to him, she struggled to express her desire to put his spiritual welfare above her own, to be the least of all his children, in a self-oblation that shows both the sincerity and love, and also some of the excess (as perhaps Mary Hale might have regarded it, and as a critic of today would certainly regard it) of an emotional and not over-humorous nature.

> I do not want even to know God in any way; even to think of such things is ridiculous of course – that would not leave my Father unattainably above.
>
> . . . if one realized the Divine – but even in that moment I cannot conceive of perfect bliss without the assurance that his was greater.
>
> I used to think that I wanted to work for the women of India – I used to have all kinds of grand impersonal ideas – but I have steadily gone on climbing down from these heights, and today I want to do things only because they are my Father's will. . . .

The letter continues in a gush of emotion that was as sincere in its adoring desire to humble herself by putting him far above her, as the next argument or clash of swords in which she did not in fact always 'do things because they were her Father's will' – would certainly prove to be. The pendulum was swinging again.

The completely open way in which she displayed the maddening, as well as the great aspects of her own character, is shown perhaps at its clearest in her book *Kali the Mother* which she had just completed at Ridgely Manor and was soon to see published. It was a book which made considerable impact in India, and was admired by many thinking people including Aurobindo. Reading it today, it shows, so frankly, so many aspects of a complex and many-sided nature, that it is worth reading from that point of view alone. It is almost inconceivable, to a modern reader, that its different sections could all have been written by the same woman.

A literary criticism of that, or any of the books she wrote later, is an entirely different matter, and much less important. In all her writing, she used too often the fashionable literary jargon of the day. This was the age which had been influenced by Tennyson and the Pre-Raphaelites. There was a constant usage of 'Fain would I' and 'Could we but' and 'Nay, foolish one' in her writing which is irritating to us today. But the late twentieth century has bred its own jargon, and the Freudian–existentialist–sociological clichés of our own age will possibly cause a similar embarrassed wince, or amused annoyance, to future generations. The discrepancies go deeper than that.

The opening pages of the book (which consists of a series of essays approaching the Kali-theme from different angles) are written by Nivedita the journalist, and they go straight to the point. 'Our daily life creates our symbol of God. No two ever cover quite the same conception. It is so with that same symbolism which we know as language.' The essay is straightforward, and apart from an almost inevitable quotation from Rossetti's sonnet, with its angel-watered lily, and the use of 'nay' rather than 'no', here speaks the journalist and the concise writer, and she deals with Shiva even better. Passing on to an essay on Sri Ramakrishna, who worshipped Kali, what she has to say is interesting and incisively expressed. She uses the touches of colour and detail of which she was so fond, but in which she often went over into excess, in their best proportions. She paints a picture in loving detail; a picture of the poverty of Sri Ramakrishna's room and the impression it made on her when she visited it.

The lamp was lifted, and the long shadows seemed to come down, from some dim upper abode, and prostrate themselves in worship. All was as he had used it, the lounge beside the bed, a huge water jar in one corner, a few religious pictures on the walls and nothing more. Outside, the heavy rain of June fell steadily, and below the terrace the Ganges moaned and hastened on. I have seen it in other moods – seen it when the oleanders whispered to the roses on the terrace, when the great mango groves behind were full of blossoms, and the clang of the bells for evening worship broke the silence to make the place like a smile at the time of prayer. And I have seen it in the terror of an Indian noon, full of coolness and flower fragrance. But never did it look so poor as that June night, and never was poverty made so beautiful.

From that point on, in the final essays, the Nivedita who could be irritating and who was not always able to laugh at herself, took charge and galloped ahead. From 'Arise, my child, and go forth a man! Bear manfully what is thy lot to bear; that which comes to thy hand to be done, do with full strength and fear not' through a touching appeal to the Ishta for those who suffered, couched in heavily biblical language, she leads us into an embarrassing soliloquy. 'Mother! Far away, one whom I love is very sad today. His heart calls to mine for help, but though I tell him how I love him, I leave him still uncheered.' To the very Nivedita-like touch, 'Give *him* that inner peace! Let me win it for him, if Thou wilt be kind!' Kali replies, 'Ah foolish one! Every thought of love that you send out to answer his, becomes a fetter of iron to hold him in life's anguish!'

It was not the journalist who wrote the early essays (yet it was the same woman, incredibly enough) who wrote the last chapter in the book, written in fact for 'Baby Leggett', of Ridgely Manor, beginning 'Baby darling, what is the very first thing you remember?' and developing into 'The little birds come, and the wee lambs love you, and the wild rabbits touch your feet . . . And you love all the people mother loves, – don't you dearie?' Certainly mothers and aunts by the pram talk like that to its occupant on occasion, even today. What is startling about Nivedita is that she wrote it down, pages of it, in an adult book on Kali-worship. Her later book for children, *Cradle Tales of Hinduism* is very different and less whimsical. Here in *Kali the Mother* she is Nivedita in many ways, and not all of them are wise, but every one of them without exception is honest. She hurls on to the page, without over-much discrimination, whatever she felt at that moment. If she had been more discriminating, more cautious, and a little less emotional, she might have been a better writer, but on the other hand, she might not have waded out into floods to feed famine victims, or held in her arms children dying of the plague. It is a part of her whole character which does not appear on the postage stamp and which is so often forgotten; that whole-hearted and unashamed mixture of opposites. She took everything that she was, noble or difficult, understated or gushing, and used it all. In *Kali the Mother*, she wrote it down, and those who accepted Nivedita had to accept her as she was. She did not present a carefully revised version for public display. And since she had to face very diverse audiences, her own diversity had its uses. She was speaking to the intellectual when she wrote, 'We have seen that anthropomorphic representation of the Divine is absolutely necessary to human nature. But to learn the manner and method of that expression, we must know the whole heart and feeling of a people.' But the more simple would probably prefer her in her more personal moods. 'And so everyone of us, simply by thinking his own thought, and living his own life to the full, may be answering his brother's cry for God in ways beyond the dreaming of the world.'

She was determined to live her own life to the full. During her American tour she was often weary, but she kept going.

However far apart their paths lay, Vivekananda knew what was going on in her life, and compared it constantly with his own problems so that she never saw herself as entirely alone, or her difficulties as unique.

You are learning your lessons. That is all I want. So am I. . . . Between my nerves and your emotion we may make a mess of everything just now, so Mother is curing my nerves and drilling you into level-headedness – and then we go. This time, good is coming in chunks, I am sure. We will make the foundations of the old land shake this time. . . .

Good certainly came, if not always in chunks. Nivedita returned to Chicago, then in February (of 1900) on to Kansas City, Minneapolis, and Boston. After a few months, she was able to form 'The Ramakrishna Guild of Help in America' with Mrs Leggett as President and Mrs Ole Bull as secretary, and representatives (including Joe MacLeod) in Chicago, New York, Boston, and Detroit. Mrs Leggett gave a thousand dollars to help start Nivedita's school work and Mr Leggett helped with the publication of a booklet in which Nivedita set out her aims for the Ramakrishna School for Girls.

The school was to be built – if money could be raised – on the banks of the Ganges near Calcutta, for twenty girl widows and twenty orphan girls, under the guidance and influence of Sarada Devi. The English and Bengali languages and literature would be taught, with simple mathematics and science, and handicrafts bearing on the revival of the old Indian industries, so that each girl could eventually earn her own living without leaving her home. The girls must choose for themselves whether they would prefer 'the life of marriage, or consecrated national service'. Those who preferred national service might eventually start new Ramakrishna schools in other places.

She ended the booklet by explaining that she was not putting the duty of Americans to people overseas above their duty to their own country, but since commerce and finance were international, service too should be mutual between countries. She added a quotation from Whitman: 'Are all nations communing? Is there going to be but one heart to the Globe?'

She was also trying to publish her book *Kali the Mother* and her lecture tour continued. She had some success, some despondency. 'Some leader had said that a new truth before it is accepted must meet with ridicule, argument and opposition. When these three are present you know that you are about to win. Oh dear! Come on all three, as hard as you can. I don't mind *how much*, if only you are not everlasting.'

Letters from Vivekananda were now all directed towards cheering her on. Often he described his own health as 'improving' and even spoke once of 'such fine *sleep*!' 'We put all our energies to concentrate and get attached to one thing; but the other part, though equally difficult, we seldom pay any attention to – the faculty of detaching ourselves at a moment's notice from anything: both attachment and detachment perfectly developed make a man great and happy.'

He was frank about his own difficulties. He did not find 'rapid attachment and detachment' easy, either. He wrote always as one sharing the heat of the battle rather than as one merely commenting on or advising on it. 'All blessings on you . . . Don't despond in the least . . . You come of the blood of a Kshatriya. Our yellow robe is the garb of death on the field of battle. Death for the cause is our goal, not success . . . Steady, child, don't be bought by gold or anything else, and we win.'

Josephine MacLeod ('Yum-Yum' or 'Yum' to Nivedita, who had no objection to whimsicality) kept her in touch with Vivekananda. There was Mrs Blodgett, for instance. While Vivekananda had been staying at Ridgely Manor, a message came for Joe MacLeod to tell her that her brother was very ill in Los Angeles. She went to him at once, and found her brother, whom she had not seen for ten years, dying in a small cottage on the outskirts of the city, tended by his landlady, Mrs Blodgett, aged seventy. To her amazement, over his bed hung a life-size portrait of Vivekananda. She asked the old lady if she knew him, and Mrs Blodgett replied, 'I was at the Parliament of Religions at Chicago in 1893, and when that young man got up and said, "Sisters and brothers of America", seven thousand people rose to their feet as a tribute to something, they knew not what; and when it was over and I saw scores of women walking over the benches to get to him, I said to myself, "Well, my lad, if you can resist that onslaught, you are indeed a god".'

Joe explained to her that not only had he resisted the onslaught, but that she herself was staying with him at her sister's home in the Catskills. 'He will come here, if you ask him,' she said.

In three weeks, her brother was dead, but Mrs Blodgett's kindness, and her enthusiasm for Vivekananda, did not diminish. He came some weeks later and stayed in her tiny cottage for months, while he lectured on the Pacific coast.

Nivedita was not there, but she heard all about it from Joe. Vivekananda got on with Mrs Blodgett as though he had known her for years. She made him pancakes for breakfast, which they ate at the kitchen table, 'and such discourses he would have with Mrs Blodgett, such repartee and wit, she talking of the villainy of men and he talking of the even greater wickedness of women. . . . Mrs Blodgett seldom went to hear him lecture, saying her duty was to give us delicious meals when we got back . . .'

So, though the ways were parting, Nivedita was still kept in touch. His lectures in California were – by request – often full of instructions about meditation (Raja Yoga). Inevitably the subject must have presented him with many difficulties, because meditation, as he told them, is a very individual matter; the guru knows the potentiality and the natural tendencies of the disciple, and instructs accordingly. He insisted on purity and chastity as an absolute basis for meditation, for the married as much as for monks, and his audiences accepted his 'bomb-throwing', as he called it, when he thundered his total repudiation of the teaching of some medical men in the West, that 'chastity was against the law of nature, and resulted in ill-health'. He accused doctors (of whom there were several in the audience) of being animal in their morals, 'with the morals of a tomcat, if that is the best you have to say on the subject!'

The 'bombs' did not upset them; they listened endlessly, as long as he would teach them to meditate. They loved his jokes; on a freezing cold day, questions about Hell were followed by 'if *this* isn't Hell, I don't know what is!' In reference to his own unmarried state, 'The one thing that I have against the monastic system is – that it takes the best men away from the community!'

Some of his lectures at the Washington Hall, San Francisco, were taken down by a disciple and published fifty years later, though she commented she would have needed a speed of at least three hundred words a minute to catch them all. 'And his stories and imitations absolutely forced one to stop writing, to enjoy watching him . . . Swamiji's speaking style was colloquial, fresh, and forceful . . .' Fragments of these notes give glimpses which were obviously familiar to Nivedita, and on which her own meditating would have been based.

How is it to be attained? In a dozen different ways. Each temperament has its own way. But this is the general principle: get hold of the mind. The mind is like a lake, and every stone that drops into it raises waves. These waves do not let us see what we are. The full moon is reflected in the water of the lake, but the surface is so disturbed that we do not see the reflection clearly. Let it be calm. Do not let nature raise the wave . . . Just this moment I think I am all right and I will meditate upon God, and then my mind goes to London in one minute. And if I pull it away from there, it goes to New York to think about the things I have done there in the past. These waves are to be stopped by the power of meditation.

He explained that all depended on the power of concentration; and that all must be built on a basis of morality.

Here comes Miss So-and-So. She says, 'I am going to be a Yogi.' She tells the news twenty times, meditates fifty days, then she says, 'There is nothing in this religion. I have tried it. There is nothing in it.'

The very basis of spiritual life is not there. The foundation must be this perfect morality. That is the greatest difficulty . . .

The Hindu boy or girl gets initiation. He gets from his Guru a word. This is called the root word. This word is given to the Guru by his Guru and he gives it to his disciple. One such word is OM. All these symbols have a great deal of meaning, and they hold it secret, never write it. They must receive it through the ear – not through writing – from the teacher, and then hold it as God himself. Then they meditate on the word . . .

He taught that bathing and cleanliness is considered vital for meditation; that posture is important, the spinal column being left perfectly free of the weight of the body, since yogis believe that a hollow canal called the sushumna runs through the middle of the spinal column. The power of meditation opens the column and when energy is sent to the base of the spine the Kundalini rises. Sexual activity, he said, uses the power which would otherwise be used in meditation; therefore continence was necessary, or, in the case of married couples, faithfulness and chastity and a slow progress to a relationship of spiritual companionship and eventual continence later in life. To equate a permissive, frequent or excessive sex life with any hope of progress in meditation, he regarded as impossible. And for full and total 'realization', he taught that absolute continence would be needed. For this reason, monks were regarded with especial respect in India; from their ranks came the greatest ones of all: Christ, Buddha, Chaitanya, Ramakrishna, were all living lives of celibacy when they reached the heights of meditation. He taught the necessity of simple breathing exercises, usually given by the guru, at the beginning of meditation; of training the mind to remain still and watch the flow of its own thoughts until one began to see that one was not identified with the mind, one was *not* the mind. Something was watching the mind, and its thoughts.

Then, with the repetition of the mantram which in itself was a form of 'That', ultimate Brahman, and was a link with the ultimate, when the waves of thought were stilled, concentration deepened, and finally by a deep concentration on the object of the meditation, often visualized as being within one's own body as a flame is within a lamp, one eventually 'becomes' the object of concentration. One does not 'think about'; one 'becomes'. The object of concentrated meditation will vary, he said, with each person, and may in some cases be a great soul, or the spiritual heart of such a one within one's own heart, but the ultimate object will be to get beyond mind and body, and realize what one, in truth, is. This was his teaching in his lectures and in his books – and here in Washington he summed it up again.

Excepting the infinite spirit, everything else is changing. There is the whirl of change. Permanence is nowhere except in yourself. There is the infinite joy, unchanging. Meditation is the gate that opens that to us. . . . In the long run this power of meditation separates ourselves from the body, and then the soul knows itself as it is – the unborn, the deathless, the birthless being.

His audiences were fascinated. Both as a personality and as an instructor in meditation, which was new to them, he caught and held them.

He gave them love. 'All faces are dear to me,' he said, and reassured those who doubted their own powers of meditation. '*I* am with you now. Try to have a little faith in me.' Then, afterwards, he meditated with those who wished to do so. 'Seated cross-legged on the divan, clothed in Sannyasin garb, with hands held one within the other on his lap, and with his eyes apparently closed, he might have been a statue in bronze, so immovable was he. A Yogi, indeed!'

11

Vivekananda's exhaustion was growing, and though in public he appeared to be the same as ever, his detachment was increasing. At Los Angeles, he spent some time with an American disciple. Her mother, very old, and blind, was approaching death. He sat often and for long periods on the floor beside her; he explained that the contemplation of death, to the Hindu, was not a morbid idea but as important as consideration of birth. To this moment, the whole of a life led up; the eternal soul picked up and dropped many bodies in reincarnation after reincarnation; 'the body comes and goes'. Before death, the preparation began; a slow detachment, a loosening of bonds, and in old age or illness, a very natural and good retreating within, which was only sad to those who watched it without understanding what was going on. The soul progressed like the leech which caught on to the next blade of grass, before it left the blade to which it had been clinging. An entire life's experiences and values were brought to a point, and on that point the soul passed forth; if re-birth lay ahead in another body, then the life, body, even the parents to come were at this point being decided as a result of what had gone before; even in senility, or death or stroke, the true life was not touched. The body and mind (as in meditation), he said, were dropping away; the personal identity of that life was ebbing, but the life within was not.

He remained in silent contemplation.

Nivedita, her life mounting and moving forward at last to its exciting future, with hopes of a return to India ahead of her – busy, vigorous and less depressed and uncertain than she had been before – could not entirely understand his apparent lack of involvement. As she rushed forward, he was beginning to slow down.

He struggled on 'sometimes well, sometimes ill', as he said in his letters. There were signs of weariness. 'Sturdy and Mrs Johnson got disturbed by Margot, and they fell upon me.' One has the impression from his letters that on all sides complaints, arguments or queries were touching him less and less.

In April 1900 he wrote from California what was perhaps the most beautiful, certainly the most well known, of all his letters, and he wrote it to Joe MacLeod, his friend whose commonsense and loyalty had never failed him; 'one familiar face which never had a line of discouragement, never changed, but was always helpful, cheerful and strengthening', as he had written of her four years earlier.

And now, in April, he sent her the letter which was perhaps the greatest gesture of friendship he could have made. His *nunc dimittis*. It was a very quiet letter.

The battles are lost and won. I have bundled my things and am waiting for the great deliverer.

'Shiva, O Shiva, carry my boat to the other shore.'

After all, Joe, I am only the boy who used to listen with rapt wonderment to the wonderful words of Ramakrishna under the Banyan at Dakshineswar. That is my true nature; works and activities, doing good and so forth are all impositions. Now I again hear his voice; the same old voice thrilling my soul. Bonds are breaking – love dying, work becoming tasteless – the glamour is off life. Only the voice of the Master calling . . . 'I come, my beloved Lord, I come.'

Yes, I come. Nirvana is before me. I feel it at times – the same infinite ocean of peace, without a ripple, a breath.

I am glad I was born, glad I suffered so, glad I did make big blunders, glad to enter peace. I leave none bound, I take no bonds . . .

. . . The world *is*, but not beautiful or ugly, but as sensations without exciting any emotion. Oh, Joe, the blessedness of it! Everything is good and beautiful; for things are all losing their relative proportions to me – my body among the first. 'OM' That Existence! . . .

In June, Nivedita returned to New York and so did he. He was to lecture at the Vedanta Society of New York; she was to speak there, also, on two occasions.

When she attended his first lecture, she found that she had instinctively taken the seat at the left end of the second row, which had always been her place at his London lectures. Inevitably her mind went back to those days and to all that had happened since. Had she been wise? Was it a mistake? As she (typically) wrote in a letter to Joe MacLeod, 'My own life, – where was it? Lost – thrown away like a cast-off garment that I might kneel at the feet of this man.' The sheer drama of that sentence shows how far removed she was from understanding the detachment towards which he was moving; there was always, perhaps, a touch in her of the Margot who declaimed Mark Antony's speech to young Richmond. But she went on to say, 'I read in his glance what I too felt in my own heart; complete faith and abiding comprehension of purpose – better than any *feeling*.'

The Leggetts had left for Paris to attend the Congress of the History of Religions, arranged in connection with the Paris *Exposition Universelle*. Vivekananda was going to join them there; he was to speak at the Congress, and as they were anxious about his health, they asked him to stay and rest at their house. Nivedita was also going to attend, but she left America before him because she had promised to work with Professor Patrick Geddes, the British sociologist, who was organizing the various sessions of the International Association at the Congress. She had met Geddes and heard him lecture in New York and was delighted to collaborate with him. She was hoping that a chance to study his ideas on sociology would help her in her understanding of Indian life.

What happened, on the contrary, was that it helped her in her understanding of her own limitations.

She found the work of assisting in cataloguing, indexing and reporting his lectures not at all to her liking. Worst of all, she had been accustomed to absorb Vivekananda's words and then give them to audiences in her own phrasing; Vivekananda gave – and indeed encouraged – liberty to express whatever truths she discovered in her own way. One can imagine a social scientist confronted by Nivedita's prose at its most flowery, and one can also imagine Nivedita faced with work which she detested and which she knew was unsuitable for her; and sympathy for them both is inevitable. The clashes that arose were probably also inevitable, but they depressed her considerably. 'I feel torn to pieces. He wants a voice that will utter his thoughts as he would have done. I try then to make a mosaic in which the bright bits are his words, and I provide only the grey cement of mere grammatical context.'

She had always preferred bright bits to grey cement. After many difficulties, she gave up the work. But their friendship remained for the rest of their lives. She recorded her thanks to him in her introduction to her book *The Web of Indian Life*. She was always loyal to her friends; working with them was often a different matter.

In August 1900 Dr and Mrs Bose came to Paris; this botanist and his wife, whose acknowledged success delighted Vivekananda, were to become close friends of Nivedita's. Vivekananda, who had recently learned to speak French, gave his lectures at the Congress. He stayed with the Leggetts at 6 Place des États Unis, and Nivedita often met him there. It was here that one of his funniest letters was written, about the 'Congress of Cranks'.

The letter, after giving a comic caricature of everyone present, ends in a positive riot of mixed metaphors, with Joe 'yearning to chase them all out of the house if they did not stop their nonsense'.

But Vivekananda's detachment, even his humour, were not in accord with Nivedita's depression and her increasing desire to be 'up and doing'. Her conflict with Geddes worried her. Mrs Ole Bull, who was staying in the village Perros-Guirec, near Lannion in Brittany, invited Nivedita to stay with her, to rest, walk, and take some much-needed fresh air and quiet. Mrs Bull was regarded by Vivekananda as a mother, 'the steady mother'. Certainly she mothered Nivedita.

Nivedita's health improved, but in the quietness of Brittany she brooded on her guru's apparent indifference. Did his detachment mean that she had offended him? And why did he criticize her attachment to various friends she had made? She wrote him a letter in which she complained and blamed, and asked for advice and understanding.

The reply she received was weary, quiet and, to a distraught Nivedita, alarming. From this distance of time it seems mild and straightforward; to his devoted and perhaps excitable disciple fretting away in the quiet village in Brittany, its mildness and weariness were the last things she had hoped for.

He told her that he had at last resigned the Presidency of the Ramakrishna Mission, and the Belur Math (monastery) now belonged to the immediate disciples of Ramakrishna exclusive of himself. The new President was Brahmananda, his great fellow-disciple of Ramakrishna. 'I am so glad a whole load is off me, now I am happy. I no longer represent anybody, nor am I responsible to anybody.'

As for his friends, he had given his best energies nearly to death, and 'received only hectoring and mischief-making and botheration . . .' He informed her that her letter to him indicated that he was jealous of her new friends. 'I never directed you before: now, after I am nobody in the work, I have no direction whatever. I only know this much, so long as you serve "Mother" with a whole heart, She will be your guide.'

He told her flatly that he had no jealousy of any friends she made.

Only I do believe that Western people have the peculiarity of trying to force upon others whatever seems good to them, forgetting that what is good for you may not be good for others. As such I am afraid you would try to force upon others whatever turn your mind might take in contact with new friends. That was the only reason I sometimes tried to stop any particular influence, and nothing else. You are free, have your own choice, your own work. . . .

He signed it 'With all love and blessings', but Mrs Ole Bull, who saw the result of it in Nivedita's increasing anxiety, invited him to come and stay a few days.

Nivedita was about to return to England to try to find means for the Indian work; she had no plans; she had no idea how long she would have to stay in England. Vivekananda came to stay, with a friend, at a cottage nearby; he gave her a poem of benediction.

On her last evening in Brittany, after supper, he called her out into the garden, and told her that there was a sect of Muslims who are reported to take each new-born babe, and expose it, saying, 'If God made thee, perish! If Ali made thee, live!' 'I say, but in the opposite sense, to you, tonight – "Go forth into the world, and there, if I made you, be destroyed. If Mother made you – live!" '

He blessed her, and she assumed that this was his farewell blessing on this occasion.

Next morning, however, just after dawn, she left the cottage, sitting in a peasant market-cart. Her last sight of him then was as he stood on the road outside the cottage, with hands lifted in 'that Eastern salutation which is also benediction'. He returned to Paris, and eventually, to India.

She returned to England, but whether wisely or not, she was not at all sure.

12

She saw question marks in whichever direction she looked. Joe MacLeod received several of them. 'Have I any business to go on in England? . . . As far as *wishes* go – my whole soul is in India. I am more and more convinced that there is nothing to be done outside, and what I am doing here is the merest fancy-work.'

Was she a practical worker? Founder of a school? Earner of money for the school? Lecturer? Nun? 'I have only one wish in the world, and that is to live a nun's life perfectly. But every day the golden apple of my desire seems to slip further out of my hands. I wish the Swami would bless me and send me out to seek it.'

He had already blessed her and sent her out; which golden apple she sought, he left to her. Her closest friends must have found it difficult to imagine Nivedita living the silent and withdrawn life of a totally world-renouncing nun; as Vivekananda had once said of her, she took things up with overwhelming enthusiasm for a time, and for a while nothing else mattered. She was also loyal in her friendships; a friend was a friend for her life; she may have struggled with the effort to maintain a dispassionate and equal love for all beings, but her nature was against it. She met the Boses in London soon after her return. Dr Bose was ill and was operated on at the end of December. During his convalescence Dr Bose and Mrs Bose, Mrs Ole Bull and Nivedita stayed with Nivedita's mother at Wimbledon. Dr and Mrs Bose became friends both of Nivedita and her family and remained so even after her death, when they continued a strong friendship with Richmond.

Nivedita was already known in some circles in London, as a speaker and journalist. She decided to accept any requests for a speaker that came her way and see where that led. In January and February 1901 she gave on average three lectures a week, including a lecture in Edinburgh. In England, she spoke strongly against the false accounts of Indian life given by Christian missionaries. She did not attack their religious teaching, but in a lecture she objected to their accounts of India and of Hinduism. They replied by asking a young Christian from Madras to speak next, but he stood up and supported Nivedita. He stated bluntly that he did not care to call himself a Christian since reaching Europe.

She began to consider writing a book against the missionary propaganda in India, and in May she met Professor Geddes in Scotland. He offered her a chance to lecture at the Indian section of the Glasgow Exhibition, and when she told him about her idea for the book, he offered to write an introduction to it.

She was inevitably plunged more and more into activity. The journalist William Stead asked her to write a life-sketch of Dr Bose; *Kali the Mother* had been published and was favourably reviewed; Romesh Chandra Dutt promised to publish another book, and at his suggestion she wrote some chapters of *The Web of Indian Life*.

But her homeland was not here; she did her best but she chafed to get away.

'Plague must be raging in Calcutta, I cannot bear to be away . . .' That sentence contains much that won the respect of her friends and enemies over the years; though she may not have realized it, it showed all the single-pointed dedication of the nun, which she thought she was losing. It may even, perhaps, move us more than those ever-mounting passages of prose which usually began simply and then wound up to a colossal and sometimes self-conscious climax of poetically balanced sentences. It is in her simplest, most straightforward words that she suddenly shines out clearly.

By May, she was worn out. Mrs Ole Bull invited her to Norway, where a bronze statue of Ole Bull was to be unveiled.

She camped in Lassoen, not far from Bergen, on a rock by the sea. 'It is a green gem set in a blue sea, and carved with roads and rocks and pines and filled with delicious odours of the forest. It is more like Achhabal than anything else.'

The Boses stayed there with her for some days; R. C. Dutt, the Indian liberal leader, visited her and discussed *The Web of Indian Life* with her; he was writing a book on Indian economics. The reply to the missionaries, called 'Lambs among Wolves', was published in England in the *Westminster Gazette*.

She returned to England after three months: in September 1901 she spoke at Glasgow, and in October she passed a week in the Home of Retreat of the Sisters of Bethany in London, which she loved, and she found the atmosphere and the daily round of devotions very reminiscent of life in the house of Sarada Devi, 'The Holy Mother'.

In November she met Professor Geddes again, and also edited Dr Bose's book *The Living and Non-Living*.

But during this year of 1901 she had reached the great cross-roads, and throughout the year, her future attitude to her life in India, to her own life, to her dedication (dedicated to *what?*) was changing, crystallizing; and worrying her, with a mixture of growing impatience, longing for political action, and guilt.

She was furious at the treatment meted out to Dr Bose by English scientists; he had been honoured in Paris, and in universities throughout the world, including America. In England his treatment was very different. She felt that his work was not appreciated, that it was suppressed and spoiled and that he himself was not given the honour that he received in other Western countries. She regarded this as anti-Hindu prejudice. There may have been several factors at work, including his linking of science with religion, but to Nivedita the issue was one of colour-bar, and nothing else.

Any attack on her friends was liable to start a fire smouldering. 'As for England, this "Bose War" seems to spell individual and general degradation." She talked to Indians in England. Dutt asked her to address a group of Indian students, and this time she chose a very different subject from her usual talk on Indian woman, or Indian Art. This time, it was 'The Reawakening of India'.

She became very interested in the Indian National Congress and once even thought of joining it. In London she met the Russian revolutionary leader Prince Kropotkin. She had read Kropotkin's *Mutual Aid* in America, and had been attracted to his ideas.

> He knows more than any other man, what India needs.
>
> What I specially dwell upon is the utter needlessness of governments . . .
>
> I have said a good deal about the hopelessness of the Mutiny, because there was no continuous policy looming beyond. But the village system supplies machinery of self-government enough, and the grim conviction of the people that all other things are unnecessary is the only policy that could possibly prove permanently continuous. So I see now what we have to work for. As India is already the most civilized country in the world, I see clearly that she is at this moment the only country where a gigantic race is employed, as a body in working this out . . . We shall one day peacefully wait upon the Viceroy and inform him, smiling, that his services are no longer required. The great *means* of doing it will be elaborated by degrees, as we come to have what Mr Geddes calls 'a theory of the Pacific Life'.

It is startling, on reading those words, to realize that she had not yet met a young man called Gandhi, who was already beginning to think about India and its future. She had seen what was going on in India; she had heard Vivekananda publicly rousing his people to a consciousness of their own nationalism; but he had never preached politics, and indeed had said repeatedly that if ever India sacrificed her deepest religious experience and philosophy to politics, she was doomed. He was concerned with the spirit of man, which might inspire different kinds of action; she herself was a nun, not a politician. 'Do you think I do not know that the great message of Swami is unique? That I could never forget, but beyond that I do not understand. For all this last year I have been going through experiences that lie far outside his course for me.'

The last sentence is crucial. The battle of conflicting loyalties was beginning, and it was doubly and trebly complicated by the fact that she had seen his own torment concerning his own people, the potential warrior in him held back by the monk. She knew, too, that things in India were getting worse. He had written to Mary Hale:

> Even education will no more be permitted to spread; freedom of the press has stopped already (of course we have been disarmed long ago) . . . For writing a few words of innocent criticism, men are being hurried off to transportation for life, others imprisoned without any trial . . . There has been a reign of terror in India for some years. English soldiers are killing our men and outraging our women – only to be sent home with passage and pension at our expense . . . Mary, you can afford to be optimistic – can I? Suppose you simply publish this letter – the law just passed in India will allow the English government in India to drag me from here to India and kill me without trial.

Nivedita knew only too well from her discussions with Indians in England that this was true. Even had she believed that the British rule was entirely benevolent it was still patriarchal; her militancy and fury were beginning to mount, and they were never far below the surface of her nature. She saw that what she had discovered in teaching children, was true for communities; they must learn for themselves, and make their own mistakes. 'You may employ artists to teach baby painting, and they may touch up her work so that it seems marvellous, but one little scrawl that is really her own is worth thousands of such pictures.'

In this letter to Joe MacLeod the militancy rang out clear. She referred to the British in India as a gang of robbers: 'anything that is Indian and for India I touch the feet of, however stupid and futile. Anything else will do a little good and much harm, and I have nothing to do with it. Yes, my way will do some harm too, but it will be vital to the people themselves. Good and evil of their own, not any other's, and for such harm I care nothing. They need it . . .'

She saw much potential goodness and goodwill in England, and felt that if people like Vivekananda, Dr Bose, and Dutt, could come to England, friends for India would be made, so that when '. . . in twenty years from now, the blow is struck (I *know* that will be) there will suddenly be a body of men and women in England, to rise up and say "Hands Off! This people shall be free!" '

So far, so good. But now she began to move on to a programme that certainly does seem to suggest an approach that 'lies far outside his course for me'. The next passage in this very crucial letter (and it is significant that it was written to her friend Josephine MacLeod, not to Vivekananda) went on:

To me, now, a missionary . . . the better he is doing, the worse he is . . . The English official is a fool, playing amidst smoking ruins and crying on the highway that he builds well. The native Christian is a traitor to his own land. For these and for all other bought men, paid spies, mercenaries, India has no use and no time. Very different work they must be at, who would save her, or show her, rather, how to save herself.

The last sentence brings her right over the borderline to political action, but still wearing her nun's garb; it is, in that sense, masterly. The change from 'save her' to 'show her, rather, how to save herself' fits not only the teacher, the lecturer, and the nun, but also the Hindu mother who sends her sons out to battle, acting as their inspiration rather than their leader. Vivekananda had himself said, in America, that India lay like a giantess asleep; supposing the original metaphor of her vocation and her dedication – to 'call and call to the sleeping god within, till the god wakes and makes answer' – should now apply not, as Vivekananda originally intended, to the 'god within man' but to the sleeping god that was India?

Somebody had to rouse the nation. Was she to be the one? Her entire nature fitted her for it; all the 'fighting Irish' in her was awake; she had already proved that she could rouse large Hindu audiences to enthusiasm; she had the undoubted asset, in India, of being a disciple of their much-loved leader; she was a woman and nun, and therefore a mother-figure and liable to be treated with respect; she was a member of the ruling nation by birth, who had become totally a Hindu in thinking and loyalties; that in itself was enough to bring them rallying to her cause. And she longed to fight for India as Vivekananda could not do; fighting for India was, in a sense, fighting for him.

Or was it?

What was he going to think about all this? To say that the path she was now considering – wherever it took her – lay outside his course for her, was something of an understatement, and she knew it. Even if her 'fighting' was largely verbal, she could not deceive herself into thinking that the one who points the way has no responsibility for the results. And what was all this going to do to her school-teaching, her work for women, her lectures on religious subjects, such as Kali-worship, in India, her work for understanding between Eastern and Western women, in America and Europe?

There was one obvious solution. If her conscience was torn between what he would wish her to do and what she would *like* to do – why did she not ask him?

> I am afraid . . . I shall want my Mother to stand between me and my Father's wrath . . . To my great horror, freedom has meant something to me, for my life has come to include many elements that Swami would probably not have put there. They are all for him, however, I trust, in the end – and he will not hold me less his child than before. . . . And I belong to Hinduism more than ever I did, but I see the *political* need so clearly, too!

'I am afraid' was honest; indeed, her letters were always honest, but 'my Father's wrath' and the obvious intention to go ahead where he might not approve (since words like 'wrath' were typical of Nivedita at her most dramatic) contrasts oddly with that earlier letter of hers to Vivekananda himself, 'today I want to do things only because they are my Father's will . . . one longs to serve for serving's sake, for ever and ever, dear Master.' The continual swing of this emotional pendulum was obviously very clear to Vivekananda, and had been very clear for a long time. Josephine MacLeod can hardly have failed to notice it, either. ('My own life – where was it? Lost – thrown away like a cast-off garment that I might kneel at the feet of this man') and her enthusiasm expressed in other letters, for total self-oblation to the guru, for the passive sinking of one's own will in the will of the guru, of becoming merely his hands and feet – the sincerity of this was total. If there was one thing that both Vivekananda and Joe MacLeod detested it was insincerity, and neither of them ever doubted Nivedita's integrity and loyalty. But the two strands in her, were pulling against each other

Left to right: Sister Nivedita, Mrs Sevier, Sister Christine and Mrs Abala Bose at the Mayavati Ashram, 1907

Sister Nivedita

Sister Christine

Sri Sarada Devi (the Holy Mother) and Sister Nivedita

again; one was gentle, and submissive, and the other was very militant indeed.

Why she did not simply ask him, there and then, is a question to which we can never know the answer. Certainly he was not too ill to be expected to take any interest in a vital question which must affect the future of his disciple, and possibly the future of India also. On his return to India, he had not retired to bed as a sick man who must no longer be bothered with the things of this world. That was not in his character, and she knew that it was not the case at all.

On return to India, he occupied himself mainly, at first, with the private teaching and training of monks and lay disciples, and writing letters, as usual, all over the world. He took his mother on a pilgrimage; it was the wish of Hindu widows to make a great pilgrimage, and since he rarely saw her and his monastic life had caused him to leave the family, he wished to take her on her pilgrimage before his death. As usual, he was besieged by crowds of people, and at Dacca lectured to two thousand people, and on the next day to three thousand, speaking for two hours.

But on his return to the monastery at Belur, his health was worsening. Asthma and diabetes were giving particular cause for concern. He lived very quietly indeed, much beloved by his fellow-monks who had been fellow-disciples of Sri Ramakrishna and who understood, as Nivedita with all her devotion could not do, the constant interplay of the different sides of his nature. They knew the human side, which could be exhausted beyond endurance and sometimes angry and must now be protected from too much work; they saw the withdrawn moods of total deep meditation in which he must be left alone for hours at a time, perhaps sitting under the Vilva tree or the mango tree by Sri Ramakrishna's temple: they watched him organize the life of the monastery although he no longer had chief responsibility for it. He joined in everything, he was the heart and soul of the place, and they knew his joking and teasing moods as well. He loved the animals kept by the monastery, and mock-disputes raged between him and Swami Brahmananda, the Head of the Order, with regard to the boundaries between livestock and vegetable and flower gardens, and who was trespassing where. He attempted to sink an artesian well for purifying the water, he made bread (not always successfully) and went for walks. His collection of animals was large, including a she-goat, some cows, sheep, ducks, geese, an antelope, a stork, and a kid which followed him wherever he went.

So life continued busily. Vivekananda was beginning to suffer also from general dropsy, but in his monastery he was busy and at peace, and free to walk about barefooted, wearing his Gerua cloth, without the coat, waistcoat, trousers – and without the collar, which he had particularly disliked – of his life in the West.

On 7 September 1901 he wrote to Nivedita from the monastery. It was a 'Dear Nivedita' and signed 'Yours etc. Vivekananda' letter – friendly, brisk, amusing, but certainly not suggesting that it came from a man too weak to be asked a question about his disciple's future work. He told her that it was the season of rains again, the river was rising and flooding the banks, the ponds and tank had overflowed. He had just returned from lending a hand in cutting a deep drain to take off the water from the monastery grounds.

He did not write about politics, or about India. He told her, of all things, about ducks.

> The rain-water stands at places some feet high. My huge stork is full of glee, and so are the ducks and geese. My tame antelope fled from the Math and gave us some days of anxiety in finding him out. One of my ducks unfortunately died yesterday. She had been gasping for breath for more than a week. One of my waggish old monks says, 'Sir, it is no use living in this Kali Yuga [Age of Kali] when ducks catch cold from damp and rain, and frogs sneeze!' One of the geese had her plumes falling off. Knowing no other method, I left her some minutes in a tub of water mixed with mild carbolic, so that it might either kill or heal: and she is all right now.

So the question remained unasked. All that Nivedita wanted was to return to India; she was homesick. And her work, whatever it was to be, lay there. Not in the West.

On 31 December, she sent her luggage on board the *Mombasa*. On 9 January 1902, she boarded ship at Marseilles and began the journey home.

13

So she returned home to India, and received an enthusiastic ovation at Madras. She travelled with R. C. Dutt and Mrs Ole Bull, and they were all three given a public reception. When Dutt had spoken, Nivedita addressed the huge audience in words which did not tend to endear her to the British government, but which went through her audience like a flame, and later caused Vivekananda to write to Mrs Ole Bull, when he read Nivedita's address in a Madras journal, that 'the reception Nivedita had in Madras was for the good of both Nivedita and Madras. Her speech was indeed beautiful.'

The speech was later published in the Calcutta daily newspaper, *Amrita Bazar Patrika*, and from then on the British government began to watch her movements and censor her letters, especially when it became clear that she was often visited by national political leaders, including Gokhale and Dutt. The speech itself makes it clear that now she was in no doubt as to where she stood.

> Just as it has been realized that in religion you have a great deal to give, and nothing to learn from the West, so also in social matters it will be well to understand that what changes are necessary you are fully competent to make for yourselves, and no outsider has the right to advise or to interfere . . . These changes must be original, self-determined, self-wrought.

She spoke of Vivekananda, and of her own good fortune in being considered 'his daughter', and praised Dr Bose and his achievements in the West. In conclusion she said:

> I come then, to the application of all that I have said – your national customs require no apology. Stand by them. Your great men yield in nothing to the great men of other countries. Glory in them, love them, encourage them to the top of your heart. They will never give you cause to be ashamed.

Such words today would be regarded as the mildest commonsense, as applied to *any* country. Spoken under the circumstances of that time, and by an Englishwoman who thought, behaved and lived like a Hindu, they were revolutionary. The audience knew it: the spark was smouldering. It was still smouldering mainly beneath the surface; but it was there.

She was home again, and the welcome home was tumultuous. But her feelings were mixed. As usual, she saw the left and the right hand of 'Mother Kali' at work in her life in equal measure. Many flocked to hear her. But to others, she could say what she liked about her status as the daughter of Vivekananda, she could claim to speak as a Hindu, but to the orthodox she was still unclean, a foreigner, and with no possibility of ever being recognized as a Hindu nun.

Swami Atulananda, a Western Swami of the Order, writing to an old lady in England years later describing his own difficulties in this respect, makes it only too clear that Nivedita endured much from the Hindu side of the fence, at a time when the British were beginning to regard her with suspicion from the other side. The 'fighting Irish' in her nature is unlikely to have worried overmuch; but when we watch the militancy growing in her, it is as well to remember that she faced not only overwhelming tropical heat but the small miseries of personal rejections by the orthodox also.

> Western Sannyasins [monks] are not of Hindu caste [wrote Swami Atulananda]; Orthodox Hindus will not eat with them, they are not allowed in Hindu temples . . . When I was prevented to enter temples I argued that I was a Hindu Sannyasin. The reply was, 'Your body is from the West, so we cannot allow you in the temples' . . . And I know that there are Sannyasins who will not partake of a feast, if the feast is paid for by a Western Sannyasin. I have experienced it. I gave the money but did not come near the food. I had everything done by and through Brahmins. Did not even show myself at the feast. Still, many who heard that I had put up the money, refused to touch the food . . . When Nivedita came to India many of the Sadhus of our mission even, refused to take food with her, though she was a Brahmacharini, which is the same as a Sadhu. So though there is supposed to be no caste for Sadhus, the age-old instinct is there . . .

'Cooking-pot religion', Vivekananda called it. But, however, he defended her, she had to face it.

Again her affections and emotions were going to be torn, and she faced the fact. They had been torn when she left England; she belonged to so many worlds.

Here, she was coming back to the gentle mothering of Sarada Devi who was 'Holy Mother' to the Order and indeed to all Bengal and much of India, eventually. The gentle rituals of each day in her house were like the atmosphere of the Home of Retreat of the Sisters of Bethany which Nivedita had experienced in England. The fun and teasing were there, too. Because the ladies of the Zenana must remain at home, secluded, and could not visit theatres, Sri Ramakrishna had always encouraged the performance at home of religious plays about the gods; his niece, Lakshmi Didi, was particularly skilled at drama. On one occasion, Lakshmi Didi acted as Jagaddhatri, and Nivedita as the lion on which she rode. This so much amused 'the Mother' who was unaccustomed to seeing tall English ladies acting as lions, that Nivedita went about the room roaring like a lion to the huge enjoyment of her 'audience'. There was much there that was happy: homely, natural and familiar. But against that was set the darkening cloud of Vivekananda's ill-health.

The question of her own future career was still uncertain. She had some money for her school now, but certainly not enough to build the great school for women by the Ganges that Vivekananda had hoped for. Half a loaf was considerably better than no bread, however, and she could reopen the school in the original premises in Bosepara Lane; but who would help her to run it, who would look after it when she was not there? And as the political aspect of her future grew stronger and stronger in her own mind, the inevitable question arose: who would run the school single-handed while she travelled, lectured, and whipped up Hindu feeling into something more strongly nationalistic?

She was meeting many people who felt deeply about Indian nationalism. One of the first was a young man as yet practically unknown, who had come to Calcutta in December 1901 to attend the Congress session. His name was Gandhi.

It was not at the time a meeting which seemed to mean very much. Their ways did not lie together but though they did not know it then she was one of those who prepared the road which he later trod, and in after years he acknowledged it fully. He was then a very young man, in South Africa. He described his meeting with her in her 'place of residence – a Chowringhee mansion'. He said that he was taken aback by the splendour that surrounded her. He did not find much meeting ground in their conversation, and when he spoke to Gokhale about this, Gokhale replied that he was not surprised that 'there could be no point of contact between me and a volatile person like her'. But, like others who could not find any agreement with her, he added that he noticed and admired her 'overflowing love for India'.

She was then staying as the guest of Mrs Bull and Josephine MacLeod; the 'mansion' was theirs: he did not see the little house in Bosepara Lane, and assumed that all this splendour was Nivedita's. When his attention was drawn to this mistake, after her death, he corrected it at once.

> I never knew the fact, till I saw the note in the *Modern Review*, that I had met the deceased not at her own place but at a guest's. The reader has to recognize my painful limitations. My reading is so poor that I have not read, much though I should like to have, the lives even of those who have contributed to the making of modern India . . .
>
> I have a full recollection of the conversation between Sister Nivedita and myself. But I do not propose to describe it. No fault in the translation or the original can possibly damage the memory of one who loved Hinduism and India so well. It will ever be cherished with gratefulness.

The humility and gentleness of Gandhi's immediate correction of his earlier mistake, and his probable reaction against her militancy, shows as clearly as any longer account might have done how totally different their personalities were, and how very much both were needed at different stages of India's struggle. Gokhale's comment is shrewd; 'volatile' in its meaning of 'lively and changeable' is based on a close and friendly knowledge of Nivedita. And the meeting was so brief that Nivedita had no chance to learn what potential lay hidden in that apparently mild young man; and he did not see the gentleness behind the sparks and the fire. It is probable that he would have been much more at home with her in Bosepara Lane. It is fascinating to speculate about what might have happened if she could have heard him, later, addressing audiences, or if he had seen her in famine or plague, but it can only be speculation. Their meeting was brief.

She was, in any case, busily establishing her own life's work. He, much younger, was still earnestly seeking for his.

As soon as Nivedita was back in 17 Bosepara Lane again, she wrote to Vivekananda suggesting that she should reopen the school. His reply left her in no doubt about his confidence in her:

> May all powers come unto you! May Mother Herself be your hands and mind! It is immense power – irresistible – that I pray for you, and, if possible, along with it infinite peace . . .

If there was any truth in Sri Ramakrishna, may He take you into His leading, even as He did me, nay, a thousand times more!

The Mother and Sri Ramakrishna. His life's loyalty went to both. He could not have given her a greater blessing. As usual, he left matters in her hands, and did not interfere. He wrote to Brahmananda, now Head of the Order: 'Regarding Nivedita's School, I have written to her what I have to say. My opinion is that she should do what she considers to be the best.'

She opened her school on the Saraswati Puja (feast) day, and invited the ladies of the neighbourhood to attend the function, and many of them did so.

In April one of her greatest problems was solved. Christine Greenstidel came to India; she lived with Nivedita at Bosepara Lane and became her assistant in running the school.

Sister Christine, as she was officially called, had been born in Nuremberg in 1866; when she was three, her parents settled in Detroit and she lived as an American. She had met Vivekananda in America and became his disciple. In England she met Nivedita, and helped her in her work in Detroit. Vivekananda trusted her faithfulness and dedicated loyalty to her work, completely. Once he had said of her, 'I need her for my work in Calcutta.'

She has recounted the strictness of his methods with his disciples, and yet the complete freedom he left in their hands when it came to decisions about their own actions (which must have been one of the reasons why Nivedita did not ask him his opinion about her own future career).

His respect, nay, reverence, for the divinity within was so sincere and so profound that his mental attitude was always, 'Hands off'. He did not ask for blind submission. He did not want slaves. He used to say, 'I do not meddle with my workers at all. The man who can work has an individuality of his own, which resists against any pressure. That is my reason for leaving workers entirely free.' Imperious though he was, he had something which held this quality in check – a reverence for the real nature of man.

These words of Christine's make much clear to us, including the unquestioning confidence with which she came to India. She wrote, also, of his attitude towards the education of women:

No man can do this work. It must be done by women alone. On this point he was stern. 'Am I a woman that I should solve the problems of women?

Hands off! They can solve their own problems.' This was consistent with his unbounded faith in the power and greatness latent in all women. 'Every woman is part of the Divine Mother, the embodiment of Shakti [Divine energy],' he believed.

When she arrived in India, Nivedita was delighted and relieved. Christine's nature was in many ways the opposite of her own, which perhaps was just as well. Nivedita wrote of her, 'She is absolutely staunch. She is gentle and clinging, and not too dominant, but she is loyal and sympathetic and generous. Perfect in sweetness and perfect in trustworthiness, and so large in her views.'

Vivekananda's letters to Christine were always full of trust; she seems to have been a woman of gentleness, but quietly unshakeable. He wrote to her, after her arrival in India,

> I know you are great, and my faith is always in your true heart. I worry about everything except you. I have dedicated you to the Mother. She is your shield, your guide. No harm can reach you – nothing can hold you down a minute. I know it.

In March, Nivedita spoke at the Classic Theatre on 'The Hindu Mind in Modern Science'. Miss Bett, who was Nivedita's old nurse, had come with her from England; in the early days of the reopened school, she seems to have been the chief standby in running it. In the school holidays (beginning in May) Nivedita and Christine stayed at Mayavati, the ashram established for Vedantic meditation in the Himalayas by Captain and Mrs Sevier; Vivekananda's health was not good enough to allow him to accompany them this time.

In the years that followed, Nivedita and Christine often spent their holidays at Mayavati. In running the school, they became friends as well as colleagues. It is from Christine's description, spoken to a monk of the Order later on, that we learn that Vivekananda in fact became increasingly angry as he watched Nivedita's political work increasing while she still remained a member of an Order committed to non-involvement in politics, and that he scolded her thoroughly for it, and insisted that she must choose one path or the other. Since he gave freedom of choice, she knew that either she must accept that freedom, and make her choice, or else ask him the direct question in the Hindu spirit of obedience from disciple to guru, 'Which path do you wish me to take?' Her doubts and self-questionings at this time must have been anxious and painful.

Certainly the only project lying ahead about which there could be no doubts was the school. She had returned from America with several thousand dollars which had been donated for the school, and now a start could be made. She returned to Calcutta in June; but so much was to happen in the immediate future that it was not until early in 1903 that she worked in the school herself.

14

Very reluctantly, those who knew Vivekananda were beginning to admit to themselves that there was little hope that he would be with them for many years longer. Asthma, diabetes, kidney and heart trouble, and now dropsy, which made his feet tender and swollen so that walking was difficult for him; it was a combination that would have killed most men already. And he took very little rest; in 1902 he hardly slept at all. But there were days and weeks when he seemed almost completely well again and in the peace of the monastery, with the heaviest weight of responsibility lifted from him, he was nevertheless the centre and heart of the place, and passionately concerned with the daily life and routine. Once he stood at the window with Joe MacLeod, when she was visiting, as they watched Nivedita distribute school prizes on the lawn outside.

'I shall never see forty, Joe,' he said suddenly. He was thirty-nine. She did not take the remark seriously, and he did not refer to it again. People flocked to the monastery to receive his blessings and instructions; there were furious arguments on the boats, when the orthodox objected to his unorthodoxy; but the worst of the grumbling died down when he arranged a feast-day in the orthodox manner. The respect which he gave to both the extreme formality of conventional worship, and the warnings he gave against overmuch attention being paid to the minutiae of rituals, were difficult for many Hindus to grasp; his greatness as a national hero whom they regarded as a patriot-saint was constantly being threatened in their eyes by his alarming habit of eating with untouchables and foreigners, or of worshipping with Christians or anybody else.

He even, on occasion, shocked the lowest castes. He was fond of some simple Santal labourers who worked in the monastery grounds. Once he offered them a feast, but they explained that if they ate food cooked by him, with salt, they would lose their caste. He promised that the salt should be served to them separately, and at last they agreed. They said afterwards that they had never tasted such food before; it was a highlight in their lives, to eat as much well-cooked and well-flavoured food as they wanted. They were so simple and guileless that, as often before, it tore open his feelings and he longed to live longer, to serve God in the poor, and *somehow* to leave this yearning for service, with the others. He addressed the monks and novices in an outburst that Nivedita, when she heard about it, knew was typical of him.

See how simple-hearted these poor illiterate people are! Can you mitigate their misery a little? If not, of what use is your wearing the Gerua? . . . Sometimes I think within myself, 'What is the good of building monasteries and so forth? Why not sell them and distribute the money among the poor. What should we care for homes, we who have made the tree our shelter? Alas! Nobody in our country thinks of the low, the poor and the miserable! . . . How I wish to demolish the barriers of 'Don't touch-ism' and go out and bring together one and all . . . unless they are raised, this motherland of ours will never awake! . . . In the whole history of the world have you ever seen a country rise without a free circulation of the national blood throughout its entire body? If one limb is paralysed, then even with the other limbs whole, not much can be done for the body – know this for certain.

A lay disciple protested that it was a hopeless task to establish cooperation amongst all the varying creeds and sects in India, to make them act in unison for a common purpose.

He was asking for the lion's roar, and he got it. 'Don't come here any more, if you think any task too difficult!'

Nivedita heard much of all this; she saw him in glimpses; like everybody else, she had very little long-term hope for his life, but she was convinced that there was some time to go yet.

Sometimes he would wander along the village paths that led from the monastery gates to the high road, or would meditate wherever he happened to be, by the Ganges, or under the branches of a tree in the monastery compound. His room was on the second storey in the south-east corner of the monastery. In the middle of the room was an iron bedstead fitted with a spring mattress, given to him by one of his Western disciples, but he preferred to use a simple bed on the floor. His desk and a small table, with a rack on which to hang his Gerua clothes, were all the furnishings of the room, which is now kept exactly as it was, and has been visited by thousands of pilgrims. The most important object in the room, to him, was a picture of Sri Ramakrishna. In this room he wrote, studied, gave instruction, received his friends, sometimes ate his meals, and meditated. It was the nearest thing to a fixed home that he ever knew. It comforted many people, including Nivedita, to know that he was there, and he wrote to his monastic disciples, asking them to visit him there. And, from all over the world, they came. Nivedita wrote, 'Visits were paid and farewells exchanged that it had needed voyages half round the world to make.'

He dropped hints enough of the approaching end. 'How often,' he said, 'does a man ruin his disciples, by remaining always with them! When men are once trained, it is essential that their leader leave them, for without his absence they cannot develop themselves.'

'I am making ready for death,' he said. 'A great tapasya and meditation has come upon me, and I am making ready for death.'

Nivedita wrote that 'Once in Kashmir, after an attack of illness, I had seen him lift a couple of pebbles, saying, "Whenever death approaches me, all weakness vanishes. I have neither fear, nor doubt, nor thought of the external – I am as hard as *that*" and the stones struck one another in his hand – "for I *have* touched the feet of God!" '

Sri Ramakrishna had promised that when he knew who, and what, he was, he would die at the time of his own choice. He could no longer be interested even in the question of rain-scarcity, and possible famine. 'You may be right,' he said, 'but I cannot enter any more into these matters. I am going down into death.'

Nivedita touched on the question of her political future. He disagreed with her on a question of education. She replied, 'Yes, don't you see! That's exactly why I say that the *other question* must be answered first! Then all questions of education.'

He knew that by 'the other question' she meant 'political freedom'. But he answered, as he answered all questions now, 'Well, well, Margot, perhaps you are right, only I feel I am drawing near to death. I cannot bend my mind to these things now.'

Still nobody expected that his death was nearer than a matter of a few years. 'There was nothing sad or grave about the Swami, during these days . . . Never had one felt so strongly as now, before him, that one stood on the threshold of an infinite light.' She recorded that he seemed, especially on the last day, stronger and better than he had been for years.

Even then, in the week before he died, he was anxious about his work, and said to her, 'You know, the work is always my weak point! When I think *that* might come to an end, I am all undone!'

She described her last meeting with him.

On Wednesday of the same week, the day being Ekadasi [a fast day] and himself keeping the fast in all strictness, he insisted on serving the morning meal to the same disciple [Nivedita]. Each dish as it was offered – boiled seeds of the jack-fruit, boiled potatoes, plain rice, and ice-cold milk – formed the subject of playful chat; and finally, to end the meal, he himself poured the water over the hands and dried them with a towel.

'It is I who should do these things for you, Swami! Not you, for me!' was the protest naturally offered. But his answer was startling in its solemnity – 'Jesus washed the *feet* of His disciples.'

Something checked the answer, 'But that was the last time!' as it rose to the lips, and the words remained unuttered. This was well. For here also, the last time had come.

That was Wednesday, 2 July 1902. She later wrote to her friend, Mrs Hammond:

On Wednesday morning I went again, and stayed three hours. I think now that he knew I would never see him again. Such blessings! I cannot tell you. If I had only known! As it was, well as he looked, I was so full of the idea of the care he required, that I introduced no topic lest it might agitate him, and I dreaded over-staying lest I should make him tired. If I had only known, how precious every moment would have been, but Oh! how unbearable.

Friday, 4 July, was a quiet day. It was the American Day of Independence; and Vivekananda had taught, said and written often enough that the independence of a nation in freeing itself from bondage was as nothing to the glorious independence of the soul freeing itself from the body. He did not regard the succession of lives through which the soul passed in various reincarnations as short pleasant interludes from which it was unwillingly torn away. The old metaphor of life as a warm room into which the bird flies, and stays there for a brief while before flying out into the storm again, he regarded as the exact opposite of his own belief. He had written to Mrs Ole Bull, when her father died:

Coming and going is all pure delusion. The soul never comes nor goes . . . The earth moves, causing the illusion of the movement of the sun; but the sun does not move. So Prakriti, or Maya, or Nature, is moving, changing, unfolding veil after veil, turning over leaf after leaf of this grand book, while the witnessing soul drinks in knowledge, unmoved, unchanged. All souls that ever have been, are, or shall be, are all in the present tense . . . Because the idea of space does not occur in the soul, therefore all those that were ours, are ours, and will be ours; *are* always with us, *were* always with us, and *will be* always with us. We are in them. They are in us.

So he taught that the soul, remaining always where it stood, dropped its body at death like an old coat, and the slow detachment that took place before death was the preparation.

By his constant turning to the super-conscious as the only content of consciousness to be desired . . . Vivekananda built up in those around him some sort of measure of Real Existence, and the idea that the mere fall of the body could seriously interrupt this, became impossible . . . Yet the Swami laid down no hard and fast conclusions on these subjects, for others to accept. He carried those about him at any given time as far as they could go, by the force of his own vision, by the energy of his effort to express in words the thing he himself saw. But he would have nothing to do with dogma. Each one, to his thinking, must work out his own belief, basing it on the data of his own experience.

On 4 July he rose early. Swami Brahmananda, the Head of the Order, and Swami Saradananda were away in Calcutta on business. They were not worried about his health, which seemed to have improved. On that day he showed no sign of illness. Of the senior monks, who had been disciples of Ramakrishna, only two were present in the monastery. One was Swami Advaitananda, an old man who had been older than Ramakrishna himself by several years. The other was Premananda, a man of great gentleness who had been praised by Ramakrishna for his purity and love. Because of his devotion to the monks and to the householder devotees, he was sometimes known as 'the Mother of the Math'. It is from his letter to a brother monk in America, written the following month, that we know in detail what happened on that day.

After Vivekananda's meditation he teased and joked with Premananda, as he often did, making them all roar with laughter. He ate fruit and drank warm milk as usual, but on that day he insisted on feeding Premananda and serving him, himself.

At half past eight in the morning, when he went to the shrine to meditate, he was alone. At half past nine, Premananda went to the shrine to perform the morning worship. Normally, Vivekananda sat in a corner of the shrine meditating while the worship was performed. This morning he asked Premananda to have the mat on which he sat in meditation placed in the room next to the shrine; in this room a photograph of Sri Ramakrishna was kept on a bed during the night; the room was known as 'the bedroom' of the Lord, so that his presence was remembered there as realistically as in the room in which he had, in fact, lived. The mat was put in there, and he asked Premananda to close all the doors and windows as he meditated alone in there. This had never been done before.

At eleven o'clock he rose from meditation, and came out, singing softly to himself the hymn, 'Who says my Mother is black? The Black One with flowing hair lights the lotus of my heart.' The song of the Mother expressed the heights of both devotion to the personal God and the Ultimate. It was a summary of the truth taught by Sri Ramakrishna, and a favourite song of his.

Afterwards he walked to and fro in the courtyard, talking to Premananda. He ate his lunch in the refectory with the others with great relish, saying that he was hungry, and at the meal he was light-hearted and amused. After lunch he rested. At one o'clock he woke Premananda and said, 'Come, let us read something. I couldn't sleep today. I got a headache after meditating. My brain seems to have become weak.'

For three hours he gave instruction on Sanskrit grammar to the novices, illustrating the lesson with jokes, puns and stories. Afterwards he went with Premananda for a walk along the road outside the monastery garden, describing to him the Leggetts' garden in America, and the American use of machinery in gardening.

At half past five they returned to the monastery, and he continued to talk to Premananda, explaining in considerable detail the history of European civilization, and the history of colonialism.

At dusk Premananda returned to the shrine room to perform the Vesper service. Vivekananda talked for a while to the father of Ramakrishnananda, a brother disciple of Ramakrishna. Then he went to his room.

He said to his attendant monk, Brajendra, 'I feel very light in body. I feel very well.' He asked for his rosary for meditation, and said that he wished to be left alone until he called.

After an hour he called Brajendra, who fanned him, and then he seemed to doze for a while. His hands trembled for a few minutes. He seemed to Brajendra to be in meditation. He gave a deep sigh and became very still. This was not unusual in meditation. Brajendra waited. He waited for some time. Alarmed, he ran to fetch the elderly Swami Advaitananda. A couple of minutes later, Premananda came to the room. He saw that Vivekananda's eyes were open. His expression was radiant.

He called for the father of Ramakrishnananda, who chanted Ramakrishna's name, which always brought Vivekananda back to normal consciousness. But there was no return. The radiant expression on the face did not change. It was still there next day.

Doctors were sent for.

The two Swamis returned in great haste from Calcutta.

At midnight the doctors pronounced that life was extinct. Death had apparently occurred just after nine o'clock, but so accustomed were they to his deep meditation that hope was not given up until midnight.

That night, Nivedita went happily to bed. He had sent her a message earlier in the day to say that he felt a great deal better.

During the night, she dreamed that Sri Ramakrishna had died once again.

And woke, to face the morning of Saturday, 5 July.

15

In the morning, the news was brought to her. She went at once to the monastery.

The monks sent messages to spread the news across Calcutta. It was sent by telegraph to other parts of India, and across the world. Some of the monks were sent out for incense and sandalwood. Incense was burned in the monastery. Flowers were gathered.

When Calcutta recovered from its stunned disbelief, the crowds began to pour in. They came by boat up the river, and landed at the Ghat; carriages arrived at the monastery gate. The grounds were crowded from end to end with those who came to mourn, and still the people came.

The body lay in state in his own room, where he had died. They queued in an unending file to pass the body. Beside the body sat Nivedita, fanning it, all through that endless morning in the heat of a Calcutta July.

At two o'clock in the afternoon, the body was brought down to the porch leading to the courtyard. There the Arati service was performed. Lights were waved, mantras recited, conch-shells were blown, bells were rung, and incense was burned. At the end of the ceremony, the vast crowd, with one movement, bowed low. Many fell prostrate, and those who were his disciples touched his feet with their heads as the final gesture of devotion, self-oblation and dedication.

A procession was formed. The body was very slowly lifted, and with the shouts of triumph which showed that death was a liberation and that this life had been a triumph, the procession moved slowly through the courtyard and across the monastery lawn.

Behind the procession walked Nivedita, barefoot. She knew where they were going – towards the Vilva tree standing in the south-east corner of the grounds. There, slightly to the left, was the spot where Vivekananda himself, a few days before, had said, 'When my time comes, cremate me here.' And here the funeral pyre had been built.

The body was placed on the pyre. Reeds were lighted, and not only the monks but scores of the people of Calcutta, lighted the pyre until it was ablaze from end to end.

Today a temple stands on the spot, and the altar of the temple is built exactly where the body lay on that Saturday afternoon. But all that Nivedita could see on that day were the flames. The body was covered by the Gerua cloth which he had been wearing when she saw him last. When she said so, Swami Sadananda offered to give it to her; but she refused. To take it from the pyre did not seem right to her. So she watched it burn.

She had wished that it were possible to send a piece of it to Josephine MacLeod, the most trusted of all his Western friends, who was not in India.

At six o'clock in the evening, she still sat by the pyre. Out of the embers and blackness a small piece of Gerua cloth blew towards her, and fell at her feet. The monks told her to keep it. It was big enough to send to Joe. Everything else was burned.

As the evening came, the monks poured Ganges water over the smouldering embers of the fire, and the people went home. They were still stunned by the death. It was as though a mountain had fallen, and the whole landscape had changed.

Nivedita went home to Bosepara Lane. She took out her diary, and under 4 July, she wrote two words: 'Swami died.'

16

Now she needed to work; now was the time for action. It was not only self-preservation that stopped her sitting quietly to think and to remember. There was also the absolute certainty, common to anyone who had ever worked with Vivekananda, that sitting about and brooding on the past was the one thing above all others that he would have despised. He had made it clear enough: 'It may be that I shall find it good to get outside my body – to cast it off like a worn-out garment. But I shall not cease to work. I shall inspire men everywhere until the world shall know that it is one with God!'

To get outside his body. To cast it off. A typical phrase. He had taught that the soul stood where it always did, eternally unchanging, and body after body, in incarnation after incarnation, picked up, used, and dropped; and in the slow withdrawing from activity at the very end of life, a moving towards freedom from bondage. On the night of his death, a boyhood friend had dreamed that he had come to him in triumph, calling, 'Shoshi! Shoshi! I have spat out the body!' 'Spat out' is a long way from the Western idea of clinging to the body, of longing to remain; and equally far from the despair of the Stoic. Use it, detach from it – then cast it down, spit it out: it is finished. Since at last he was free, mourning was pointless. She wanted no pity. She wanted to work. She wrote to her friend Mrs Hammond, 'Pray that I may have strength and faithfulness and knowledge to do this, and ask no other blessing for me. I want no other. He is not dead, he is with us always. I cannot even grieve. I only want to work.'

She had passed the crossroads, and had made her decision. What he would have said about it she could never know, and she had left it too late to ask him. But she was going to move beyond the bounds of an Order which had no politics. Vivekananda had expressly stated in the rules and regulations he drew up: 'The aims and ideals of the Mission being purely spiritual and humanitarian, it shall have no connection with politics.'

The wisdom of this for the Order was obvious. But to remain a member of the Order would hold her back from any hope of political action.

Indeed, looking at the matter from the point of view of the Order he so much loved, why should they be dragged into action she might undertake politically, why should the Order be judged harshly because of anything she might decide to do? As long as she bore their name, any action she took, any speech she made, would naturally be assumed to carry their approval, and to speak for the whole Order. In all honesty, she could not remain within the Order and still speak as freely in public as she chose.

Yet how could she leave? She was devoted to the Order, and to the monks, many of whom were her personal friends. Their devotion to her and their concern for her well-being, was not only a matter of respect for the 'spiritual daughter of Vivekananda', but also of very strong concern for a brave woman who had left the comforts of her own country to live in poverty and heat and devote herself to India. Her lack of care for her own health worried them constantly; and for her to move about the country, lecturing – a woman, alone, in India, where such a thing was unthinkable – without one of the monks to accompany her and thus give an assurance of the Order's blessing and an indication of respectability which the Hindus would honour, this would worry them even more. Then there was Sri Sarada Devi, who was, in her seclusion, the spiritual fountain-head of the Order; in every direction Nivedita was bound to the Order by ties of mutual affection and respect. She had no nuns to consult; it was not until many years after her death that a totally independent convent, with its own rules, was established. She was answerable only to herself, in any step she took now.

She wrote in a letter at that time, 'I belong to Hinduism more than I ever did. But I see the *political* need so clearly, too!'

Politically speaking, Calcutta was at that time the heart and focal point of any struggle for Indian independence that might arise. It was the capital city of India, the capital of the whole Indian Empire, and the second largest city in the British Empire, second only to London. It was famous also as a great port and a jute-milling centre. Government House, in Calcutta, ruled the three hundred million inhabitants of the Indian Empire.

Not only was the legal system and the civil service centred there, but young men from all over India poured into Calcutta to the universities.

Without the university examinations of Calcutta, they had no hope of posts as white-collar workers or in the professions. Calcutta daily papers were published in four languages: English, Bengali, Hindi and Urdu.

Among the poor, it was in some respects a city of migrants. In the quarter of the city in which Nivedita lived there were still the mansions of distinguished high-caste families, often reduced to poverty without loss of respectability. Between these grew up clusters of tiny huts, the bustees of the very poor. And along the riverside thronged not only Bengalis but Hindustanis, Chinese, Eurasians and others. The white dome of the Post Office dominated the crowded quays and shipping of the riverside. Government House more dramatically dominated the European quarter; here were the parks, gardens, museums and theatres. It was a confused, straggling, overcrowded city, and the seeds of revolt might have grown there long before, but the administration was fully in control, and the population apathetic, poor, and anxious only to stay alive, where possible. The tax-collector and the bubonic plague were more immediate dangers than the British government, in the eyes of most of the population. But administration was not as centralized as it might have been; this was Curzon's main worry, as Viceroy, and he was concerned to unite the Indian Empire more firmly under a more exclusively British executive, reducing Hindu representation in local government and insisting that committees should have a British majority; the control of higher education, in particular, he proposed to reorganize.

Vivekananda's triumphal tour of India in 1897 had roused India to a consciousness of nationalism, but not of politics. National pride, however, was growing, and Congress was restless. If political action started anywhere, it was likely to be here.

Nivedita visited the Math once or twice soon after the cremation, and discussed her problem with the head of the Order, Swami Brahmananda. No amount of discussion could alter the basic fact which she already knew; Brahmananda could not tell her what Vivekananda would have wished her to do; equally, however strong his sympathy for her, he could not allow his Order to be dragged into politics in any way whatever.

He left the decision to her. Finally he wrote and asked her what conclusion she had reached.

On 18 July she wrote her reply to him.

Dear Swami Brahmananda,

Will you accept on behalf of the Order and myself my acknowledgement of your letter received this evening. Painful as the occasion is, I cannot but acquiesce in any measures that are necessary to my complete personal freedom.

I trust, however, that you and other members of the Order will not fail to lay my love and reverence daily at the foot of the ashes of Sri Ramakrishna and my own beloved Guru.

I shall write to the Indian papers and acquaint them as quietly as possible with my changed position.

Yours in all gratitude and good faith,

Nivedita of Ramakrishna

Up to that moment, she had always signed herself, 'Nivedita of the Ramakrishna Order'. She now changed her title to 'Nivedita of Ramakrishna', and finally, to 'Nivedita of Ramakrishna-Vivekananda'. She was still the friend, colleague, and, in some ways, the honorary daughter, of the Order; the ties of friendship, concern and fellowship would continue; but formally and in the eyes of the public, the break must be made clear. Whatever she did, the monastery would no longer be held responsible.

This also meant, of course, that there would be no further instruction or official expectation of obedience from the Head of the Order; though he would continue to give advice or assistance. The daughter of the house, so to speak, had left home; but only nominally. She had not gone very far away from them in her adherence.

The *Amrita Bazar Patrika* of 19 July 1902 published a news item:

Sister Nivedita

We have been requested to inform the public that at the conclusion of the days of mourning of Swami Vivekananda; it has been decided between the Members of the Order at Belur Math and Sister Nivedita, that her work shall henceforth be regarded as free and entirely independent of their sanction or authority.

On 24 July she wrote to Joe MacLeod, worrying. Was she a school teacher or a nation-rouser? What about the school, and the work for women? Was the task for which she had come to India, big enough?

We talk of 'woman-making', but the great stream of Oriental woman's life flows on. Who am I that I should in any way seek to change it? Suppose even I could add my impress to ten or twelve girls, would it be so much gain? Is it not rather by taking the national consciousness of the women, like that of the men, and setting it towards greater problems and responsibilities that one can help? . . . I don't know. This may be all my own sophistry, I cannot tell. Only I think my task is to awake the nation, not to influence a few women.

The phrase 'add my impress to' is not one that Vivekananda himself would have used; his attitude of 'calling to the god within' and his 'hands off' to any suggestion of moulding or stamping a character, does not seem to be echoed here. But she knew only too well for how short a time her girls were likely to be at the school. Education for women was not taken very seriously by most of the parents, attendance would be irregular and could not be enforced, and when a girl showed intelligence and promise of becoming a teacher or leader herself in the future, it was of very little use, as she would be married and disappear into the Zenana in her early teens. To 'put an imprint on' a child before she was removed for ever, was the most Nivedita could do, in many cases, towards fostering a little independence of thought, or any sturdy nationalism, which might perhaps be passed on in time to each girl's own children.

It is significant that her first action was not to return to the school but to address large adult meetings.

On 19 July 1902 she left Calcutta for Jessore to address a memorial meeting in honour of Vivekananda. Next, she addressed a similar meeting at the Classic Theatre in Calcutta. And now she began to plan an extensive lecture tour of different parts of India. Not only did she hope to address the people, but she also needed money for the future, not just for the school, but for the many calls on her pity and her charity. Out of her tiny earnings she was already helping some poor women of the neighbourhood by paying them eight annas a week. The only way open to her at the moment appeared to be the finishing of her book *The Web of Indian Life*, which carried some hope of earning money; so she faced that task as well as the lecture tour, immediately following this time of emotional strain, tragedy, and the nagging worry of her final decision.

It is not surprising that all this – on a diet of fruit and milk, in the heat of an Indian summer in Calcutta – brought her to a state of physical weakness that caused collapse and illness during the first week in August.

As soon as news came to the monastery that she was ill, Swami Brahmananda, the Head of the Order, and a brother monk, went to visit her. It was an immediate example of what was to be the new shape of her life. She was independent, she lived her own life, but in illness or trouble, the 'daughter' was still a member of the family, in fact if not in name, and the Head of the Order who had agreed to her absolute right to run her own life, now exercised the right of a father to insist that she ate chicken and eggs, to gain a little strength, whether she liked it or not.

She did not like it. She had trained herself to live on the very simplest and most meagre vegetarian diet, and this new arrangement, even as a temporary measure, struck her as being shockingly extravagant and most unorthodox. But chicken and eggs she was given nevertheless, and she did what she was told, meekly enough. She rested and she ate well. Prolonged illness and weakness had thoroughly alarmed her. This was no moment to drop out of the battle. All that she cared about now was a return to health and vigour.

As soon as she was well, she began her lecture tour, and the monastery sent one of the Swamis to accompany her. It is probable that he kept a fatherly eye on her tendency to work herself to death on remarkably little food, and that she accepted his help or suggestions when she was unlikely to have listened to advice from anyone not connected with the monastery and with Vivekananda. But certainly her tour would not have been the success it was, and she might not have been so readily accepted by Indian audiences as a disciple of Vivekananda, with some right to speak in his name, without the presence of a representative of the Order, whose appearance with her underlined the Order's knowledge of her tour, and gave some official status to her lectures. It was a particularly opportune moment for the tour, when Bengal in particular and India in general was still stunned by the loss of its great patriot saint, and uncertain where to turn next.

The Swami who accompanied her, and was often her friend and adviser in time of need, was Swami Sadananda, and a better choice could not have been made, for the two had a great deal in common, both in their approach to religion, and in the life they had chosen to live. His first approach, like hers, had been through a simple and fervent personal devotion to Vivekananda; like Nivedita herself, he had been caught by the man's personality and character and had 'left all, and followed him'.

After the death of Sri Ramakrishna, before Vivekananda went to America, he spent much time wandering around India as a roving monk, uncertain how to spread his master's work, or how to help his own people whom he saw everywhere destitute and without leadership. Sadananda had then been a young station master at the Hathras railway station. The whole town became devoted to Vivekananda when he stayed there briefly, and when he left finally, Sadananda, now with begging bowl, left his job and went with him as his disciple. He found that a monk's life, wandering in the Himalayas, was a life of extreme hardship; when he was weak from hunger and thirst, Vivekananda looked after him, led him on horseback across a flooded river, and when he was too ill to stagger, carried his clothes, shoes and belongings.

When, after his American tour, Vivekananda, seated in his carriage of honour in Madras, saw Sadananda standing in the thickest part of a dense crowd, he stopped the carriage and shouted, 'Come, Sadananda! Come, my boy!' and made this gentlest of disciples sit with him in his carriage. So Sadananda was now linked with Nivedita in a common personal devotion to Vivekananda; both had left their lives, their careers and homes, and come to the point of no return; each had listened to Vivekananda's words on the subject of Indian servility to the British and lack of spiritual cohesion or any national unity; each had every reason to respect the other. In particular, each was deeply concerned about the young people of India, and anxious to strengthen the fibre and determination of the young. The ignorance of young Indians about any part of their country but their own, and the poverty which caused them to spend their lives in total ignorance of the world outside their own front door, and so made them dangerously easy to govern and direct, and all too easily deluded, had worried Nivedita for some time, as it had worried Vivekananda. Sadananda agreed with her. Quietly and in the background, he determined to do what he could.

On 22 September she left for Bombay, and began her lecture tour at the Gaiety Theatre, Bombay, where she spoke about Vivekananda. She followed this by two more lectures in the same theatre, with average audiences of a thousand on each occasion. Her lectures were widely reported, in Indian papers of repute, including the *Bombay Gazette* and *The Times of India*. Her subjects were religious and philosophical. There was nothing in them that could be regarded as even mildly revolutionary. What was revolutionary was the fact that a British woman, a disciple of Vivekananda, accompanied by a monk of the Order, was addressing them at all. And her words, her manner, her obvious passion for India, were more colourful than anything to which the audiences were accustomed.

She gave lecture after lecture, including talks to women; her welcome everywhere was overwhelming. On 1 October she wrote to Josephine

MacLeod: 'I was precipitated upon the task somewhat more suddenly than we expected, as you see. Oh! It is good to hear the news you tell from Swami – "India shall ring with her". Is that the plan which is now being fulfilled?'

She travelled on with Sadananda to Nagpur, and stayed as the guest of Justice Kohlatkar. She lectured on each of the four days of her stay and on her last day she crammed in four engagements, all with students, and addressed students' meetings. She moved on to give a series of lectures at Wardha and Baroda. It was at Baroda that she met Aurobindo Ghose, later to be imprisoned for nationalist activities, and the stories which eventually grew up concerning the meeting of these two, first in Baroda and later in Calcutta, became more and more fantastic as time went on. Indeed, those who regarded her chief claim to respect and adulation as being the doubtful honour of achieving status as a bomb-throwing revolutionary, refused to the end to believe that nothing very sinister had happened on either of these occasions in spite of Aurobindo's denial of her involvement.

Then followed more lectures, further visits to other cities, and at last a return to Calcutta on 7 November. Then, later in the month, three more lectures, and, in early December, on to Madras with Sadananda. Here she stayed at a monastery established at Castle Kernan by Swami Ramakrishnananda, one of the great giants and stalwarts of the Order, and one of the original disciples of Sri Ramakrishna. She held him in the greatest respect, and he and many of his groups of students attended her lectures. He had already started groups called 'Vivekananda Societies' at various places throughout the Presidency. These societies were organized for purposes of religion, and of educating and feeding the poor. The students and the workers met with her often in discussion groups to discuss not only the Swami's idealism and the Hindu religion but also the unity of India and nationalism.

On 20 December, she spoke on 'The Unity of India' to a large audience of educated Hindus, and it was a lecture of considerable significance.

She pointed out that 'We in India have a great synthesis, an unparalleled synthesis, full of strength, majesty and potentiality, and hope that the day would come when we should understand and know that, and act on the strength of it'.

There was no indication of exactly what meaning she implied, in her use of the word 'act'. Everything that she wrote and said at that time suggests that she was not concerned with the form action would take, her task was to call India into one undivided whole; she was preaching a conscious, proud and dignified sense of nationality. Until that became a reality, there was very little point in looking into the future.

She tore to shreds the British doctrine that what had united India was cheap postage, extended railway services, and the use of a common language – English.

If India had no unity herself, no unity could be given to her. The unity which undoubtedly belonged to India was self-born and had its own destiny, its own function and its own vast powers, but it was the gift of no one.

She knew her audiences. As usual, she spoke incisive sense with a strong emotional involvement that touched their hearts; typically, she wound up into a repetitive crescendo which may sound excessive when written down, but which brought her listeners to a pitch of fervour which neither intellectual statements, nor unfelt emotionalism could have done. She cared, and cared passionately and very obviously, about her subject and about every word she said.

Yet again shall come the great re-establishment of Dharma when the whole of this nation shall be united together not in a common weakness, not in a common misfortune or grievance but in a great, over-flowing, complex, actual, ever-strong, ever-living consciousness of the common nationality, the common heritage, the common struggle, the common life, aye! the common destiny and the common hope . . .

The lectures, discussion groups – mostly on Indian unity – and further travel fill her diary for the rest of the month. 1902 was a year of much stirring in India; Congress leaders were already issuing petitions and protests. She could not have started her work at a more opportune moment.

Nivedita's *bête-noire*, Lord Curzon, took a step in 1902 which infuriated her more than anything else he could have done. It brought in protests from all over India. He appointed a Universities Commission, on the basis of which a Universities Act was later passed in 1904. He 'officialized' the universities, and thus brought all education under the control of the British government, rather than the local municipalities. Nivedita was an educationist, in every sense of the word; indeed, whenever she was asked what was her function in India, she replied, 'a teacher'. Now she wrote furiously in a letter:

We have had a Universities Commission lately, which has done its very best to kill all education, and especially all science education. This is *the* point in India's wrongs that fires me, the right of India to be India, the right of India to think for herself, the right of India to *knowledge*. Were this not the great grievance, I might be fired by her right to bread, to justice, to other things, but this outweighs all.

She was watched by the police, and her letters were censored, but she expected this. The police did not necessarily assume that she was making bombs. She tried, even now, to be fair to the British. A report in the *Madras Times* on 28 December quoted her statement that 'the crowning glory of the British Empire was that it was conscious of treating India as a whole from one end to the other. The fault under which many Indians were labouring was that they concerned themselves solely with their village or their province.' With a sense of justice that must have cost her a good deal, she added that 'Lord Curzon, the present Viceroy, was showing a wonderful energy in that direction'.

Before 1902 – that vital year in her life – was over, there was one memory added to many others of the past which she recorded in the last chapter of the book she later wrote, *The Master As I Saw Him*, and it is a chapter of gentleness and religious faith which make all implications of 'bomb-throwing revolutionary plans' so out of key as to be ludicrous.

A little before Christmas, as her Madras programme was fixed for Christmas itself, she went with Swami Sadananda and Bramachari Amulya, then a novice who afterwards became Swami Sankarananda, the seventh President of the Order, to Khandagiri, and sat on the grass by a lighted log among the hills and caves at the edge of the forest.

Since Hinduism accepts all Incarnations, Christ was worshipped; and just as the great Hindu religious epics are acted and dramatized, so the two monks of this Hindu Order 'kept Christmas Eve' by acting the part of the shepherds in the Christian gospel, one of them carrying a crook. They had a copy of the Gospel of St Luke, and read it aloud in the relevant passages, but they did not stop there. They went on to read of the death and resurrection of Christ, and to discuss it.

But the tale sounded as never before, in our ears. Instead of a legal document, dated and attested, whose credibility must stand or fall by the clearness and coherence of the various parts, it read now like the gasping, stammering witness of one who had striven to put on record the impalpable and the intangible. The narrative of the Resurrection was no longer, for us, an account of an event, to be accepted or rejected. It had taken its place for ever more as a spiritual perception, which one who had experienced it had striven, not always successfully, to put into words. For had we not had our own glimmerings of a like back-coming to put beside it?

17

The school had reopened in February 1902, but it had seen very little of its headmistress. In the last week of January 1903, Nivedita took over from Miss Bett, who had been looking after things, and in March she was joined by Christine.

The education was founded on the system in which 'knowledge is supposed to receive a foundation in concrete experience, and all work to appear to the child as play'; drawing, brush-work, clay-modelling, mat-weaving, paper-cutting, sewing and games were included, with the more formal study of Bengali and English, Arithmetic, Geography and History. Nivedita wrote to Joe MacLeod in April:

> I really think you would be charmed with our little house. Our first courtyard is quite a vision of red brick and green plants, and we keep it exquisitely clean, and two or three good airy rooms.
>
> Sometimes, after dark, ladies come in to see us, and they sit down in basket chairs with cushions, while we often sit on the floor to talk with them. I know they like it, and they are so fine they never show the least surprise or shyness about foreign ways. . . . We are just living here quietly, and letting things grow about us.

The change to living there quietly and letting things grow about them, after the determined and emotional strivings of that colossal lecture tour; the needs of one or two little girls after the arguments and even greater needs of audiences of thousands; it was a glimpse of peace, with its courtyard and airy rooms. The women who came to visit them (after dark, for it was not respectable to be seen on the streets) showed how far her influence had spread, and how greatly the trust was growing. Until Nivedita arrived, education had been in the hands of Christian missionaries, who insisted on converting (or, as the Hindus saw it, 'perverting') their pupils, and who would not believe that Hinduism could accept a worship of Christ without giving up its own faith. But these two disciples of Swami Vivekananda followed his own instructions 'never to teach against the aspirations of the taught'; and trust and neighbourliness grew stronger.

There were forty-five girls in the school in that small house. Nivedita kept a careful record of each child, and the records are illuminating, starting with the child's caste and then abruptly turning into a vivid cameo portrait of a real child who springs out of the page at us, not a number on a school register but a complete and individual personality.

Shubashini Datta

Caste Kayastha. Attended 51 times out of 60. Shubashini is said to resemble her grandmother in being witty, sociable, agreeable and utterly superficial. It is a very clever and happy kind of superficiality, however. I like the child. She picks up English well. Her colour work is excellent. She has an intense love of manual occupations, in which she becomes perfectly absorbed and never tires of repetition. Learns good manners easily.

Bidyutmala Bose

Caste Kayastha. Attended 45 times out of 60. One of the strongest characters I have ever seen. Her courage and determination are wonderful. And she has exquisite taste. She was troublesome and disobedient till I had a quiet talk with her the other day – since then a smile has been enough. And the daintiest offerings have constantly arrived. She has fire and will enough for anything but will be smothered in marriage, of course. Her sewing is particularly good. Let me make special memorial of the garland of pink and white flowers in the green plant lying solitary in its basket.

Gynandabala

Caste Koyburtho. Attended 22 times. A funny low-caste child, with the kindest of hearts and a mania for homework. She never liked lessons and could hardly be taught to read but if she could clean the schoolroom or help Bett she was in clover. Afterwards, in the days of plague work, she would dog me on the inspection round. It turned out that she kept a little shop for her mother. She wanted to be much more liberal than her mother one day when I went to buy bananas – and I cannot forget the quick flush of shame with which she received the mother's restrictions.

All the little girls. Bright-eyed, eager, full of promise; and nearly all destined to be snatched back, half-educated, to live out the rest of their lives hidden away. The gentle, self-effacing life of the Hindu wife was one of the nobler aspects of Hindu life that drew Nivedita most to India; but she was depressed that it must start so soon, that there was no choice; that those who, like herself, might have been leaders, nuns, or teachers, or even in some cases educated married women, marrying later in life, had no hope. She wrote of one child, 'She is determined not to marry and has told someone that, if forced, she will commit suicide. She has tremendous conscience and most refined feelings and plenty of commonsense. She takes quickly to great ideas, and must be saved from marriage!'

One of her pupils, Saralabala Dasi, became in her later years the first Head of the Woman's Convent (dedicated to Sri Sarada Devi), many years after Nivedita's death. As a child, she watched and remembered. She noticed, for instance, that unlike most Westerners, Nivedita had no punkha or whirling fan in the room to make the heat tolerable. She kept a hand-fan near her, and went on working. As time went on, she was usually in her study, writing her books and articles, and concentrated too deeply to notice the heat. When she left her room, her face and eyes would turn red with intense heat, and she went from room to room to see what the students were doing, and how the work was proceeding. Often she held her hands to her head, and if asked why, replied, 'I've a bad headache.' Then back to her writing she went, and the headache went with her.

In an age when children were seen and not heard, and Indian girl children more so than most, Nivedita believed with a passion that almost rivalled her passion for India, that a child's work was its own Karma-yoga as truly as an adult's dedicated work should be, and that work done for God should be reverenced and valued, even if the hand that fashioned the work was a child's hand, and the work itself, 'frightful'.

Bringing for modelling a mound of clay and some patterns, she would gather the girls together. 'We will all learn,' she would say, and with great enthusiasm, sit for modelling. . . . No matter how frightful might be the figure made and brought to her by any girl in the early stages, Nivedita with great respect would take it, and just as one touches the deity's prasad [food blessed and offered to the deity] to one's forehead, she would touch it to her forehead, and decorate her room with it.

The little girls used to shape tiny dolls and bring to her; these she kept in a box. In this way all the things fashioned by her pupils' hands lay on display in her room, in layers. . . .

She kept a painting of a hundred-petalled lotus, surrounded by small jasmine flowers, hanging in her bedroom. She was extremely proud of it; one of her girls had painted it.

The children were always a little in awe of her; her manner could be severe, and she would punish by simply ignoring altogether a child who was a nuisance; but her enthusiasms, her way of clapping her hands like a child and saying 'Right! Right!' when they had done well, and her reverence for their efforts, whether frightful or otherwise, won them completely; they made tiny dolls for her, they followed her round, they remembered the days in the school for years afterwards.

But Nivedita was still constantly pulled in her interests and anxieties towards the larger field of work. In April she wrote in a letter, 'The whole task now is to give the word "nationality" to India in all its breadth and meaning. The rest will do itself. India must be obsessed by this great conception . . .'

'India *must* be.' Startling words to come from the tiny building in Bosepara Lane. But the theme of nationality, nation-making, was never out of her mind. She said that she spoke it with every breath she drew, like a mantra.

In July, when the school was closed during the intense heat of the Calcutta summer, she visited Darjeeling, in the foothills of the Himalayas. Every year, throughout her life, she took holidays with her close friends, Dr and Mrs Bose; on this occasion Christine went with them, and they were joined by Mrs Ole Bull. It was a gathering of friends, and Nivedita wrote to Alberta Sturges, the Albert of the Ridgely Manor days, Joe MacLeod's niece. She told her that she was busily writing her book, *The Web of Indian Life*. She had a great hope that after that she might begin a book about Vivekananda. '*That* ought to be a great Nation-Maker, if one is found worthy to write true things in a true way. And Nation-making seems now the one and true task.'

She was happy among the mountains 'with a great morning vision of snowy Kinchinjunga'. When she became tired she went for a twenty-mile ride on horseback 'to get over the fatigue of writing', which probably did not surprise her friends. Mrs Ole Bull mothered Christine, and Nivedita remarked, 'I think Christine never felt "mothered" in her life before.' The whole letter suggests a time of peace and refreshment, in so far as Nivedita was capable of peace; she seemed to catch at it in snatches, in the intervals of writing and horse-riding and making plans for the school and the campaign for nationalism.

Plans were already in her mind for starting a Woman's section in the school. In November the women's section was opened, and the only hours possible for it were between noon and four o'clock when the women were free from household duties, and could spend what might otherwise have been the siesta hour in learning, reading and writing (taught by the sister of Dr Bose). Classes were held on religion, and needlework was taught to them by Christine. The school report mentions how the women tried to finish their housework early in order to attend the school in time, and how they behaved with almost saintly amiability to their families and did double the amount of housework so that nobody should prevent their going to school. To these young women it was a revelation. Nivedita told Joe MacLeod that it was unheard of that married zenana ladies should leave their homes and come to lessons at the house of a European. 'But they do it, and there never was a moment's difficulty.'

Much of the success of this new project was due to Christine. Nivedita said, 'The women's work is a wonderful success. But *she* is *more* wonderful. Her whole time is given up to study, work and visiting. She lives here, without fuss, without complexity. I look at her and feel that I never knew my own measureless inadequacy before.'

There was always a touch of something very like guilt in her praise of Christine. This was the humble, steady, behind-the-scenes worker and teacher, dedicated to her one job only, and getting on with it, silently, which Nivedita always felt that Vivekananda had intended she should be herself, and which in some moods she longed to be. Certainly she knew that without Christine her work would have been impossible.

As the numbers continued to grow, 17 Bosepara Lane became altogether too small. They rented the old house at Number 16 as well, and it was kept entirely for work; this was Nivedita's old house, her first home. Classes were held in the outer rooms. In the two large rooms upstairs, Christine held her sewing classes and in Nivedita's old bedroom Christine now slept. Nivedita and her one servant stayed at Number 17.

Nivedita taught sewing and needlework and gave teachers' training classes for the older girls; an optimistic step. The work of the school began every day with the chanting of Sanskrit prayers, and

'Bande Mataram' in front of a decorated picture of Sri Ramakrishna. 'Bande Mataram' ('I salute the Mother') was a song which later became the national anthem of India, before independence, and as a slogan it was eventually prohibited by the British government.

So the little school flourished, and was often visited by Sarada Devi; but Nivedita was not content. She never was. She dreamed of its becoming the nucleus of a huge educational movement, the centre of a University Settlement to promote the cause of national education. She also planned to start a Boys' Home, in which the boys could study for six months, and spend the other six touring the country, so that they might learn to know and love their own country, since most of them had never been outside Calcutta. Ultimately, they might become a new kind of monastic order dedicated to the service of the country. She said that she was 'bubbling over' with the idea, and somehow she would rent a house in Baghbazar.

A Home could not, in fact, be started. But Swami Sadananda, as enthusiastic as she was herself, took some boys of the Vivekananda Home to the Pindari Glacier, and Rabindranath Tagore sent his young son with them. Indeed, Sadananda made several such tours with the boys over the next few years, and wore his already frail health to a state from which it never recovered. But, like Nivedita herself, and like their Master before them, he had never been much concerned with preserving his health to a comfortable old age.

During this year, Nivedita was not only teaching – one job was never sufficient – but she also had a heavy programme of lectures, both in Calcutta and outside Bengal, and she was writing regularly for twenty-one newspapers and journals.

As well as this, she added one more responsibility to her home life, which many people would have regarded as a burden. To her, it was a joy.

Gopaler-Ma – the venerable old lady, the child widow who had lived as an isolated nun at Kamarhaty, who so often visited Sarada Devi, and was treated by them all with the utmost respect, for she had treated Sri Ramakrishna like a son, seeing in him the 'Baby Gopala' whom she worshipped – she, at the age of ninety, had fallen ill. Nivedita begged to be allowed to have the old lady in her own house, and to nurse her until she died. This most orthodox of women, who had been shocked to find a European staying at Sarada Devi's house, willingly agreed to stay with Nivedita, who called her 'dear little grandmother' and 'dearest treasure'. Special arrangements were made for her food, and a young Brahmin widow, Kusum, stayed in the house to look after her. But Nivedita loved, tended, and cared for her personally whenever she could, for two and a half years until she died, and served with the absolute humility of the young to the old (and in this case to the saintly old, blessed and venerated by Sri Ramakrishna) which was very Hindu indeed.

And so, when she travelled and lectured, in India or abroad, she had a home in Bosepara Lane, and now it was a busy home. No longer solitary, she had an ever-growing family. Christine, the children, the women who came in the afternoons, her own servant, Kusum the attendant of Gopaler-Ma, and Gopaler-Ma herself. And in her own room were the boxes of tiny dolls that the children had made, and their clay models – all their early efforts – lying on display in layers. She had, at last, the joy of a family of her own; and, like most families, it brought with it anxiety, responsibilities, and problems as well. But it was a home, a focus, and a centre; in time it became known as The House of the Sisters and a little black plate on the front door of Number 17 bore the words 'Hours of Call – 7 to 9 a.m.' In the cool of the early morning, before the work of the day began, men, women and children – and, later, statesmen, writers, and thinkers of many nationalities, though most frequently Indian – called, and talked, and discussed. This small beginning was to grow and grow; by the end of 1903 it was beginning, and Nivedita felt herself totally a Hindu, with a Hindu home, even a Hindu 'grandmother' and many friendships. Perhaps peace was not at the moment on the agenda, but activity and hope certainly were.

18

In January of 1904 she hurled herself into a series of lectures; at first at Calcutta, then on to Patna, and a tour of Bihar. Education was her special theme, especially in relation to Lord Curzon's Universities Act. At Bankipore she turned her fury on the audience. 'It is for you to do, and you should not crouch before the Government like monkeys to get done by the Government what you ought to do for yourself... You must not sit back and thank the Government. You must work, work and work and remake the meaning of Education.'

Far from resenting, the audience loved it. Next day the *Bihar Herald* wrote, 'We wish there were more persons amongst us of the type of Sister Nivedita to rebuke and chide us as she has done and for which she can but have our sincere gratitude.'

Her appearance impressed them. Abanindranath Tagore, when he met her first at the house of the American consul, described her long white gown (made of flannel or light wool) and the rosary of Rudraksha beads around her neck; her brown hair tied in a high knot. The dress was a sensible and practical variant of the long European dress of the day, shorn of its hour-glass shape and distortions, with sleeves that were loose and full at the wrists; suggesting both the nun's robe and the sleeves of a simple Western dress, and probably cooler than the tight wrists of some dresses of the period. The Rudraksha beads (the rosary used for the repeating of the mantra) made it clear where her religious allegiance lay, and it was a characteristic gesture of hers to finger the beads when she spoke in public. She was a striking figure, and described by a A. J. F. Blair as 'a tall, robust woman in the very prime of life. Her face in repose was almost plain. The cheekbones were high and the jaws were square. The face at first glance expressed energy and determination, but you would hardly have looked at it again but for the forehead and the eyes. The eyes were a calm deep blue and literally lit up the whole countenance.'

Her friend H. W. Nevinson cut this detailed description out and went straight to the point which struck her audiences. 'It is as vain to describe Sister Nivedita in two pages as to reduce fire to a formula and call it knowledge . . . Like fire, and like Shiva, Kali, and other Indian powers of the spirit, she was at once destructive and creative, terrible and beneficent. There was no dull tolerance about her, and I suppose no one ever called her gentle . . .'

Gopaler-Ma might have disagreed; so might Sarada Devi, and the children who died in her arms in the plague epidemic; but she was mother and matriarch, and what India was seeing then was the matriarch, who buckled on her son's shield and sent him out to the fight. In these moods they did not want gentleness; they needed fire, and she gave it to them. She continued her lecture tour to Rajgir, Nalanda, Bodh Gaya and Banaras, on to Lucknow and returned to Calcutta in February. She desperately needed a rest.

She rested by giving five very forceful lectures to huge audiences in Calcutta, and went on to tackle the vital problem of Hindu–Muslim unity in the face of British domination.

> What then was the duty of the Indian Mussalman? It was not to relate himself to Arabia. He had no need of that; his relation to Arabia was of his very life-blood; it had been accomplished for him by the faith and patient labour of his fore-fathers. No; his duty was to relate himself to India – his home by blood or by adoption and hospitality . . .

She saw the necessity of 'divide and rule' as a policy for governing an Empire; it was useful to the British. This was no time for Hindu–Muslim riots. Unity and nationalism gave her the answer, and she never ceased to hammer it home. In March she was invited to Banaras, and gave three lectures. There was no concealment about any of her lectures; indeed, concealment would have been impossible, and all the lectures were reported widely in the newspapers. The British government had no illusions whatever about her views, and what she was doing. She was watched, but that was all.

At home, a more gentle life continued. In February, Sarada Devi came to Calcutta, and Nivedita met her. Sarada Devi returned constantly to her own village, to help her old mother, to cope with a sometimes difficult family of younger brothers, to work in the fields like any village woman, and then in Calcutta she lived the life of a great spiritual figure, however hidden; always open to those who wished to visit her. Nivedita wrote to Joe MacLeod:

> The Holy Mother is here, so small, so thin, so dark, worn-out physically I should say, with village hardship and village life. But the same clear mind

the same stateliness, the same womanhood, as before; Oh, how many comforts I would like to take to her. She needs a soft pillow, a shelf, a rug, so many things. I would like to give her a beautiful picture, a piece of bright colours. But I suppose I must wait.

Christine continued to run the school; Gopaler-Ma, in contented senility, lived quietly in the house with Nivedita. In the summer holidays, Nivedita and Christine, with Dr and Mrs Bose, went to stay at the Ashram of Mayavati in the Himalayas, established at Vivekananda's wish, by Captain and Mrs Sevier, and now still run by the widowed Mrs Sevier. In Mayavati, Bose began writing his well-known book *Plant Response*. On return to Calcutta, the lectures began again.

During this year (1904) she wrote to Alberta Sturges, the niece of Josephine MacLeod, who had written to her in some anxiety because she could not reconcile her experience of Vivekananda's teachings with her present feelings of devotion to Jesus Christ, and was taking spiritual instruction from a Roman Catholic Priest, Father Powell. He did not at all approve of Nivedita's religious belief.

Why, dear Alberta, you *could* not change your Master for Him whom the Indian woman names. Every word and custom, every discovery and prepossession of your life makes you a Christian, and correspondingly every moment here makes of one born to it something which is *named* differently. That is all.

To Father Powell it was not all, by any means, as she knew.

I am so grateful for this sight of Fr. Powell's letter. If only he cd. have *in*cluded, instead of excluding me, I shd. have felt so thankful! For I feel always like an exiled and repudiated child of the Church Catholic.

I think you know how my intellectual life of many many years might be summed up as a wild longing to be restored to her, combined with a hopeless inability to subscribe to the doctrine of the objective and exclusive truth of her Creeds. And then came Swamiji . . . But since then, no priest, no nun, has been able to include me, and endorse my life. And for that I have often been sad.

She was unsurprised by the priest's rejection.

After all, we are in opposite, or at least different, camps. It is useless to forget it. Yet I can love and understand his, though *he* cannot, mine. But in India – ! He forgets his Religion here is not of 'the poor and lowly' but the Faith of the alien Government – rich, powerful, not trusted or loved.

She was aware that Father Powell and other orthodox Christians would not have approved of one of her great enthusiasms which dominated that year for her. She visited many places associated with Buddha; Bankipore, Rajgir, Nalanda, Sarnath and Bodh Gaya. She believed, as Vivekananda did, that Buddhism was not a religion separate from Hinduism but only one of many sects within it, whose followers worshipped their great Hindu teacher as higher and holier than others, just as the followers of Ramakrishna worshipped him, but also accepted the greatness of Buddha. Time, she felt, has crystallized Buddhism into something that was often too 'exclusive' and 'separate', just as Christianity, too, had crystallized into the view which Ramakrishna jokingly described as 'only *my* watch tells the correct time!'

She longed for a revival of Buddhism within India, and made several visits to Bodh Gaya, and in October went there for the third time, this time with a party including, amongst others, Dr Bose, Swami Sankarananda, and Rabindranath Tagore. They were all lodged in the house of the Mahanta (abbot).

Nivedita read to them daily from Warren's *Buddhism in Translation* and sometimes from Edwin Arnold's *Light of Asia*. There were songs and recitations by Tagore. In the evening they meditated by the Bodhi tree.

But the heights threw her to the depths again. The greater the inspiration, the further from the goal India seemed to her to be. On the last night at Bodh Gaya she cried all night.

'We have failed. The country has not been roused from its slumber. We have been able to do almost nothing.'

On the way home, she was still depressed. At the Gaya station the party, including Rabindranath Tagore and his son, and Dr and Mrs Bose, awaited their trains. Dr and Mrs Bose were going to Calcutta by the Bombay Mail. Their train came in first. Two Englishmen were seated in a first-class compartment. When Dr and Mrs Bose tried to get into the carriage, the Englishmen objected violently; they were not going to travel with Indians. One of them went to fetch the station master to remove the Boses; the station master was unwilling to take action.

When the Englishman returned, he found Nivedita telling any Englishmen who cared to listen, exactly what she thought of their behaviour. It is unfortunate that her words have not been recorded; they would have been worth hearing. The carriage door was opened, and the Boses were allowed into the carriage, at the last moment, as the guard blew his whistle.

When the train left, a furiously angry Nivedita was still raging against her countrymen's impertinence. When her own train arrived, she found that there were only two first-class compartments in the train. One was occupied by an Englishwoman, the other by a man – an Indian. Her luggage was taken to the Englishwoman's carriage, and Nivedita, still simmering, said, 'I am not going in there.'

Her luggage was taken to the other compartment, where the Indian helped her and made room for her. She called her companions and said grimly, 'Now you see the difference between barbarous Englishmen and the civilized Indians.'

It is very possible that exhaustion took a heavier toll of her than she would ever admit. As well as the lecture tours, the pilgrimages, the school, the nursing of Gopaler-Ma, and the work with Dr Bose on his books, plus her own writing, she also addressed, inspired and took under her wing some of the many groups of nationalistic young men which began to spring up.

There were many groups of this type, the Young Men's Hindu Union Committee, the Gita Society, the Dawn Society, the Anusilan Samity and the Vivekananda Society. Of them all, the Dawn Society and the Anusilan Samity drew the biggest numbers, had the most influence, and were begun and guided by some of the most well-known Hindus of the day.

Aurobindo was impatient with the Congress, which he regarded as too timid and moderate. At this stage he was in favour of revolutionary propaganda in the hopes of eventually using armed force against the British. In his autobiography, he stated that he found small groups of revolutionaries in existence, but as they were scattered and disorganized he tried to unite them under one leader. To help in this organization in Bengal he created a central council of five people, 'one of them being Nivedita'. After the council had ceased to exist, he became busy with his own work and she with hers, and they had no consultations about the revolutionary movement.

His idea of unification did not succeed; the various groups and societies could not agree with each other; the council was abandoned. Nivedita's role was chiefly confined to giving her books to the Anusilan Samity; books which she thought might inspire them, including volumes on the Irish Revolution, the History of Mutiny, the American Wars of Independence, the lives of Mazzini and Garibaldi, and books on economics. She also addressed the young men and became practically a guru to them. She had doubts as to whether passive resistance alone would be enough, and she made no secret of the fact that if passive resistance failed, Aurobindo's ideas might be needed. A picture of her role as being that of a Mother of Revolution – the power behind the throne, inspiring Aurobindo – has been depicted by some of her admirers as well as by those who disapproved of her, in spite of Aurobindo's flat denial. The moderate leaders of Congress, R. C. Dutt and G. K. Gokhale, were equally friendly with her, and both consulted her about their policies; she took great interest in their ideas and ideals, though she supported the views of the extremists. Gokhale came to visit her at Bosepara Lane when he stayed in Calcutta, and they talked at length about national politics. If the police were watching her, and they undoubtedly were, they must have regarded her friends as a very mixed bag: revolutionaries, extremists, liberals, moderates, and non-political monks. Anybody, in fact, who was sincerely concerned with the welfare of India. It would have been easy to arrest her. They saw no point in doing so.

As her battle for India increased, her gentleness became deeper, the fury became more militant. Even her closest friends had to go through the verbal sword-play, which could be unpleasant, before they were accepted into friendship. As Nevinson said, 'Even with her friends, her disagreement could be vehement, and her contradiction was very direct. . . . Her scorn of presumptuous ignorance and her indignation at wrong were blasting. . . . No one would call her gentle. But of all nobly sympathetic natures, she was amongst the finest.'

She was conscious of the two strands in her own nature, and even in 1903 she had written: 'Let me plough my furrow across India just as deep, deep, deep to the very centre of things, as it will go. Let it be either as a hidden voice sending out noiseless things from a cell, or as a personality romping and raging through the big cities – I don't care!'

'Romping and raging' may be a sideways blow struck at her own most typical activities; a hidden voice in a cell is perhaps less typical, and she finished the paragraph in true Nivedita style: 'But the God of my own strong right hand grant that I do not have to waste my effervescence in Western futilities. I think that I would rather commit suicide! India is the starting point and the goal, as far as I am concerned. Let *her* look after the West if she wishes.'

That was the note that the young Indians and the older politicians crowded to hear. And she continued to give it to them, as often as they wished, whenever she was asked to do so.

In The House of the Sisters, with the little black plate on the front door, they came to talk quietly. Fairly quietly, at least. The historian, Sir Jadunath Sarkar, wrote:

> Many of our educated countrymen – I narrate it with shame – used to call on her at every hour of the day and disturb her meditation and work, thoughtlessly, out of a frivolous spirit of enjoying the fun of talking to a remarkable newcomer and a 'pacca memsahib' too! Some begged for money at the end, or literary contributions from her pen, or letters of recommendation to someone in power! Very few offered her the assistance of their own labour or money.

But she did not mind. This was home, and she enjoyed meeting her friends there. Even the lane was homely, and she loved to walk up it, tired out after a day's lecturing. In the spaces between the larger, older houses, once the property of great families, little villages of mud huts with red tiled roofs had grown up, sheltered by coconut palms, where the washing hung out to dry. And in her own home, not only her study, but the roof of the house enchanted her. That roof was very much home. To the neighbouring women, secluded in the zenana, the rooftop was the place to gather in the coolness of the evening, and to talk to women on the other roofs. The girls of a family were often allowed to sleep up there, when the heat was so intense that it was impossible to breathe in the house. In the court of each house, in the open, the evening meal was cooked over a small fire. Nivedita sat on her rooftop in the evenings, looking down at the smoke rising from the little fires, and looking out at the Ganges, which could be glimpsed from the roofs of Bosepara Lane.

19

These were the years of ferment and agitation, of discussion and argument and the making of future plans based on present ideals. The Sunday morning breakfasts in The House of the Sisters in Bosepara Lane became well known. On Sundays there was no school, and the early morning, before the burden and heat of the day began, was the best time for the journalists, members of Congress, scientists, and men of ideas in all walks of life, to meet and talk. S. K. Ratcliffe, the editor of the *Statesman*, cycled down with his wife from their own house every Sunday morning for breakfast. He wrote afterwards in his *Margaret Noble: In Memoriam* that breakfast was served very simply on the little verandah, and those who talked there could never tear themselves away until the sun had become too hot for a comfortable journey back through he blazing streets.

Certainly Nivedita was under surveillance, but no move was made by the police. She spoke in support of the extremists rather than the moderates; she was known to be a friend of Surendrenath Banerjea, at that time an extremist in Congress, but also of R. C. Dutt, the economist and liberal. More dangerous to her was her friendship with Aurobindo. His aims were frankly revolutionary at this period of his life. He was also enthusiastic about Kali-worship. Nivedita's book, *Kali the Mother*, inspired him. He knew that Hindus would need a rallying-point, in which he proved to be a true prophet, but his choice of symbol was unfortunate. Even amongst Hindus, Kali-worship was a hotly controversial issue. Nivedita's famous Kali-lecture brought a flood of protest as well as great approval. The horrors associated with the worship had gone too far for many Hindus to accept, as she did, the great philosophy which lay behind it, and the rock which finally smashed the Kali-symbol as a rallying-point for a united India was Muslim abhorrence of the whole blood-soaked ritual, which they could not accept; they also regarded it as far too Hindu in its religious application to be a suitable symbol for a united India.

In 1905 Nivedita designed a national flag, which was embroidered by her girls in scarlet and yellow, and was displayed in the Exhibition organized by Congress in 1906. The symbol she used was the Vajra or thunderbolt, which represented 'selfless man'. Many people accepted the symbol and began to display it, but in fact the symbol which was to unite India many years later proved to be Gandhi's Charkha. It was the spinning wheel, not Kali or the thunderbolt, which led India to independence.

During these turbulent years, Nivedita continued to encourage anything that might unite the country in a common strength, in any sense of manliness or purpose as one nation. 'It begins to be thought that there is a religious idea that may be called Indian, but it is of no single sect; that there is a social idea, which is the property of no caste or group; that there is a historic evolution, in which all are united; that it is the thing within *all* these which alone is called "India".' They are Nivedita's words, but they might well have been the words of Gandhi.

The economist Benoy Sarkar said of her that she was 'the philosopher of romantic nationalism and aggressive Indianism'. Her longing to turn Indian apathy into something united and aggressive, something full of a passionate life of its own, poured out during those years into a concern for education, for art, for a renaissance not only of Indian art but of thought and culture and aspiration of any kind which might bring vitality to a nation that appeared to be withering.

Curzon's determination to unite India more closely met with her approval, his method of achieving this end by bringing the nation more firmly under British rule did not. When she crossed swords with him, she did so in the columns of the newspapers. As Chancellor of the University of Calcutta, he stated in his convocation address that truthfulness was primarily the virtue of the West, not of the East. His educated Indian audience, including Sir Gurudas Banerjea and Nivedita, felt deeply insulted. Two days later, the *Amrita Bazar Patrika* published two quotations, under the heading 'Lord Curzon in Various Capacities'. Both were provided by Nivedita, anonymously. The first was the long quotation on Western truthfulness, taken from his recent speech to the University, the second was a quotation from his own book, *Problems of The Far East*, in which he gave an example of his own untruthfulness, used cynically for the furtherance of his career. Nivedita pointed out that a recent edition of the book omitted the incident.

The *Statesman* reprinted both quotations next day, with an editorial comment, 'The pure fun which these two pictures have given in India and will ere long give in England was worth the whole performance.' But Nivedita was less concerned with fun than with anger towards the audience who had taken Curzon's remarks so quietly. In the columns of the *Statesman* she accused them of having lacked manhood in failing to leap to the defence of their nation and their ancestors. This evidently had its effect, for in March a huge mass meeting was held at the Town Hall with Dr Rashbehari Ghose in the chair, in protest against Curzon's convocation address.

Two days later, Nivedita fell seriously ill. The doctors diagnosed meningitis. After prolonged nursing, she left, with the Boses, to recuperate in Darjeeling, and did not return to Calcutta until July.

On 20 July, Curzon announced the partition of Bengal. The area had become too large for efficient administration; he intended to enlarge Assam by transferring several large Districts to it. This was to be done by drawing a boundary line through central Bengal. It gave a majority to the Muslims in the new Eastern Province, and to Biharis and Oriyas in the West. The Muslims had supported the British rulers throughout the decade, and it was hoped that they might form some bulwark against Hindu nationalism, which was rising in Calcutta and might begin to spread.

The blow united Bengal as never before. The people had not been consulted; their feelings had been ignored; they were humiliated. On 7 August a protest meeting was organized at the Town Hall. Nivedita wrote in her diary on that day, 'Partition of Bengal Meeting. The black shadow.'

Surendrenath Banerjea led protests and petitions, and was heartily supported in them all by Nivedita. It became increasingly clear that these methods would not put back the boundaries where they had been – and yet, though Nivedita never saw the results, the clamour of public outcry and anger eventually produced exactly that result. In 1905 Curzon resigned the Viceroyalty. When George V, then Prince of Wales, visited India in 1905–06 he became convinced that partition had been a mistake and one of his first acts as King in 1911 was to reunify the Province. Lord Minto, who succeeded Curzon as Viceroy, thought Curzon totally mistaken in forcing the matter through against all the wishes and hopes of Bengal, and in the teeth of united Hindu opposition, and he began to work behind the scenes with John Morley, who became the new Secretary of State for India in 1906. Morley was already a fighter for Irish rights; he and Minto were both concerned that Indian public opinion should be consulted. They knew that the day of totally autocratic and paternalistic rule was over for ever. It was the first step towards the final realization that the day of imperial and colonial rule of any kind was drawing to its close, but there was a long way to go yet.

Nivedita approved of Minto and his reforms; but those reforms too were still to come. In 1905, and in the years that followed, it was the flame of bitterness and anger that she fed, and she gave her help to all those who were feeding it; what lay beyond did not concern her. She had been trained as a Karma yogi, in the yoga of selfless work which cares nothing for the fruits of work. 'To work you have the right, but not to the fruits of work.'

One new weapon came into Hindu hands; the Swadeshi movement. This was a boycott of British products and an insistence on purchasing only Indian-made goods. In the long term it might be difficult to sustain, but Nivedita saw that for the moment it would bring the markets to a standstill and would certainly cause permanent injury to the fortunes of many British merchants. Above all else it would unite the Hindus and give even the poorest and most illiterate a chance to experience, and to show publicly, a little national pride. It was no accident that it coincided with the singing of the forbidden song 'Bande Mataram' on the streets. She wrote in *The Indian Review*:

> The note of manliness and self-help is sounded throughout the Swadeshi Movement. It is precisely in a matter like the keeping of the Swadeshi vow that the Indian people especially can find an opportunity to show their true mettle . . . The Swadeshi Movement has come to stay, and grow, and to drive back forever in modern India the tides of reaction and despair.

The day of Partition, 16 October, was observed as a day of mourning and fasting amongst Hindus in Calcutta and Congress decided to raise a national fund to help home industries.

The 1905 session of Congress was held at Banaras. Nivedita was invited by Gokhale, the President-elect, to attend. She attended all the sittings, and her house in Tilbhandeswar was a meeting place of the leaders of various shades of opinion. The members from Bengal were by now divided into extremists and moderates. Nivedita supported the extremists, who were determined to gain acceptance for the Swadeshi Movement. They were led by Bipin Chandra Pal, and Gokhale, as a moderate, opposed him. Gokhale stated that Indian destinies were now permanently linked with those of England, and advance must continue within the Empire itself. Nivedita disagreed with him, and supported the extremists, but both men were her friends, and met at her house in a common unity. The extremists' resolution was accepted unanimously. Nivedita wrote 'The one thing that strikes a first-time visitor to the Congress, for instance – a visitor who goes with a determination to ignore preconceptions and judge as far as possible from facts – is the extraordinary agreement of all members, from extreme right to extreme left.'

In the Calcutta session of Congress in the following year, however, she was forced to change her mind. The split between those who would accept British rule and those who were determined to break it for ever, grew wider. The extremists, led by Bipin Chandra Pal and Aurobindo, organized a new party to join in permanent battle with the moderates.

After that, she attended no more sessions of Congress, and spoke again and again in favour of unanimity. The split, however, continued to widen and deepen, and the extremists moved towards more revolutionary activities, while the moderates, encouraged by Minto's reforms, saw some hope in cooperation, and none in a defiance of the whole might of the British Empire.

Inevitably, Nivedita found less and less time for teaching the children. As she became more closely involved in her fight for nationalism, she delegated more of her personal work to other people. But, in spite of all the activity, an emotional and sometimes lonely woman continued to write letters to Joe MacLeod. When young Alberta, no longer hoping to be a nun, and no longer writing about Father Powell, decided to marry George Montagu, who later became the ninth Earl of Sandwich, Nivedita wrote a series of letters which gush with all the joy of an excited mother who can hardly believe that the child has found so much happiness. The first, to Josephine MacLeod, was written on 6 July, 1905.

How happy I am over the news! I kept waking and sleeping all night to think and then dream of it. I received your letter, on coming in from Dakshineswar and seeing Shiva's moon there, high over the Ganges. They are both – both – both blessed amongst mortals.

Happy as she was as a nun, she admitted at last the problem left by Vivekananda for his women-disciples who were not nuns, but had been constantly urged by him to remain unmarried.

It has always seemed to me that there has been one great danger in the high ideals we have drunk in. We have rated nunhood so high that wifehood has seemed low beside it. But more and more I have come to feel that this is untrue. In the one vow as in the other there is a daily faithfulness of word, thought and deed required of us – and the fulfilment cannot be too austere.

She even admitted a certain disagreement with Vivekananda.

. . . who was a *man*, and could see women only from the outside. All that he taught was true, of course; because he made the highest demands of women, and assumed that they were selfless, his demands were answered. For him, and because he expected it, they became selfless. Why should they not be equally selfless in marriage? So to me Alberta remains the same Alberta always, – a nun at heart, though she be a wife – just as ideal when worshipping in her home as when worshipping in a church.

She set out her own ideals for marriage, and they were very much the ideals of a nun. 'No yielding to a thirst, no yielding, or self-indulgence of any kind. It is a great *giving*, an infinite tenderness, a solemn quiet and joy – and *such* a compassion . . . much reserve, much silence, much prayer.'

She was thinking, probably, of the life of the zenana women, and of the gentle saintliness of Sarada Devi. Whether the life of the eventual Countess of Sandwich would be quite the same, does not seem to have occurred to her. The English pattern of marriage, in which a close friendship and companionship in daily life replaced the more secluded pattern of the Hindu wife, is perhaps a more different life than she realized. In her letter to the bride-to-be ('dear one, in everything the words of your heart's joy have been ringing across my ears . . . and to-morrow you will be married!') the ideal of the wife's devotion to the husband she is describing to Alberta is very much the attitude of the self-oblation of the dedicated religious devotee to her god. 'Make *him* all things, in fierce forgetting of self . . . to stand back and see the Beloved receive the uttermost vision, the vision which without her he could not have reached, yet in which she herself is seen as only the handmaid of God. Surely *that* is the culmination of all marriage.'

It is difficult to see why the husband, whether Hindu or Western, could not receive the 'uttermost vision' – assuming him to be as spiritually advanced as Nivedita seemed to expect – without the self-less oblation of his wife; but here again it is very much the nun speaking. The naiveté, the intense emotionalism, and the loving concern for Alberta, on the other side of the world, carried more of Nivedita with it than any formal cheerfulness she might have sent.

In her letter to Joe, after the wedding ('How empty the house must have seemed last night when they had gone away, and the revels were over! I could scarcely have felt closer if I had been on the spot'), she refers to some unhappiness, some frustrations, in her own life. Her relationships were often stormy; her friendships deeply devoted and any hurts inflicted on her by her friends involved her feelings more than, as a nun, she felt they should. She was living such a mixture of lives; detachment was almost impossible in her life as she was living it now.

Must one *always* be ready to give up *everything* with a smile? I am afraid I am growing fearfully attached. There are some things that I *cannot* give up. . . . Would you not *feel* hurt if someone you loved never said a word about wanting your presence; or would you only never let the pain be seen? I used to think and talk about renunciation. I very much fear that I actually know about it less and less.

She had always been easily hurt; and to the end of her days she was easily depressed if a relationship did not go well. How far the clash of her own sword caused these problems, it is difficult to say. She could be hard and soft at once, as her friends sometimes said of her. Extreme gentleness and considerable aggressiveness were always there, under the surface; always the two strands.

A. J. F. Blair described his meeting with her, which shows the other side of her nature so clearly that it is difficult to realize, at first, that this is the same woman who wrote the letters about Alberta's wedding.

We met at a friendly tea table, and as I was the only other guest, Sister Nivedita addressed herself directly to me. Our hosts knew what was coming, and chuckled quietly in their sleeves. I did not, and proceeded to indulge unsuspectingly in the amiable banalities which do duty for conversation at nine hundred and ninety-nine tea tables out of a thousand. The host and hostess, I am sorry to say, maliciously led me on.

The tranquil enjoyment of the situation ended with startling abruptness. Sister Nivedita suddenly whipped out a metaphorical rapier, and was under my guard before I could utter a gasp. I felt it to be a cowardly attack, and looked appealingly at mine host for protection. But his unfeeling grin conveyed the coldly comforting assurance that I was about to be carved up into small sections, and that he and his wife were prepared to survey the operation with the keenest enjoyment.

Faint, and bleeding internally from my cruel and unexpected wound, I next appealed *ad misericordiam* to my assailant. But she was inexorable, and followed up her first advantage so remorselessly that in five minutes I gave up the ghost. It was a rude awakening, if the metaphor is not too mixed. I thought her an angel until she slew me. But I saw that she could be an angel without mercy.

As for me, the encounter raised the devil within me. I forgot that she was a woman, and thirsted for revenge. Rendered careless by her easy victory she presently gave me an opening of which I took advantage in her own coin, and we became friends from that moment. That, as a matter of fact, was the motive of her sudden onslaught.

Friendship with Nivedita was not a slow growth. It sprang to maturity at the first meeting, or not at all; and I do not know that anyone was ever privileged to know the depths of her womanly kindness without first being subjected to that moral test. . . .

20

Nivedita stayed at Banaras after the Congress session, but she was not staying there in order to rest. The list of her activities there during January 1906 include the collecting of funds for a small Home of Service started there by a group of Vivekananda's disciples, the writing of the Report for the Home, making a tour of Rajputana, delivering several public lectures on her return, and meeting Mrs Annie Besant.

Her relations with Mrs Annie Besant had always been cordial, and she heartily approved her support for Indians, her lonely fight, and her struggles; but she remained detached from Theosophy. Vivekananda had lectured to Mrs Besant's group whenever he was asked to do so, and had met her on many occasions. He had once expressed his opinion of her, frankly, in an interview, 'Her knowledge of our religion is very limited; she picks up scraps here and there; she never had time to study it thoroughly. That she is one of the most sincere of women, her greatest enemy will concede.' He also spoke of her in a public lecture at Madras, saying that every Hindu should be grateful to her as a sincere well-wisher of India. 'For that, the eternal gratitude of every true-born Indian is hers, and all blessings be on her and hers for ever. But that is one thing – and joining the Society of the Theosophists is another.' Mrs Besant was one of a long list of friends of India whom Nivedita met and encouraged as a friend – but did not support in religious matters. Mrs Besant remained a European; she defended the Indian cause, but very much from the outside, and Nivedita now regarded herself as a Hindu. Her own dedication to India was total, and her knowledge was expert. Time was pressing; she had no wish for long discussions on Theosophy. She met her when she could, exchanged friendly greetings as Vivekananda had done, and went on her own way.

Nivedita returned to Calcutta at the end of January and as usual plunged into activity. But during 1906, one great bond with the past was broken. Gopaler-Ma had reached the end of her days; it was time for her death. This was not a moment of sadness, but the peak, the climax to which her whole life had led. In extreme old age she had become like the child whom all her life she had worshipped; she had been 'baby Krishna's mother', and now her life was narrowing down to that one thought which had been the dominating thought of her life, the summing-up of all her days; God worshipped as a child; the innocent, the simple, the beautiful.

All devout Hindus longed to die beside the waters of the Ganges, sprinkled with Ganges-water as they died, for this was the holy river. Their relatives carried them there as the end approached. Nivedita herself decorated Gopaler-Ma's bed with flowers, garlands and sandal-paste according to custom, and went with her, barefooted, as the bed was carried down to the Ganges. It was mid-July, in the very height of a Calcutta summer, and the heat was at its worst.

For two days and nights, Gopaler-Ma lingered. Nivedita and attendants, and some of the monks who had known Gopaler-Ma when, even then an old woman, she had come to Sri Ramakrishna and worshipped him as Gopala, waited and watched unceasingly in the heat beside the river. On the last morning, a Brahmin chanted over her, Shlokas from the Upanishads, and she stirred and responded visibly to the familiar words. But, beyond that, her consciousness was suspended, and still they waited.

We, the waiting women, could hear from without the long low lapping of the Ganges against the foot of the bathing stairs, and the moaning whisper of the rain-winds as now and again they swept down and caught the surface of the waters. And once in the midst of the silence came a rushing and swirling of the river beneath the cloud-veiled moon, and the little boats lying at anchor on the Ganges knocked against each other, and the word went round, 'The tide is coming in.'

Hour upon hour had gone, and still no change. Some who had rested, rose and plied little offices of tenderness beside the sick, and another lay down to snatch a spell of sleep. Suddenly there was a stir. 'Call the bearers,' said one, 'for the end is come.'

The cot was lifted on to the shoulders of the monks and the attendants, and one of the monks, who had known the old lady in her visits to Sri Ramakrishna when he was himself a boy disciple of Ramakrishna, bent over her, whispering the words that the dying woman would love to hear, 'Om Ganga Narayana Brahma!' And as she lay with feet touching the water in the high tide as waves washed against the banks, there was a triumphant shout of 'Haribol!' for the last breath had gone.

Nivedita wrote, 'Gopaler-Ma had died indeed at the moment of dawn, on the very turn of the outgoing tide.' But the 'little treasure' of Nivedita's house was gone and she had been a link with Sri Ramakrishna and Vivekananda. Only two weeks previously Swami Swarupananda, the monk who had befriended and taught her at Almora in her tour with Vivekananda, had died of penumonia. This was another severe blow.

But, as usual, she had no time to stop for grieving. There was work to be done. During the last months of 1906, Barisal in East Bengal became famous; and Nivedita entered into one of the greatest experiences of her life. She saw suffering and beauty together, on a scale that nearly overwhelmed her; her reaction was characteristically vigorous, practical, and assured. She did not merely act, her mind was busily noting, assessing, and advising; she drew her conclusions.

Barisal protested against the partition of Bengal, the Gurkha occupation, and the methods of Lieutenant-Governor Sir Bampfylde Fuller, who came to Barisal to make a personal inspection which would decide whether or not a state of famine could officially be said to exist.

He decided that it could not. In September, all official famine relief stopped.

The people of East Bengal thought differently. The cities began to send help; in Calcutta, schoolchildren saved their luncheon pice 'for the famine' and in the town of Barisal a relief organization with Aswini Kumar Dutt at its head was able to open relief centres in 160 different places and scatter the young men of the city to give help. The organization was voluntary, unrecognized by the government. Bampfylde Fuller had been an appointee of Curzon's. His ruthless measures did not endear him to the people, and he resigned under the more humane rule of the new Viceroy, Lord Minto. Minto saw little hope of reform without such resignations; but in the meantime the famine continued, albeit unofficially. Funds poured in from the people of Bengal themselves, and though it was impossible to reach all the starving, thousands of lives were undoubtedly saved. Nivedita's opinion of the British government's inaction in the matter did not stop her doing justice to individual Englishmen who had a heart, and showed it. She heard, with considerable approval, of an English magistrate who helped to stop a European firm of rice dealers from raising the price of grain. When the magistrate protested, they replied simply that they were not in business for sentiment, and this was their chance to make a profit.

The people replied by announcing that they would break open the rice warehouses, and loot.

The firm appealed to the English magistrate for the protection of the law against the mob; and Nivedita recorded dryly, he 'very properly' declined to take any notice of an appeal based on a vague threat. The firm was forced to promise to keep the price down to its normal level, and a small deputation, unarmed, called on them in acknowledgement, 'and also perhaps to let them see what they might have expected had they proved more obdurate'.

The people of Barisal were not at first too willing to allow Nivedita to visit, with the voluntary young workers, the distressed areas. It was only 'after considerable difficulty', she records – a sentence that she had recorded once or twice before – that she was able to persuade them.

She went, of course. Shooting across the flooded rice fields in a boat made of narrow planks of palmwood, in which seven or eight people could sit one behind the other, so long as one or two of them continuously baled out the water which was regarded as a natural part of the navigation, or wading out in the water above her knees into the floods. For flood had followed famine on the breaking of the monsoon, and the rivers, swollen by heavy rains and melting snows in the north, poured into the delta. The river country of the delta, canals and water lanes known as the 'Granary of Bengal' had once again betrayed its people, justifying the village proverb, 'With kings, with horned beasts and with a river, a man may never be friends.' The south wind blew and the waters remained. The rain drizzled endlessly out of grey mists, and all that could be seen was the spread of waters. 'Suddenly a great wind would catch the jungle-belt about us, and all the mangoes and palms respond, moaning and wailing. Then again it would pass, and silence come once more, upon the infinite monotony of our level world.'

It was a delta country which, under normal conditions, she loved; it stretched for two hundred miles or more in each direction, a vast triangle, fringed by jungle, coconut palms, and banana plants. The farm houses were built of mats woven out of bamboo splinters, the rafters and posts made of bamboo, the floor made of silver river-clay; as well as the farm, a barn for a couple of cows and a hayloft filled with rice straw was all part of the same building. Outside there was usually an open verandah which was used as the family reception-room, always on the far side, away from the river, facing the farmyard and outbuildings, the husking shed, the dovecote, the herb and fruit garden. Palms and jungle growth surrounded the houses, which were well spread out, across the rice fields, in each small village.

Now it was very different. But there were moments. Even in the midst of horror, there were moments.

There was dawn on 8 September, for instance. She remembered that, afterwards.

> One of those dawns of pearl and opal that come to us in the Indian autumn. The water lilies lay open still, as they had lain all night long on the surface of the waters. Here we paddled up to a cluster, lying touching one another, as if with their heads on each other's shoulders, with golden hearts, and rose-tinged petals. And we counted them, and found them seven. The air was cool but not chill, and full of quiet and fragrance. And all around us in every direction – inwards from the edge of the river-current behind us, to the distant line of farmstead groves, and right and left, all the way from one dark jungle-border to another – stretched the smooth silver water, pierced by the upspringing spears of the young rice which here and there was so scanty that each upright blade was companioned in its own reflection in the water-mirror underneath. A world full of the joy of the senses, . . . for him whose body was fed, and mind at rest.

She remembered, long afterwards, the bamboo hut lined with corrugated iron in which the whole party spent the night, with one of the helpers sitting throughout the night on the top step of the front door, which was just above the flood water level, watching the moonlight on the river and splashing the water with his hands whenever he saw water snakes swimming towards the house to feed on the rats and mice which lived under the platforms.

She sympathized with the tears she often saw in the eyes of the young student relief-workers who accompanied her. She saw the sense, even, of the workers' insistence that when help had been given to the starving, they must in their turn give a hearty cheer, however weak and hoarse. But the cheer itself struck her as 'unutterably ghastly'. 'I would rather not have heard it,' she said.

She set herself to do all she could for (and afterwards to recount only) those individual cases which in a sense represented all the starving, and always to see them as individuals. And all the time her practical and energetic mind was assessing the reasons for the horror, struggling to find some way of preventing it in the future, going to the roots of the problem which could be set out later in articles, lectures, or books. A little isolated compassion and the presentation of a tin of biscuits or a handful of fruit did not appear to her, under the circumstances, sufficient.

A mother and three children were found in a rotting and flooded cottage. The three children, starved as they were, looked far better-nourished than their mother. Then she found the eldest son, a boy in his early teens, hiding in a corner, ashamed because, like the youngsters, he had no clothes. He was as emaciated as the mother. These two had been starving themselves to feed the little ones, for many weeks.

Nivedita could not stand it. The principle that every ounce of food they had brought must be doled out with scrupulous fairness she entirely accepted, but this time she could not bear it any longer. Somehow she had to convince this mother that for her childrens' sake she must stay alive. She had a spare tin of biscuits, and another full of almonds and dried figs, which the party had brought for their own food if they could not get back that day. She took a biscuit and ordered the mother to eat it, adding sternly that she intended to stand there until she was obeyed.

'She obeyed me, poor soul, for little option was given her.' But the children had to be given nuts and fruit. Now Nivedita had to face the fact that they were followed by boat-loads of the starving, who saw food being given.

There could have been trouble, and very serious trouble. The people in the boats stretched out their hands, crying that they were hungry. They were asking for the judgement of Solomon in a fair division where no division could be made.

She did her best, and then waited for the riot.

First she gave a biscuit to each of the children in the crowd. Then one to each of the women. Then, to each man she gave one for himself, and one for each of the children at home.

Their reaction brought the realities of famine home to her, more than all the tragedies had been able to do. They were overjoyed. This was not the usual ration, this was *extra*! 'Whole boat-loads of grown-up men and women turned homewards with the hurry and excitement of happy children, under the unwonted good fortune of having received one-eighth of an ounce of extra food apiece!'

The visits continued; she was not submerged by the suffering. She trained herself to see what had to be done, and then to get on with it. Journalism there would be, and she was preparing for it, but that could come later.

In Barisal they insisted now that she should see one of the worst villages in the delta, Matibhanga. 'There,' they said, 'are people clothed in banana leaves and living on weeds.'

Nivedita took that kind of remark with a grain of salt, but she went to the village. 'As a matter of fact, of course, the people were clothed in nothing of the sort,' she comments tartly, for relief-workers had given out a little cloth, though one old woman was certainly clothed only in a piece of old mosquito netting.

The village was completely flooded, and the villagers who waited to greet them stood up to their waists in water. Many of them lived in houses ruined by the floods and other cottages were obviously about to collapse. When the people saw her they cried, 'Mother! Mother! Give! Give!'

Some of these people were now living in haylofts, open on three sides, and one of the party's boats floated underneath one of these and remained there for a while, sheltering from the endless soaking rain that fell from grey skies across grey waters. The relief workers said that seven miles away, in the interior, she could see worse horrors.

> But our time was short, and for myself I had seen enough. I cannot pretend to have any fine taste in the shades of human misery. The prospect of death by drowning or exposure or inanition, or the fact that a mother is watching a child die, who might have been saved if she had proper food and medicine to give it, any one of these things is quite sufficient to convince me that the sufferer requires all that can be given. I make no distinction between bad, worse, and worst in such cases.

She went home and sitting by the window of her study she wrote it all down, while it was still vivid in her mind; even the humour of the Bengali saying, 'I dined on horses' eggs', meaning 'no food'. She had seen the 'horses' eggs', the water lilies in the dawn, the faces of the dying, the rain falling endlessly from a heavy sky, she had heard the forced cheer, and wished that she had not; she had made the best use of a tin of biscuits, and those biscuits still haunted her. Now the journalist in her began to dig to the roots, to explain, to struggle to find reasons, to suggest remedies. Action needed to be nation-wide; it needed to be political; it should take commonsense steps from what was already there.

First she listed the strata of starvation; those who were swept away at first, and then on upwards. First there were the beggars; a huge group! Then the single women, widows and unmarried girls who had nobody to work for them, and lived by husking rice; they were the gleaners, paid in kind rather than cash. Above them, the farm labourers, and then the owners of larger farms; almost small squires. Others affected were fishermen and boatmen, village priests, schoolmasters, railway staffs, clerks, doctors and others.

The peasant, by famine was turned into a labourer; his women became gleaners. The village schoolmaster, doctor, or squire, simply died. He did not wish to live. The communities dissolved, because once a farmer or labourer became a beggar, he remained one forever. The misery spread out to the cities. In Calcutta, she found as she wrote that the price of rice had doubled. In Dacca and Mymemsingh, the price had quadrupled.

She drew one conclusion in particular from what she had seen. It went deep into her thinking. She decided that in the world, there are two humanities; one, the country dweller, more or less illiterate, who pays to the centre. The city-dwellers, more literate, are paid from the centre. And between the two, she saw a great gap. There were two Indias; two nations always in other countries beside India – town and country. But in India 'the presence of a foreign bureaucracy adds immensely to the evil characteristics of the modern epoch'.

She did not suggest that the withdrawal of the British would bring in the millennium; she saw the vast scale and complication of the problem. But the presence of a foreign power, concerned, as she saw it, with its own profit and only in the case of a good-hearted individuals here and there, concerned with the good of the Indian people, overweighted the problem beyond bearing.

In India's past history, prosperity had depended on a well-filled granary. At least three years' supply of rice had to be held in reserve. But gradually money rather than grain was coming to be regarded as wealth. Nivedita saw this as the direct result of the fact that rent and taxes now had to be paid in coin. The burden of taxation was too heavy. Bengal's amount of taxation was permanently fixed, but the Road Cess and the District Cess vitiated the benefits of this, the building of roads and bridges was of less use than an understanding of the waterways and fisheries; and the cultivation of jute, encouraged by the British as it brought great profit to European firms, flourished at the expense of the rice fields which were vital to the people.

Now she began to draw her conclusions; the British could and would do nothing. Exploitation, she wrote, is always inevitable in imperialism. And in India the Christian Church, which in medieval England had at least made a force with considerable power to stand against the brutalities of the state, was useless when bishops and clergy themselves had an investment in the imperial machine; they could not stand aside from it. The Hindu religion was the soul of the people, but it was not an organization, indeed its great strength lay in its wandering monks who lived like prophets in the wilderness, with no stake in society, and the religious beliefs and practices centred in the individual homes, not in a large and organized church. So – who was to lead? 'What the Christian faith did for the English serf, that, secular learning must do for the subordinated Oriental. It is the school, moreover, and not the Parliament, which is to be the cradle of new social combinations.'

The students, she saw, were organizing famine relief under that great and kindly schoolmaster, Aswini Kumar Dutt, and were beginning to feel a sense of their own nationality; not clearly yet, but it would come. She would have liked to see them settle in the villages, forming communities, and reporting peasant needs to the cities, seeing a little more clearly what needed to be done. They could organize a boycott against the growing of jute, and explain to the peasants why it was necessary. New crafts and trades could be taught in the villages; spinning, the growing of fruit trees, the improvement of cattle-breeding. These things could be linked with the Swadeshi movement. Something must be done about the tax gatherers.

Something must be done. Always she came back to that. Her idea of student administrators was idealistic; possibly hopelessly idealistic. But who else was there? She could not forget the students, and the young monks of the monastery whom she had seen organizing the famine relief. Two things she knew; India must find a national identity, and throw off British rule; and the greatest hope lay in her educated and idealistic young men. The women were, in the main, illiterate; they were going to be essential, but in a different way. Somehow, the spearhead would be the young. In education lay the hope of the future. She was not sure how it would develop, but it was beginning.

She wrote on and on until she collapsed. The attack of meningitis the previous year, followed by recurring attacks of malaria, had worn her out. Christine nursed her, and her friends the Boses helped to care for her. Swami Brahmananda came again from the Belur Math to make arrangements for her care and tretament.

When she became a little stronger, the school was closed for a few days while Nivedita and Christine took a short holiday. On her return she concentrated on her writing. She was beginning to write her books *The Master As I Saw Him* (an account of Vivekananda) and *Cradle*

Tales of Hinduism. She also helped Dr Bose in writing his book *Comparative Electro-Physiology*.

The British government had crushed the revolutionary activities that were beginning. The arrest and deportation of Indian leaders, without trial, depressed her. On the day Lajpat Rai was deported, she wrote in her diary, 'Is the government crazy?'

When Bhupendranath Dutt, brother of Vivekananda and sub-editor of the *Jugantar* was arrested for writing a seditious article, she offered bail. Later, when he was given a year's imprisonment, she visited Vivekananda's mother, Bhuvaneswari Devi, to console her, on many occasions. It was not a happy year.

Josephine MacLeod and Mrs Bull were seriously worried about her health, and begged her to return to the West for a year or so, to gain strength in a temperate climate. She began to consider it seriously, for she had a premonition that her own death was not many years away. If she died, how would Christine continue to run the school? Nivedita had always been the provider of funds. More money must be earned. Also, she had not seen her family in England for five years, and a visit home was long overdue.

There was every reason to go. But, as always, she longed to stay. The decision was finally forced by the Boses. Close friends could sometimes persuade Nivedita when nobody else could. This time, they succeeded.

21

Nivedita's work for her friends often took up much of her time, especially when the friends were writers. During her busiest years she spent as much time on other people's writings as on her own. Dr Jagadis Bose and his wife Abala Bose were her closest friends in India; she spent every holiday with them, and in their house in Calcutta she often addressed groups and read aloud much English poetry. She was practically one of the family. Abala Bose was fascinated by her school and its work for Hindu women, which at first she had thought to be impossible; she and her husband's sister even taught there for a while. Bose himself, though he was older than Nivedita, turned to her with increasing trust for help in his work; she called him 'Bairn', and from the moment in 1902 when she came to believe that some British scientists were belittling him and ruining his work, she began to revise and edit his books with him and help him in every way possible. He came to Bosepara Lane frequently and she worked there on his books with him. The results were seen in his books *Living and Non-Living*, *Plant Response*, *Comparative Electro-Physiology* and *Irritability of Plants*; but inevitably this meant that less of her own work was produced. She taught hardly at all now; lecturing and writing took all her time. Bose knew her colourful and argumentative nature and was stimulated, refreshed and amused by it. To a protest from a friend about her verbal sword-thrusts he once answered, 'She wants you to argue and then be defeated by her in argument, and then only she will be pleased.'

But it was not only her close friends, such as Bose and the Liberal leader R. C. Dutt, whose work occupied much of her time. Dinesh Sen, who lived in Baghbazar, wrote *A History of the Bengali Language and Literature* in English, and asked her to go through it for him. It took them a year, often working all day. He, too, was mothered and encouraged by Nivedita, who scolded him for his timidity, and his lack of interest in politics, as frankly as she praised his hard work.

As so often happened, he valued her friendship and help, but did not find it easy to work with her. Arguments raged during the work. In theory, her function was confined to correcting his style and his handling of the English language, but if there was any part of the book which she did not like, she insisted that he must alter it. She held the trump card, and used it.

'Dinesh Babu, unless you change this passage, I will not read your book.' Her point was always the same; this book was intended for people who were not Indian, and therefore it must not contain anything that did not reflect glory on India.

In the story of Dhanapati, she objected that the true culprit was let off, and the innocent punished. This might lead to criticism of Indians; so it must be left out. On these occasions she may have forgotten that she was the disciple of the man who said that he worshipped truth above all else, '. . . and if I had to choose between truth and God, I would choose truth and let God go.' But, like most of her friends, Dinesh Sen did not resent her criticism; affection and sympathy were, as always, her saving grace, even at her most dominating. Writing of her, later, he said that behind her angry words he could feel her affectionate heart, 'soft as a petal'. The two strands of her nature were always there.

The arguments raged; the book progressed. When it was published she asked him not to give acknowledgement in it to her help, in any way. 'Such labour of love cannot be bought for money,' he wrote afterwards, and 'I have only read in the Gita about selfless work, but have hardly come across anyone with detachment like hers.'

Her contributions to journals and newspapers were endless; appeals for help or work were rarely refused. Her own books are inevitably short, and much in them is not new today, but the impact they made at the time was considerable. *Cradle Tales of Hinduism*, and *Kali the Mother*, were popular. Her book *The Web of Indian Life*, published in 1904, was reviewed in India, England and America – often favourably, but in England, particularly amongst missionaries and orthodox churchmen, it was received with some fury. Today it seems a pleasant book, interesting but not exceptionally exciting, and most of its conclusions would be accepted without much argument; its chief interest for us now lies, perhaps, in its flashes of vivid description; a modern reader might wish for more such flashes. Its love of India is, inevitably, extreme.

But the anger of the missionaries at this presentation of Hindu life as being beautiful and praiseworthy, continued to mount, and one missionary, Amy Carmichael, published a book called *Things as They Are* as an answer to Nivedita's book. In a letter to Josephine MacLeod in 1905, Nivedita wrote: 'We are beginning to have counter-blasts from the missionaries now, to the book. Sometimes they are very funny, and always they express more than the poor author suspects. It is for India to understand my book, and make the world admit that it is not half the truth.'

Many of her books, including *Footfalls of Indian History*, are making a point which is now already accepted; and much of her writing consists of collections of lectures and essays; readers today may regret that the detailed passages of description were not more frequent, or that her account of Vivekananda in *The Master As I Saw Him* is not longer and more illustrative of the man as well as the saint; but she was not writing for them. She had work to do for her own time, her own people, and she was literally working herself to death. The presentation of India as a noble and potentially great country, rather than as one which needed converting, reforming and governing was unexpected and startling, particularly as the books were written by a Westerner. The impact they made, and the controversy they aroused, sent out ripples that spread very far indeed.

Even when her friends who were writers, statesmen or poets did not work directly with her, she spent much time with them, and sometimes discussion and clash led to a clarifying of their thoughts, as she always stimulated them, and strengthened their own self-confidence. The poet Rabindranath Tagore was her devoted friend, but his comment on her was extremely frank. 'I had felt her great power, but with all that, I understood that her path was not for me.' He referred to her 'militancy', and to her habit of exerting her power with full force on the lives of others. 'When it was not possible to agree with her, it was impossible to work with her.'

Bose, however, worked with her constantly. And when various universities in the West asked him to lecture, in 1907, the Boses persuaded Nivedita to go with them for a rest in a more temperate climate.

When they left for Europe, they took her with them. As usual, she visited the Belur Math, and paid a visit to Sarada Devi, as well as worshipping in Sri Ramakrishna's room in the Temple Gardens at Dakshineswar, before she left the country. They sailed from Bombay on 15 August 1907. Her visit to the West was inevitably misrepresented. It was even suggested that it was dangerous for her to stay in

India, because she had helped Bhupendranath Dutt, and had offered to put up bail for him. *The Englishman* had referred to her as 'a traitor to her race', and the theory that she fled into temporary voluntary exile was an exciting and romantic one, but the truth was more prosaic and practical. She was worn out, and had been aware of the necessity of taking a rest, long before she left India. There was no question of her rushing from the country in a panic. Months previously, in April of 1907, she had written to Josephine MacLeod and told her that she would probably be going abroad in August.

The journey to England, this time, made a great contrast with the last journey. Then she had travelled with Vivekananda. This time she took the notes she had made during that greatest occasion of her life, and while she was on board she went on with the writing of her book *The Master As I Saw Him*. She had begun it, tentatively, in 1904. It is not a long book, but it took her five years to write it.

'Of course, I know that if I succeed, it will be *the* work of my life, the one thing, in fact, that I have to give. And I feel more and more that all that training was not really given to me, but to all the Indian generations through me, in some way.'

It was the most difficult task she had ever tackled, and in it she faced her own major problem; that her view of him was inevitably 'Nivedita-coloured'; that she could not be completely objective about him, or record him in any way except through her own eyes, and she had already learned from sometimes bitter experience, that each friend's view of him was different. 'To be properly written, the "life" should be *all* Swamiji. He should move through it, like Jesus through the Gospels, alone, unfettered, unshadowed. But I feel incapable of this, and capable only of telling what I have seen in him.'

The very fact that she saw her own view as being inevitably a fetter and a shadow made her more objective than was usual in her writings.

She did not attempt to record the small human details about him, and Westerners may perhaps regret that in the whole book, from beginning to end, there is not one word either of criticism or even of purely human description. But she had set herself, Hindu-fashion, 'to write down more aspects of him that are Eternal, and be able to discard remorselessly all the rest'. It remains her most outstanding book, even within the strict limits which she set herself. Only in his own letters, which she collected and gathered in later on, do we see the more human aspects. The memories and fragments written by many people, which were also later collected, together with his own discourses, lectures and writing, give the rounded picture; on this voyage she saw the necessity of completing her own part of that picture, while there was time.

When she reached Aden, she received a letter from Christine telling her that the school had reopened, all the children had come back, and there were about fifteen women in the sewing classes. She was relieved and delighted. Her usual homesickness for India was already beginning. Not for the India of the crowds and the journeys and the political anger and the endless frustrations and wearying heat, but the small, private, beautiful India which had not changed through the centuries and which now and then shines out, in vivid glimpses, in her other writings.

The ships of flowers, for instance. The tiny ships, 'the fleet of little nameless boats, floating on ponds and rivers in all the villages of Bengal tonight, each bearing its twinkling lamp into the all-enshrouding dark', which were launched on the last day of the Bengali month of Paush to celebrate the opening of the annual commercial season, 'the old-time going forth of merchant enterprise and exploration'. The little ships were loaded with Bel-leaves, flowers, and consecrated fruits and grain, as the women prayed 'with each fresh gift, for some beloved life, that through the coming year it might go safe amidst whatever tide'.

She was as homesick for that gentle clarity of Indian beauty in the well-loved festival, as the British in India who longed – with a passion that sometimes led them to build themselves imitation Tudor houses under brilliant Oriental skies – to see the blazing fires of Christmas, and the Christmas tree, in frosty weather, or English villages built of Cotswold stone under cool grey skies.

And like them, she made almost a cult of the motherland. Now under skies that were only too often cool and grey, she longed for vivid colours, and the houses of Bosepara Lane, the Neem-tree and the Ganges. So she drew together friends of India who were in England, and talked, thought, and breathed, nothing but India.

She had opened a lecture given to the Sesame Club in London, in 1900, with the words:

> Have any of us thought how much our work has gained from being done in a place where we were thoroughly at home? . . . Have we ever realized how intimate is the connection between the great interests of our life . . . and the feeling of being at home, amongst our own people? . . . But all this does not mean that we must stay in the place where we were born.

Seven years later, the dichotomy between home and the birthplace was even greater, and more permanent. So she brought her adopted homeland with her in every way that she could, and immediately began to work for it.

22

She reached England on 6 September 1907. It was five years since she had met her family, and she came laden with gifts: reed-pens, palm-leaf books, little baskets, Mala-bags, Tulsi-Malas, Rudraksha beads, incense burners, amulets and spice-boxes, pictures of the baby Gopala Krishna, and innumerable photographs. She brought, too, some Ganges water, and the rosary beads of old Gopaler-Ma. Her mother, that most orthodox of Christian women, touched the beads with reverence. 'That indiscriminating love that my mother gave me! That all-giving love!'

She stayed in her mother's house at Clapham, apart from a week in November when she met the Boses in Germany, and Josephine MacLeod in Paris. It was the first time she had met Joe since the death of Vivekananda, and there was a great deal to talk about, and much to remember.

Cradle Tales of Hinduism was now published, and well received. She noted in her diary, on 31 December 1907, 'A wonderful year! . . . Two books – *Comparative Electro-Physiology* and *Cradle Tales* out – others proceeding – Oh blessed year!'

While she was in England, she continued her usual programme of lecturing and writing. She also met Prince Kropotkin, the Russian revolutionary writer. Many of her Indian friends including Gokhale, R. C. Dutt, Bipin Chandra Pal and Ananda Coomaraswamy, were in England at the same time; so were her Western friends from India, Ratcliffe, Havell, Blair and Geddes. Inevitably there were rumours that dark political deeds were afoot. But in fact, it was a time of discussion and rallying. What they were planning was not bomb-throwing. It was a conscious shaping of an ideal, a political unity, which would be very much needed in the future, and politicians and journalists in England who were in sympathy with India's struggles talked with Nivedita, and discussed the future. Her friends in England included Sir Henry Cotton, Dr V. H. Rutherford, Keir Hardie, J. Hart Davies,

James O'Grady, Swift MacNeill and William Redmond. Stead, Nevinson, and the editor of the *Manchester Guardian*, as well as editors and journalists from other papers, met her and joined in the 'Indian struggle' in any way possible. She regarded them as friends of India, and entitled an article she wrote for the *Modern Review* 'Our Friends in Parliament and Outside'.

As she strode through London, walking – as a friend said of her at that time – with an intensity of manner, and cyclonic personal energy, she was not concerned only with Indian political ideals and strategy, or thoughts of her school. She had developed a passion for which she became well known, and unlike her feeling for science, about which she did not claim to know very much (and so accepted Dr Bose's theories and research without too much query), this was a passion for a subject about which she held very decided views and for which she waged her own battles, with allies and adversaries. She had become deeply involved in the renaissance of Indian art, which she regarded as an essential part of the reawakening of the nation.

> Art must be re-born. Not the miserable travesty of would-be Europeanism that we at present know. There is no voice like that of art, to reach the people . . . oh, for a pencil that would interpret the beauty of the Indian sari; the gentle life of village and temple; the coming and going at the Ganges side; the play of the children; the faces, and the labours, of the cows!

In this, as always, she was an extremist. In her wise and timely battle against the imitation of European art which Indian artists were then struggling to produce, she became increasingly convinced of the accuracy of her own opinions, and would brook no opposition. Possibly she never entirely comprehended the difficulty of those Indian artists who saw art as personal rather than national, and who, without wishing to imitate European paintings, nevertheless, did not necessarily wish to depict the Indian sari, the Ganges side, or the faces and the labours of the cows.

Certainly, she had made converts, and they were very influential people indeed. Abanindranath Tagore, the vice-principal of the Calcutta Art School, was still enthusiastic about European ideas, until he met Nivedita. But she changed his views, and before long he introduced a new school of art, known as the Calcutta school. Even this led to skirmishes when a group, including Gaganendranath Tagore and Sir John Woodroffe, founded the Indian Society of Oriental Art. Their views were regarded as degenerate and crude by some other schools, but Nivedita and the Calcutta school criticized the other schools for adopting Western methods of composition, and for lack of Indian feeling in their painting.

Her friendship with the Tagores, including the poet Rabindranath, and with other Hindus, did not cut her off from her feelings for European art itself, but her ideas may be open to question. She reprinted some Western paintings in Indian journals, to familiarize Indians with great European masters, and in typical Nivedita style she hurled in whatever she admired. She began fairly enough with Raphael, Michelangelo and Titian, Millet, Puvis de Chavannes (apart from his nudes) and then included in her list with equal enthusiasm, Rossetti, Morris and Burne-Jones. But at this stage of her career, it was not always wise to argue with her. On matters of art, she could be dictatorial. On one occasion she sent Nandalal Bose with Asit Haldar to accompany Lady Harringham to copy fresh paintings at Ajanta. She did not ask them if they wanted to go, she simply fixed the date, bought the tickets, and there the matter ended: they went. Their devotion to her, however, was undiminished. Years later, Nandalal Bose said of her, 'When she died, it was like being deprived of the presence of a guiding angel.'

Her great ally in this aesthetic revival in India was an Englishman, E. B. Havell, of the Indian Educational Service, superintendent of the Madras School of Art, and Keeper of the Government Art Gallery in Calcutta from 1896 to 1906; he was now in England, and one of the many friends she met there. Her support for him was unwavering, but when he pointed out to her that he could teach a man to draw and paint, but he could not make him an artist or a genius, Nivedita told him firmly that the essential ingredients were love of country, pride of birth, hope for the future, and dauntless passion for India. These, she maintained, could make heroes out of dolts, and original geniuses out of copyists.

Havell, Nivedita and Coomaraswamy attacked, in print, constantly and often under much criticism, the theory which Vivekananda also had attacked; the view that Indian art was derivative, having its roots in Greek art. They fought this Hellenic theory long and valiantly, and all three also defined the function of the art schools in India, and objected to the employment of foreign teachers using foreign methods.

Her criticisms of those of whom she disapproved could be extremely acid. She met Havell in England with his wife and little daughter. In letters to him after this visit, her praise and enthusiasm for his views mingle oddly with her comments on those of whom she disapproved, including Sir George Birdwood.

> Sir George Birdwood is indeed a fraud . . . Birdwood on Buddha!!!! . . . It takes a much more generous mind . . . to open new areas of sympathy and understanding to the world, or even to enter them himself. . . . He has a good deal of the taste of the craftsman, a dash of gall. . . . but that ends it. . . . The great intellect and heart . . . that usually do the work . . . he and his kind are incapable of achieving.

She refers to his remarks on the Buddha as 'the very effrontery of Philistinism', 'crass'. A reference to the Tagores – 'how fortunate that their clan is both powerful and enthusiastic' – suggests allies in a field of battle rather than friends who held similar views on art and aesthetics. But it was, in fact, a battleground; and that is how she saw it. A revolution in art, when art has been smothered by political pressures and historical circumstances, requires warriors. The excitement and force of her phrasing, her enthusiasm and her dislikes, even her energetic handwriting, burn out of the letters. It is clear that here again she was fulfilling her function, as so often before, of setting brilliant minds arguing, discussing, thinking out for themselves matters which they might have been taking for granted. As with Bose, and his scientific work, she helped to kindle a flame which India needed, but in art, as in science, she was concerned with Indian nationalism of which art and science were, in her view, an expression.

Now, in England, she was meeting Havell again, writing to Indian artists, thinking and talking of art; in the renaissance of Indian art she was already a very well-known figure, and in her own circles her influence was considerable. She was the art critic of the *Modern Review* from its foundation in 1907, and her reviews were didactic in the extreme, highly moral, very personal and dogmatic in their attitude and expressions. She criticized paintings which did not depict a moral view of life, or indeed any view of Indian life which was not as she wished to see it, and this went very much farther than her objection to nudes. 'Pictures of the nude and semi-nude are always best avoided in India . . . the expert rule is that the nude be passed by altogether.' But a painting of a young woman lying on the floor, writing a letter on a lotus leaf, was also objectionable. 'I ought to state here that I do not know of any country in which a young lady may stretch herself on the floor in public! . . . As if a sight that would outrage decorum in actuality could be beautiful in imagination!'

In her writings about art, morals are all-important, and here the Victorian lady is strongly in evidence. 'Had the picture been nobler, it would have ranked as a great masterpiece, but the sight of a man smoking a hookah while he is carried on a litter by women is unredeemable, and we can only praise its decorative quality.' 'Even in the hour of conviviality, there is nothing revolting in their pleasure. The beautiful hands of refinement and good birth, are very noticeable in both.'

She left Indian artists in no doubt as to what she expected of them. 'Nevertheless, we would remind all students of art that their true function is the revelation of the beautiful, the true, the good. It is not the fugitive moments of personal experience, but the eternal and universal, that come best to the world through them.' 'As a matter of personal taste, I immensely prefer Madonnas and angels to kitchens.' The difference between kitchens and stables is not explained, and her insistence on the revelation of nothing but the beautiful, the true, the good, presents a blank wall to 'worship the terrible' and 'my god the miserable, my god the wicked'. She expressed her ideas almost as absolutes, in many cases, and in view of her influence amongst leaders of opinion in the world of art in Calcutta, she might be accused of claiming expert knowledge in altogether too many fields. But by now, there was very little in Indian life which she was not prepared to take under her own banner, and she had perhaps forgotten her own rueful comment when Vivekananda took her away from plague nursing: 'Swami says that my chief fault is attempting too much, in which he is emphatically right.' But her eagerness, as always, generated new ideas and arguments, and set many artists' ideas flowing.

Her devotion to science and scientists was tempered by an admission that she herself was no scientist. Her service to Bose in his scientific work was inestimable, and he acknowledged it fully. She never faltered in her faith in the greatness of his theories and his research. How far she influenced his thinking during her constant work with him on his books, it is impossible to judge, but he tended, as the years passed, to move from pure physics to metaphysics, from pure botany to a Vedantic sense of the oneness of all life which has caused him to be accused by some of anthropomorphism. India and Kali became almost a cult in his approach to science. When his Research Institute was built, he honoured Nivedita's work for him by a bas-relief on the memorial fountain, depicting 'Woman Carrying Light to the Temple'. Since all knowledge was regarded by Vivekananda as a temple, it was a fair tribute. But in science, as in art, there was always the danger of a possible loss of objectivity in Nivedita's highly specialized nationalistic approach. In her own words, 'Art, like science, like education, like industry itself, must now be followed "for the remaking of the Motherland" and *for no other aim.*'

But the honour with which she is still remembered in India for her part in the renaissance of art and the encouragement of science, goes far beyond agreement or disagreement with her views. It is a tribute to her vigorous encouragement of individuals, who broke away from the Westernized convention of that time and found their own, truly Indian paths.

Many of her friends were there in England on that long visit. One was Havell, and another Ratcliffe, for whom she had fought so valiantly, in her letters to Gokhale, seeking a new editorship for him, writing 'When I reflect on his ability and sincerity and realize our great need of him, I cannot bear that India should stand passively and let him go!' Bose, for whom she never stopped fighting, and Gokhale himself, leader of the Moderates in Congress, and the leading Indian member of the Viceroy's Council. Her devotion to Gokhale, shown in letters to him from 1903 onwards, had both the touching and the irritating quality of self-abasement which came oddly from a woman whose attitude to the supremacy of women as against men had been noted and satirized even by Vivekananda. To Gokhale, she had written, 'I could more easily imagine myself retreating before the last ordeal, than your courage failing us, in anything you show to be right. For I, after all, am only a woman, while I rejoice to think that yours is every inch the strength and persistency of a man.'

It is almost impossible to believe that this is Nivedita speaking; but in her letters to him, over the years, there is a constant acknowledgement of his frail health, an endless apology for anything she has said which obviously offended him. She so often wounded her friends first, and then worried about it afterwards.

> You must not allow any of my hot flippancies to dim the fact of the momentous value I place upon your life, for one moment. . . . I fear, I ought to ask forgiveness for many wounds – but I trust that you will not now break off a friendship in which you have already pardoned much! . . . Will you please forgive me for my unintentional act of unkindness this afternoon? . . . There is nothing I would not do, if I could, to make up for my error, and induce you to banish the memory.

She was very conscious that he was entirely sincere in his fight for moderation, and she was always anxious to show that her political extremism did not put her against him; she worried about him constantly. 'My greatest hope . . . is that some day you may have cause to bless the memory of a few who went by my road in order that your work might be the more stable and enduring . . . But I and my methods are necessary, and you will yet say so yourself.'

So many of her friends were in England, some, like Ratcliffe, to stay, others coming and going; there were many liberal-minded sympathizers to help them, and she saw all the friends she could; she was busy too with her writing and lectures, and when she was not addressing her sympathizers in private houses, she was addressing larger audiences in the Caxton Hall.

News from India was grim. Violence was increasing. The bomb outrage of Muzaffarpore, the attempt on the life of the Lieutenant-Governor of Bengal, the arrest of Aurobindo, and, later, Bipin Chandra Pal, the deportation of Aswini Kumar Dutt; the depressing news was endless. Nivedita now stated frankly that she saw the necessity of eventual open planned revolt, but sporadic brutal violence revolted her. There were many who considered that her own lectures, in England as well as in India, must be regarded as bearing some responsibility for the darker tide of events, and this may have caused a certain sadness in her cry to that liberal moderate, Gokhale: 'Some day you may have cause to bless the memory of a few who went by my road that your work might be the more stable and enduring. . . .'

But the discussions, the letter-writing, and the lectures were not the sole purpose of her prolonged visit to the West which finally extended for two years. There were family relationships too.

In September she spent a month in Ireland with Richmond and his wife and the Boses. She never visited England without walking in the soft air and the quiet rain of Ireland, though it saddened Richmond that her heart was now entirely given to India, and Ireland no longer excited her as once it had done. But the Boses and her family were always the best of friends; they found Abala Bose gentle and understanding, and Bose's laugh rang out unfailingly at the simple, well-worn family jokes; like the joke about the man who boasted that he was often mistaken for the king; until a friend remarked, 'That's nothing. When I was in Paris, a man slapped me on the back and said, "God Almighty, is that you?" '

On one occasion, Richmond's young wife, hot and tired, remembered in the heat of a walk in Ireland that Richmond had taken her to

English pubs, occasionally, when they were walking together. She remarked, 'We ought to find a nice pub!' and the silence of embarrassment might have stretched to unbearable lengths, since in Ireland pubs were not for ladies, and Nivedita was in any case a nun; from every point of view, it was a remark from which the more Victorian element in Nivedita might have flinched. Far from flinching, the nun took one look at the embarrassed young face, and cut right across the proprieties – Irish and Hindu – with no nonsense at all. 'That's a splendid idea,' she said firmly. 'Let's find a pub and have a glass of stout.'

Her memories of England and Ireland, when she was in India, were not all concerned with art, politics, or the audiences at the Caxton Hall. And yet in the West she was still homesick for a very different scene; she had her own home now, and she was a long way from it. She had a cottage in a lane, but it was very unlike the lanes in England or in Ireland.

> Those learned and artistic persons, who now and then find their way to us in the midst of the Hindu quarter here in Calcutta, to spend an hour or two, will sometimes break off from their preoccupation with medieval art and modern monstrosity to assure us that the lane outside our door is a genuine bit of Early Italian loveliness. We like to hear this stated, though we had not needed to be told that our home was beautiful. In the mist of November evenings, when a couple of street lamps, hung from wall brackets at long distances, serve to light up the irregular house-fronts – that stand side by side as if treading on each other's toes in subdued and solemn eagerness – we could not have doubted that our lane was very lovely.

But this November she could not see the lane in the Baghbazar. She had to visit America, where after a series of visits to friends she began her usual lecture tour, and also met Bhupendranath Dutt and other young revolutionaries. She was beginning to collect Vivekananda's letters for eventual publication, and Mary Hale sent her the letters he had written to herself and her family.

Bose was lecturing at various universities in America and Nivedita had intended to return to India when one more heavy blow struck her. She received news that her mother was dying of cancer.

There was now no question of returning to India. She returned to England in January of 1909, where her mother was staying at Burley-in-Wharfedale. She stayed by her mother until she died.

The family had received communion together three days before their mother died. They had been together at the death. Now Nivedita stayed on with May and Richmond. Her mother had given her word that her husband's sermons should be rewritten and rearranged. Nivedita did this, and also, while she was still in England, collected Vivekananda's letters to Sturdy and copied them out. In April, she crossed to Ireland again with May and Richmond. This time their mother's ashes were laid near their father's grave. '. . . And the pines sing eternally about them in a circle', Nivedita wrote to Mrs Bull.

The Boses had returned to England in March 1909 and in May, Nivedita, Mrs Bull and Josephine MacLeod went with them to Wiesbaden, and Geneva. It was not until July that she returned to Marseilles, to sail for India. They reached Bombay on 16 July, and by 18 July Nivedita was at home again in Bosepara Lane.

Her arrival in India on this occasion has been coloured with all the glamour and mystery of a spy-thriller by many who have written about her. One account asserted that she used the name Mrs Margot and 'dressed fashionably to avoid recognition' – a statement which might have caused her some amusement – also that she took a separate route from the Boses and that in Bosepara Lane she remained disguised and did not move out for three weeks. Another account insisted that she confused the police by going from Bombay to Madras before reaching Calcutta, which might have confused Nivedita or the Boses but would have been of little interest to the police.

Her diary sets out her movements quite clearly, and they were exactly as might have been expected. She reached Calcutta on 18 July, visited the Boses in their house, and twice visited Sarada Devi, as she always did when she returned from a journey and more eagerly now than ever, following the death of her own mother. She visited the Belur Math, and as usual went to worship in the room of Sri Ramakrishna at Dakshineswar. Swami Saradananda and Ramananda Chatterjee came to visit her, and from 25 July onwards, Dinesh Sen visited her house each day to work with her on his book on Bengali literature.

A customary routine, in fact. Disappointing to those who would have preferred plots, counter-plots, and the heroine in hiding; but not at all disappointing to Nivedita herself. She wrote at once to Joe MacLeod, telling her how wonderful it was to be back at her desk, and near the Holy Mother, Sarada Devi. India was still there.

'The place really exists, the whole wonderful dreamland in one's heart is here.' But she was far too practical to expect the wonderful dreamland to lack difficulties or back-breaking worries.

23

Troubles were not slow in arriving. Almost immediately, rice and milk rose in price and the increasing local poverty became terrible. She went into her accounts and saw that expenses would have to be cut. There were now two small branch schools and though their weekly expenses were not more than three pounds, these had to be closed. The rented building at 16 Bosepara Lane had to be given up and the entire school was now crowded into her own small house, Number 17. Friends begged her to leave the overcrowded lane and rent a house in a better part of the city, but her answer was always the same: 'I will never leave the lane that gave me shelter.'

She had become less and less involved with the daily running of the school. She often experienced guilt as she watched Christine take complete charge. 'All the things Swami dreamt for me, *she* is fulfilling', and 'You see, I am no longer the worker. That place ought to be Christine's. Even about the school, I cannot hold it much longer; I shall have to turn it over to her.'

That had been written to Joe MacLeod in 1904; with every passing year it became more true.

She kept in close touch with the girls, however, and arranged trips for them, on which she accompanied them; a steamer trip to Dakshineswar, a day by tram to the zoo, another day at the Museum. She knew them closely as individuals.

One of the children, a child widow called Prafullamukhi, lived close to the school. As a widow, she had to fast all day, strictly, on the general fast days, which occurred every two weeks, and on which no food and not a drop of liquid was permitted. Piety was often unofficially tempered by mercy, but where it was not, Nivedita provided the mercy and left the piety to look after itself. She made it a little easier for the girl by giving her fruits and sweets. One busy day, Nivedita went to the Boses' house after school, and suddenly remembered that the child had not been fed. She rushed home and sent for her, feeding her and apologizing for her own thoughtlessness in eating her own meal, when Prafullamukhi had nothing. She struggled always to keep personal relationships and responsibilities alive even in the midst of constant work; but, like her guru, she knew that it would add to the already heavy strain. This she saw as being inevitable, just as he did. When girls were taken away or not permitted to attend the school regularly, she went to their homes and pleaded with parents or guardians on their behalf. One of her girls developed tuberculosis; Nivedita and Christine paid her medical expenses, and rented a home for her at Puri until she died.

Another grief was the appalling decline in the health of Swami Sadananda, the monk who had been her friend and helper on her lecture tours, and who had devoted his small remaining strength to the young people of Calcutta, taking groups of young men with him to see a little of their country, and to understand India's problems and needs. He had cared for the youngsters like a loving parent. Now that he was dying, Nivedita and Christine had found a small house in Bosepara Lane for him, where his band of young followers who called themselves 'Sadananda's dogs', served him with a devotion that shines out of Christine's account like a brilliant beacon-light. It was one of the greatest testimonies to Vivekananda's insistence that each monk in the monastery must follow the path that was right for him, and that exceptions to some regulations might be made for monks who were spiritually mature, that he lived and died with his boys in Bosepara Lane, and was not forced back into the Belur Math to die in more conventionally monastic surroundings among his fellow-monks.

Christine wrote, of the young men who served him:

> Their service was given without any reservation whatsoever. Those who were in college gave up their studies, and, so far as they knew, their careers... They washed, scrubbed, scoured and cooked for him. Day and night they held him in their arms when the struggle for breath did not permit him to lie down... The few minutes' sleep, which they were able to snatch now and then, were taken on the floor at his side, without pillows or bedding... When Sadananda was not in actual pain, they lived in a state approaching ecstasy. Life held nothing then, and it has held nothing since which can compare with it.... His love was unbounded, yet he did not indulge them nor even allow one careless or unworthy thing to pass unrebuked. He was severe in the extreme. An onlooker might have considered his treatment of them cruel, but these boys who were devoting body, mind and soul to his service, knew his love and never lost their joy... Their only fear was that he would leave them.... At that time they did not know that he would leave them his joy.

Nivedita visited him every day. Bosepara Lane was becoming a training ground for saints. It is not surprising that she flatly refused to leave it. A bigger house in a better quarter of the city would have been exile; and she might well have queried the word 'better'.

The political situation was as grim as ever, and for the moment there did not seem to be much that she could do about it. The revolutionaries who had embarked on murder or bomb-throwing had either been hanged or sentenced to long terms of imprisonment. Nivedita deplored their methods, and she also realized that these methods must inevitably bring a clamp-down which would crush even the more reasonable forms of protest. Bhupendranath Dutt, Vivekananda's brother, had gone to America after his release from prison; and Bipin Chandra Pal, on release, had left again for England. Most of the nationalist leaders were either in prison, in hiding, or keeping well away from political action. Many were deported without trial. The search of houses, and arrests, continued. This in itself united the people in a stronger nationalistic emotion; Swadeshi became even more popular. The national revival in art, literature and industry was growing stronger.

In all these aspects of life she did what she could, particularly in the way of discussion with possible leaders of opinion. Ramsay MacDonald, for instance, came to Calcutta in 1909 with a letter of introduction to Nivedita, from Nevinson. He visited her in Bosepara Lane and was so much impressed by her personality and ideals that he visited her again on several occasions to discuss her ideas on the philosophies and ideals of India. The fanning of sparks into flames, the exchange of ideas; these were not as spectacular as the spy-thriller activities with which she was often credited. But they were her own gift, her own particular genius, and always had been.

During a term of imprisonment, Aurobindo had studied the Gita and the Upanishads. His spiritual practices led him further than he expected; he had the nature of a yogi and for the first time he was beginning to face the fact. When he left prison, in 1909, he felt that the spirit of nationalism was drooping, and so he started two weekly journals, *Karma Yogin*, which was published in English, and *Dharma* in Bengali. The journals were not entirely political; he included in them articles on Ramakrishna, Vivekananda, and Yoga.

Minto's reforms, drafted with the help of Morley, were now being introduced. The moderates and extremists in Congress tried once more to unite, but found it impossible. Aurobindo's slogan was 'no compromise' and he stated clearly in *Karma Yogin*, 'No cooperation without Control.'

This left the government no choice but to deport him. Nivedita advised him to go into hiding, or else to leave British India and work from outside. When the threat of deportation became immediate, he left Calcutta for Chandernagore in French India, and sent a message for Nivedita, asking her to continue editing the *Karma Yogin* in his absence. She agreed to do so, and continued editing it until the government suspended it in April 1910, by which time Aurobindo was in Pondicherry. During the three months of her editorship of *Karma Yogin*, the whole tone of the paper altered. She kept the fervour of nationalism – 'O Nationality, come thou to me as joy or sorrow, as honour or shame! Make me thine own!' – but the general flavour became very much less political, and more expressive of Vivekananda's ideologies.

Much legend has grown up, and many writers have insisted – whether in praise or blame – that it was Nivedita who engineered Aurobindo's escape to Chandernagore, and who saw him off at the quay. Aurobindo himself at last flatly denied all this, and made it clear once and for all that, beyond her general warning to him previously that he would be well advised to leave the country, in fact he did not go to her house or see her, she did not wave good-bye to him at the Ghat, and that she knew nothing of the situation until he was already in Chandernagore.

Certainly she went twice to Chandernagore to visit him. As she was editing *Karma Yogin* in his absence, and as he was a friend whose policies she supported, this is hardly surprising. But, wildly as rumours circulated, she had very little part in the drama.

Throughout this period she was aware of many revolutionary plans and this must often have put her in a difficult position. Bhupendranath Dutt stated later that Nivedita asked them not to tell her about their revolutionary activities. On one occasion, two young boys of a revolutionary group planned to commit robbery in a house at Tarekswar, and asked Nivedita for her revolver. She gave them a furious scolding instead, and informed their leader of their plans, asking him to do all he could to stop lawlessness.

The extent to which fervour, anger and a passion for nationalism might have forced her, at last, to move in the direction of the insurrection which she had helped to arouse, can never be answered. Some of her statements suggest that she saw little hope in the end, for any other method. But her religion and her training were against it. And her detachment and exhaustion were growing.

From the time of Aurobindo's departure for Pondicherry, police surveillance of Nivedita and full censorship of her letters became more strict. Her letters often arrived torn open. She was not a woman to take this sort of treatment meekly and she wrote a letter to the Postmaster-General which was a model of courteous and icy sarcasm. It might also be taken as a model which illustrates an excellent way to infuriate an adversary while retaining one's own dignity. She did not make the smallest complaint about being the object of censorship; she simply complained that the censorship was inefficient.

Dear Sir,

It is, of course, easy to understand the overwhelming curiosity of some members of your staff about the confidences of my sister in regard to her babies and her cooking. I should be grateful, however, if you would kindly instruct them to *close up again* the letters they have opened and read. I should like to avoid the irritation as well as the possible loss of letters, which their present methods engender. I have been at great pains to keep the enclosed envelope in the exact condition in which I received it this morning – but I have a long list of grievances in accumulation, halves of first pages carelessly torn, with the wrappers off literary papers and so on. I shall venture to hope that this letter, of which I keep a copy, may reach you personally.

It is unlikely that the letter brought the smallest result. It is certain that she was heading for trouble, and she knew it. These were the dark days when the first movements towards an uprising had been heavily crushed, and it was impossible to say what lay ahead. She had far too much commonsense to seek a glamorous martyrdom which would wreck the school, discredit the monastery, and possibly ruin the career of Bose who was known to be her friend; his career prospects were improving, she had no wish to drag the future of Indian science into disrepute. And what possible benefit could her own imprisonment or exile bring to the cause of Indian nationalism? But to keep quiet and stave off trouble was a half-hearted way to live, and most unlike her. Tired and often ill, she became more depressed, more and more uncertain what would happen to her, and what danger she might bring to the school and to her friends.

And then a miracle happened. As Nivedita said herself, writing afterwards to Josephine MacLeod, 'You will never guess the piece of news we have for you today . . . This extraordinary thing has happened. One scarcely believes it oneself.'

On 2 March 1910 two women, looking around them a little nervously but determined to find 'the English lady who was running a school in the native quarters', walked up Bosepara Lane, past the old Indian houses and the bustees. One was an American, Mrs Phillipson. The other was British. Unquestionably British. She was, in fact, the Vicereine, Lady Minto.

Like every other crucial moment in Nivedita's life, it arrived quietly and entirely unheralded. The visitors were incognito. The English lady who was running the school received them with courtesy, and talked to them long and earnestly about India; she showed them around. They gave no indication, at first, as to whom she was entertaining. Members of the British upper classes, whoever they might be, did not as a rule walk alone in the back lanes of Calcutta at a time of insurrection. Nivedita regarded them with liking, and considerable respect.

The visitors knew her name. 'A Miss Noble, who has adopted the Indian mode of life and calls herself Sister Nivedita. She is an idealist and sees wonderful meanings in the Hindu religion, but it is difficult to follow her reasoning.'

They talked a little about politics, too, and Nivedita spoke gratefully of the reforms and the more sympathetic treatment of the Indians that Lord Minto, as Viceroy, had introduced during his regime. It was not until the visitors were leaving that they told her that she had, in fact, been talking to Minto's wife. It was not possible, they explained gently, for the Vicereine to visit that part of the town without police protection, so it had been necessary for her to remain incognito. 'In view of the present unrest. . . .' There was not the faintest hint, or suggestion, on either side, that anybody present might have been in any way responsible for the present unrest; or that the word 'unrest' was a courteous understatement, tactfully offered and as tactfully received.

They left a startled Nivedita behind them. But that was only the beginning.

The plain truth was, that the two women liked and respected each other at once, which was one of the extraordinary facts of an extraordinary situation. When Lady Minto told Nivedita that she disliked the Kali Temple, the Kalighat, Nivedita at once offered to show her the Kali Temple in the Temple Gardens at Dakshineswar.

The offer was accepted. A few days later, Nivedita took her new friend to see the Temple Gardens, and afterwards they left by river, in an Indian sampan. Lady Minto, who had previously seen the sampans only from the official launch, was delighted with the adventure, and sat on cushions with Nivedita and Christine, while tea was prepared as they were rowed downriver. 'I took the precaution of saying that I preferred it without milk, as visions of typhoid passed through my mind. The tea had a good flavour, and I think must have been the best Orange Pekoe, but they told us everything was Swadeshi, biscuits, tea, sugar, cups and saucers.'

There is a certain dream-like, *Through the Looking Glass* quality in the description of the Vicereine as she herself recalled the scene in later years, gliding down the Ganges in a sampan, far from her protective bodyguard, sharing Swadeshi tea-things, which were intended to be one of the measures for bringing down the British rule, with the woman whose life was dedicated to toppling the Viceroy and his government, and driving the British out of India. It would have delighted Vivekananda, who had always been fond of *Alice*. Certainly it underlined Nivedita's own firmly held belief, that if only a couple of friendly, sensible and practical women could get together, they would have been capable of straightening out the insaner follies of mankind, and ignoring cast-iron barriers which should never have been erected.

So on that golden afternoon the two women took pleasure in each other's company; Nivedita recited Persian poetry, and Lady Minto encouraged her to go on with her writing.

Later, she invited Nivedita to tea, privately, at Government House. She told her about the attempted assassination of Minto while he was touring Ahmedabad. Nivedita worried about him, and the Vicereine worried also about Nivedita, for she knew how closely the police were watching her. The startling irony of these respective worries did not detract from their complete sincerity. Lady Minto begged Nivedita to see the Commissioner of Police, and Nivedita took her advice. After that, things became a little easier for her.

Later, Lady Minto wrote to Christine about Nivedita, expressing her 'real admiration for her enthusiasm and single-minded desire to assist others'.

In April, Nivedita wrote to Havell in England:

When the Mintos come back to England in November you must go and see them. She is most sympathetic . . . and will I think be glad to interest herself in the Indian Art question. And you can always educate your own adherents! She says she has never had time to learn *India* all these busy years, and now she is on the eve of going! But there will be a sweet harmony, I hope, and an eager friend.

Mutual liking and respect covered the whole of that strange and gentle interlude. It had in it all the tranquillity and detachment which were slowly beginning to move across her life.

24

When Nivedita needed a rest, she plunged into slightly different work, or, for refreshment, went on a pilgrimage. In May 1910 she went once more to the Himalayas, this time to Kedar Nath and Badri Narayan. Her companions were Dr Bose, his wife, and their nephew.

At every stage of the journey, they travelled from one place of worship to another, with pilgrims from every part of India. They came in their thousands, and for the first time Nivedita saw something that until then she had only written about and striven for; a real unity of India; and it was a religious unity. On the journey she wrote 'that the Motherland is indeed one, that north and south are inextricably knit together, and that no story of its analysed fragments, racial, lingual or political, could ever be the story of India . . .'

The pilgrims, both men and women, moved from place to place, greeting each other, as though they had met before; they were in fact strangers, but here there were no strangers. Some walked in groups, some by themselves, telling their beads or lost in thought. She was particularly impressed to see that here, at least, women walked freely – hundreds of them, singly, in couples, or in groups. 'We are all out on a holiday together, and an air of gentle innocence and hilarity prevails, in face of difficulties, and creates a sort of freemasonry amongst all who seek the common goal.'

She noticed individual women, and what she saw enchanted her.

> She was a little old woman, and we caught her just as she had stepped out of her prim little shoes, placed neatly behind her, and with one rapt look, prostrated herself. Two people who were coming forward drew back at this, that she might not know herself interrupted, and then as again we stepped forward and came face to face with her, we saw that for the moment she was lost in the world of her own reverence . . . It was a sudden glimpse of the snow mountains to which she had paid involuntary homage.

The going was very tough indeed, for a woman in her early forties whose health was failing. She gives glimpses of it.

We much regretted that we had not insisted on waiting at Kund Chatty till the cool of the day, so hard and arid is the climb, in the fierce noon-sun, between it and Gupta Kashi . . . The road, on this final day, is terrible, especially the last four miles of steep ascent . . . as hard as life itself, in very truth.

In very truth. Life was becoming harder and harder. But on this pilgrimage, as usual, she was cheered by the courage of those who found the going just as tough, but who delighted in it.

Climbing over some peculiarly difficult boulders in the dry bed of a torrent, we met two old women, both almost blind, and bent almost double with age and infirmity. They were coming back from Badri Narayan. The place was terrible, and as we came up to them, one of them stumbled. But to an ejaculation of concern, they replied, between themselves, with an air of triumph at their gaiety, 'What! Is not Narayan [God] leading? And since He has given Darshana, what does this matter?'

When the Temple of Kedar Nath was in sight, a shout of triumph went up from thousands of pilgrims. They had tried to reach the temple on a Monday, the day sacred to Lord Shiva; but when it was reached, it was already midday and the Temple had closed only to be opened in the evening for Arati, the evening worship. During the afternoon, cold mists covered the pilgrims as they waited. But as darkness fell, the mists faded and the stars and snows were clear and bright. They were called to see the Arati worship. Blazing lights were waved and the bells clanged within the Temple.

It was one of the sights of a lifetime, to stand there, in the black darkness at the top of the steps, and watch the pilgrims streaming in. It seemed as if all India lay stretched before one, and Kedar Nath were its apex, while from all parts everywhere, by every road, one could see the people streaming onward, battling forward, climbing their way up – all for what? – for nothing else than to touch God.

The pilgrimage continued. On 12 June they reached Badri Narayan. Early in the morning she went to the temple to attend the worship. But the priests held orthodox views, and Vivekananda was not with her this time. She was denied entrance. At first she was distressed. To have come so far, and then to be shut out! But Vivekananda had trained her to show respect even to a narrow-minded orthodoxy, so she lost her disappointment in prayers, and joined the other pilgrims who were walking round and round the temple, outside, telling their beads.

When she returned to Calcutta, she shared her pilgrimage with as many people as possible, by writing 'A Pilgrim's Diary' for publication in the *Modern Review*. It was later published in book form. She listed, at the head of each chapter, the relative distances between the places concerned, and a few words on accommodation available for the benefit of future pilgrims. She also shared the experience with her girls; they remembered all their lives her accounts of individual pilgrims she had met, and her delight in their courage and devotion. 'An old lady, her hair all turned grey, just got up from a dip into the cold waters of Alakananda, but she did not mind the cold. Her clothes were still wet, as she stood there and offered salutations to the sun with folded hands' – here Nivedita would fold her own hands, while they watched – 'How beautiful! Oh, how beautiful she looked! I went on watching her from a distance.'

But now, after the pilgrimage the news grew darker. Mrs Ole Bull, now in America, had fallen seriously ill. She asked Nivedita to come to her, but Nivedita had just returned from Europe and was hoping to stay in India. She wrote cheerful and hopeful letters to the 'steady mother' who had mothered her, and had also mothered her guru. Nivedita, in fact, very much wanted to visit her. They had been good friends for years, and financially she relied very much on Sara Bull's generosity for Indian causes which they both had at heart. It was Mrs Bull's money which helped to keep the school going, and helped Nivedita to publish her writings and Dr Bose to publish his books. Bose's laboratory still had to be built, and money was needed for Indian art. Nivedita herself had hoped to write a biography of Bose. In September 1910 she wrote to Mrs Bull that 'My wonderful twelve years is drawing to a close and I feel that in November when the Mintos go, I shall enter on a very dark period – I have still two years left, but no more. I am so afraid that I shall not be there to write his life.'

In 1904, she had written to Josephine MacLeod: 'Do you remember how Cheiro foretold that I would die between the forty-second and forty-fourth year? I am now thirty-six. So I suppose I shall see this cycle too. I fancy I shall die in 1912.'

Her premonition of death was growing stronger, and dangers seemed to be attacking everything for which she had worked, while death struck down, again and again, those she had loved.

She had another anxiety. The school depended on the work of Christine, as much as on Sara Bull's financial help, and there were difficulties with Christine. She had gone to America for personal reasons in April of 1910 and returned to India at the beginning of 1911; however, after only a few days in Calcutta she left for Mayavati, the ashram in the Himalayas established by Vivekananda.

In the autumn of 1910, Nivedita received a telegram from Sara Bull to say that she was seriously ill, and wished to see Nivedita.

Nivedita left for America at once, arriving at Cambridge, Massachusetts, in November. Mrs Bull had changed into a frightened woman who would hardly allow Nivedita to leave her bedside. The 'steady mother' now clung to Nivedita, who saw that the one thing she needed above all else was to reach back into the great days with Vivekananda, and find again the quiet wisdom and inner certainty she had known then. So she sat by the bed, talking to her of all the beloved places: Belur, Almora, Kashmir, Calcutta. They lived again the greatness of those early times.

Mrs Bull's brother, and Olea, her daughter, came to stay in the house. Mrs Bull was a rich woman, and though Olea had always been fond of Nivedita, she was sometimes neurotic. She had often quarrelled with her mother in the past, and Nivedita had helped to bring them together. Now Olea became suspicious of Nivedita's intentions, and the atmosphere around the dying woman became tense and difficult.

If ever Nivedita had longed to walk away from a situation, she longed for it now. To leave the suspicions which were growing stronger would have been easy. But it would have left Sara Bull with no friend beside her to call her back to the certainties and peace she needed; and with the legal provisions of the will still in some doubt, it might have left the school ruined and forced to close, and the children would lose all hope of education. She had always detested money-grubbing for herself, and preferred to give, not to beg. But she had a responsibility towards the school, and whatever other legacies in the will might be contested later, legacies for India, for her relatives, whatever they might be, she could only let them go without complaining; but the school was a different matter. For that, and for the peace of mind of her own good friend, she was determined to stay.

She had sat by the deathbed of her own mother, not so long ago. It was natural that she should now write to 'mother' in India, Sarada Devi, who knew Sara Bull, and whose life stood like a rock. 'Beloved Mother . . . it seemed to me that yours was the presence that was to soothe and bless poor S. Sara's sick-room . . . You are full of love, and it is not a flushed and violent love, like ours, and like the world's, but a gentle peace that brings good to everyone, and wishes ill to none. It is a golden radiance, full of play.'

Those are almost the words with which she described the atmosphere that Vivekananda brought with him in the last, peaceful days of the pilgrimage to Almora, on the houseboat at Kashmir, and later in that last week of his life, when his detachment from life was almost complete. 'Playful', 'nothing sad or grave about him' and 'never had one felt so strong as now, before him, that one stood on the threshold of an infinite light'.

Those were the values she wanted to find in herself for Sara Bull; and as she sat there, day after day, increasingly afraid as she had never been afraid of plague or disaster or mob violence, she had to strengthen her own detachment, move forward into a simplicity and peace that was controlled and still; draw on all that Vivekananda had taught her on that voyage to England.

In December, she wrote to Josephine MacLeod, and in what she asked for herself – for Sara Bull's sake – she made it clear that she knew what she lacked, what she was reaching for, what she was approaching.

'Please pray for me, may all of you, that I may be made loving, patient, silent, of an intense reserve.' She went on frankly, 'I am frightened, but I dare not take any help but God's own.' And she asked for prayers for Sara Bull, 'that this dear one, in grave dangers, may learn to be herself, and discriminate between the Real and the Unreal.'

The end came on 18 January 1911. There was nothing more to be done for Sara Bull, who had 'learned to be herself'. Now the second responsibility, to which Nivedita felt that she owed her loyalty, was the school.

But she could not stay in the house. Olea became not only angry and suspicious on the question of legacies in her mother's will; she had now convinced herself that Nivedita had been trying to poison the dying woman. Sara Bull had begged Nivedita for an Indian herbal medicine to ease her pain, and Nivedita, perhaps unwisely, had given it to her. It made no difference, but it added to Olea's resentment and suspicions; there was even some talk of bringing the police into the matter. Nivedita left the house, utterly depressed by the whole atmosphere, worried about the future of the school, and bereft of her friend. She left the matter of her legacy, which Olea contested, in the hands of her lawyer, and returned to India. On her way home she visited England, and saw not only her family but some of her friends, including Ratcliffe and Nevinson.

It was a time of farewells, and many good-byes were said, on what seemed to be a temporary basis.

In Paris she met Josephine MacLeod. The news she had to give her was not happy. Sara Bull was dead, the school's future was in doubt, and before she had left America, she had heard of the death of Swami Sadananda, who had been lodged until his death in a house near her own in Bosepara Lane tended by the boys, 'Sadananda's dogs'. When, in March, she boarded the *Delta* at Marseilles, she knew that Bosepara Lane would be emptier than before. The boys had built a small shrine in his room, but Sadananda was not there.

She was very tired.

When she arrived in Calcutta, she went straight to Sarada Devi.

She also went to the Belur Math and met the Head of the Order, Swami Brahmananda, and Swami Turiyananda who had accompanied Vivekananda on that six weeks' voyage to England which was now so often in her mind. Afterwards she sat silently for some time in Vivekananda's room, and then left quietly.

During the summer Sarada Devi was away from Calcutta, visiting her village home at Jayrambati. Nivedita stayed at Mayavati, the ashram in the Himalayas, with the Boses and their nephew while she helped Bose with his new book. She was still worried about the school; Olea was not willing to grant any financial help for it. The government was prepared to offer a loan to help her in the interests of local education, and Lady Minto offered financial help as well. Nivedita was still determined that no help should ever be accepted from a foreign government for the school, and expressed this clearly in her own will. Indeed, whatever financial difficulties the school went through later, in fact it did not accept help from government sources until 1949, when India at last achieved an Indian government, and full independence.

After prolonged worry, Nivedita heard from her lawyer that provision had been made for the school in Mrs Bull's will, and whatever else might be contested, this would be available.

In June she returned to Calcutta from Mayavati. She was busy in the school, and in helping Bose in his work; busy, too, with her own writings. Two of her books, *Footfalls of Indian History* and *Studies from an Eastern Home*, were practically finished.

But the blows continued to fall.

On 25 July Vivekananda's mother, Bhuvaneshwari Devi, died.

Nivedita was by her side on the day she died, and followed her body to the cremation ground. Two days later, Bhuvaneshwari's own mother died. A few days later came news of the death of Olea, Mrs Bull's daughter. Nivedita's recent experiences with her had been depressing, but the completely unexpected death was a very great shock, and closed the door on any hope of reconciliation. Then in August came news of the death of Swami Ramakrishnananda, that great stalwart of the Order, whose total devotion to Sri Ramakrishna, and after his death to the young monks he left behind, had won Vivekananda's abiding respect and affection. He had helped Nivedita in every way he could, and met her whenever he came to Calcutta. It was he who had encouraged her to write her book about Vivekananda. She regarded him as the ideal Karma Yogin, finding his vocation in personal devotion to the guru and in selfless work; they had much in common.

Every tie that bound her seemed to be breaking. And the blows did not stop falling. They increased.

It was now that she received what was perhaps the greatest shock of all. The school depended for its very existence on the work of Christine. Without her, it could hardly continue to function at all, for its headmistress knew that her own life was moving to its end. Christine now informed her that she had decided to give up her work in the school, to live at 17 Bosepara Lane no longer, and to teach in the Brahmo Girls' School instead. She was still away in Mayavati, and remained there during the summer. Nivedita did not see her again.

The reason for Christine's decision is not known, but it is hardly surprising that the crowding of the whole school into one tiny house, under a headmistress who was often away and who, when she was there, did not teach, but still kept official control, in the intense heat of Calcutta, under conditions of poverty, strain and anxiety, would inevitably lead to friction.

All Nivedita's friends found it difficult, and in some cases impossible, to work closely with her unless agreement with her views was expressed and a considerable degree of control of the work given to her. Rabindranath Tagore's comment, 'She had power and she exerted that power with full force on the lives of others. When it was not possible to agree with her, it was impossible to work with her', may well have been echoed by Christine; and Tagore was, like Christine, a devoted friend of Nivedita's and one of her greatest admirers. The exception was Bose, who worked closely with her. But Bose had his own home, family and friends; he did not share a small overcrowded house with her; and as she was no scientist, she did not attempt to control his scientific research.

It is probable that a break between Christine and Nivedita, at some stage, was inevitable, and might have been healed, given time. Certainly it is a tribute to the friendship, and the devotion to the school, of those two often exhausted and overworked women, that the arrangement continued as long as it did.

Nivedita had one more hope. In Christine's absence, she usually relied upon the help of another colleague, Sudhira. But in September, Sudhira told Nivedita that she also was leaving to teach at the Brahmo school. Nivedita visited her at her home and begged her to stay. She refused.

Work, politics, her lectures which were now almost impossible because of government control, and now the school; everything she had striven for seemed to be breaking up, and death had followed death throughout that hot and weary summer. The lane would not see Sadananda again; and when the children left the school for the Puja holidays, there was now no Gopaler-Ma in the house, no Christine, and no Sudhira.

Those who were lit up by the brilliance and excitement Nivedita generated; those who almost worshipped her; those who regarded her as national heroine, spy, traitress, plaster saint or beloved mother-figure; those who crossed swords with her or were irritated by her militancy; those who, like Lady Minto, saw only her gentleness, and those who, like Nevinson, remarked even in his admiration, 'I suppose nobody ever called her gentle'; these tended often to forget, or did not see, her daily battle with her own needs, emotional and physical, the endless small sacrifices, privations, fasting, and humiliations, and the lack of any time for rest, or any peace and quiet. But she had watched Vivekananda dealing with all these things as though they hardly touched him, and accepting them as he accepted happiness – a necessary part of life, but always passing, always ephemeral. It is impossible to look at her, either at her most dedicated or in her most irritating moments, without seeing always the figure of her guru behind her, even after his death, for she accepted totally the Hindu teaching that the great guru brings the nature of his disciple to its highest potential, within its own pattern, provided – and this is the heart of the matter, which was never a part of her public utterances – that the daily meditation, and the repetition of the mantra which the disciple is given continues throughout life.

It is only possible to see the slowly deepening change in her last days, in its true perspective, if we remember that her spiritual practices and her daily meditation were kept private, a matter between disciple and guru, and however complex her nature – and she cannot be fitted neatly into any category – she herself never doubted that it was this silent and withdrawn core and heart of her existence which was her true identity. All the rest, the personality, as well as the body, must be used to the utmost, and then dropped. She had a shrewd eye for her own faults, and Vivekananda had never left her in any doubt that darkness is always self-created; this too must have been very much in her mind in those last days.

Vivekananda had a favourite parable, and she had often heard him tell it. It concerned a restless and busy bird who lived on the tree of life, moving to and fro on its branches and pecking at the sweet and bitter fruits. When the bird looked up, he saw on the topmost branch of all a golden bird who remained there always, radiant, serene, content in its own existence. Gradually the active bird moved nearer, and the light from the golden bird illuminated him, but nothing could be forced before its time; the sweet and bitter fruits had to be tasted, until the bird came so close to the luminous one that he realized that it was, in fact, himself; as in all Vivekananda's parables, it was a question of identity. Even the selfless service of others, which burned away the ego, was incomplete without the constant turning towards the true identity; for in serving others, the great identity – 'That' – was also being served.

Her thinking, and her experience, were so impregnated with this teaching and all that it implied that she had seen clearly in the long days by the bedside of Sara Bull the importance 'that she may learn to be *herself*, and discriminate between the Real and the Unreal'.

The very name, 'Vivekananda' signified exactly that power of discrimination. 'From the Unreal to the Real' as the Rudra prayer put it; and she believed that she was moving now from one to the other. She had always intensely disliked cowardice, or the smallest suggestion of fuss; but it was not a stoic courage that lit her last days. It was contented and quiet acceptance.

25

As soon as the school closed for the Puja holidays, Nivedita began to make preparations for her usual summer trip to Darjeeling with the Boses. Her forty-fourth birthday lay ahead, on 28 October 1911. Her years of active and political work in India, which began after the death of Vivekananda in 1902 had numbered only nine, of which two were spent in Europe. As she walked up and down the lane, paying last-minute visits, she was never entirely alone. She was well known in the lane now. And sometimes the children came back to see her.

She was visited by some of the senior students. They told her that Prafullamukhi, the girl widow whom Nivedita fed on fast days, was ill with a fever. Would the Sister visit her? The Sister would, and did. She hoped to obtain permission from the girl's family to take her to Darjeeling, to recover in the clear Himalayan air, but that too was impossible.

She was always content to be at home in the lane, even now that the building was empty except for the servant; indeed, this time she delighted in it more than ever. She knew so well the daily, unvarying rituals of the lives of her neighbours that at any moment of the day she could summon up a mental picture of what was happening at that moment in the women's quarter of the houses around her – the life moved to a rhythm she knew and loved. The lives of the zenana women had all the religious dedication of a nun's; she could not have found anywhere to live, in any country, where she would have been more in tune with her surroundings, and yet where, as she was British and not herself in purdah, she was able to come and go as she wished, to travel abroad, and – when she was at home – to inspire the brilliant men who had come to the Little House of the Sisters. Then there were the poor, in the bustees, literally at her doorstep, to be served and helped. Sarada Devi's house was nearby; to 'Sadananda's dogs' the lane was still a place of pilgrimage since his death. Nowhere else could she have had the best of so many different worlds. Nivedita and Bosepara Lane suited each other perfectly.

She rose early, when she was at home as she was now, but her neighbours rose earlier. The cleaning of each woman's own room, and the zenana department generally, began, she knew, somewhere near four o'clock in the morning. Then followed an hour's meditation, during which time the sun rose. Then a visit to the Ganges for one of the many daily bathes. She was familiar with the saying, 'Without praying, no eating! Without bathing, no praying!' 'Little companies of women of high caste begin to leave their houses on foot for the bathing-stairs . . . Every moment of the ablution has its own invocation, and the return journey is made, carrying a brass vessel of the sacred water which will be used all day to sprinkle the place in which any eats or prays . . .' On return there would be a prolonged ritual of worship, at the altar or holy place within the home, in its daily ritual, and the ritual was in the care of the women. Then at last, the first meal of the day was eaten though beggars might arrive at the last moment, and a portion of all food must be given to them first.

No nun in a convent lived a life of stricter seclusion and ritual than did her neighbours. She never forgot her introduction to India on her first morning in a Hindu home, when she had arrived, hot, dusty, and weary after days of railway travel and after a short sleep on a mat on the floor, had turned to the tea-basket she had brought with her, for breakfast, at about eight o'clock. 'Suddenly a little boy stood before me like a young avenging angel. His great brown eyes were full of pain and surprise, such as only a child's face adequately shows. He did not know much English and spoke deliberately, laying terrible emphasis on each word, "Have – you – said – your – prayers?" he said.'

That might not have delighted a typical Englishwoman newly arrived from Wimbledon, but it delighted Nivedita, and he could not have given her a happier welcome to India. The daily rhythm of life fitted her own.

The unending work of her zenana neighbours also appealed to her; the lady of the house, she discovered, whether wealthy enough to employ servants or poor enough to rely solely on the help of daughters-in-law and female relatives, who all lived always in the same house with her, had an exhausting day of it, even if there were no children to be given endless ablutions by 'drowning in the tank' as the local phrase put it. Not only must she supervise all work, and do some of it herself, but she must never eat till all members of the household and all visitors had eaten, and if visitors were late or did not arrive she did not eat. 'In this way it is often two o'clock, and I have heard of its being eleven at night, before the head of a large household will breakfast, and this would not count as an austerity.'

At half past twelve or one, the lady of the house took a couple of hours' sleep, and, as Nivedita remarked with fellow-feeling, 'she sadly needs it'. Then she sat up to read, talk, or sew a little and there followed a prolonged period with the rosary, in which the mantra or name of God was repeated on every bead, and at dusk more small rituals, and another period of meditation, in the time called candlelight, or the hour of peace. It would be quite late before the second meal of the day was taken and before that, friends or neighbours attended by women servants carrying lanterns, often arrived for a chat and gossip. The day, which had begun at four o'clock in the morning, finished at ten at night, and Nivedita had seen this daily routine carried out, not only in the houses of her neighbours, but in the house of Sarada Devi, who was not at that time in Calcutta but staying in the village of her birth, where the hard work of village peasant life was still woven into the daily rituals, and husking paddy could alternate with preparing flowers for the family worship.

But Nivedita could not bring herself to leave Calcutta without at least a visit to Sarada Devi's home. Any time spent in that house increased her own peace. She visited the house, and prostrated herself, as custom required, at the feet of Jogin-Ma, honoured friend and devotee of Sarada Devi.

'Jogin-Ma,' she said. 'I feel that I shall not return.'

Jogin-Ma became anxious, and asked her what she meant, but she could not explain her own certainty. She said, only, 'I do not know. I feel so, somehow. This is the end.'

She returned home and continued her preparations for the holiday.

When she left Bosepara Lane at last, to begin the journey to Darjeeling, she was moving towards the postage stamp, though she did not fully know it, and we at this distance of time perhaps know it a little too well.

The danger of thinking in terms of a success story lies in the possibility that we may forget that the success is seen largely by those who witnessed it, or by those who came after. We can take a god's-eye-view of the whole unwinding path of events, but the person most concerned died in the valley, and could not see beyond the mountain ahead. It is only by looking at what we now know, and then putting aside that knowledge, that we can join her in the valley where she then stood, and see the autumn of 1911, and her own life, as she saw it then.

The visitor of today, who finds that Bosepara Lane is now called Nivedita Lane, and that where the small house once stood stands the Nivedita Girls' School, a sign of the return of Christine and the eventual growth of the school into a large building in which generations of Hindu girls have grown up, will not be seeing it as Nivedita saw it then. Every inch of the lane as it then was, was home to her. 'Everywhere the happy laughter of children in the sunlight, everywhere the flutter of newly-washed drapery hung out to dry, every here and there a cow or two . . .'

But as she left home in 1911 she knew that the house was old and badly needed repair; and it stood empty, except for one servant. With the departure of Christine and Sudhira the school could no longer continue after Nivedita's death. The one task which Vivekananda had left in her hands, for which she had always accepted responsibility and which was to have been a centre of hope for the education of Hindu women, had now no future whatever, as far as she could see. She had failed, apparently, and it was a bitter failure.

Looking towards India, the outlook was more black then than is sometimes realized. The visitor who has seen the memorial on the hillside in Darjeeling, bearing the words 'Here repose the ashes of Sister Nivedita, who gave her all to India', and who is told that she was given the largest funeral procession the hill station had ever known, and that half Calcutta mourned her even if most of the British had never heard of her, will credit her with a fame and an Indian expression of love and hope for the future which she did not herself see. All that she knew then was that the partition of Bengal had taken place, there was a repression of nationalist activity, and an apparent quiescence; therefore she did not now often appear in public. Most of her friends who had been leaders of public opinion were out of the country, in prison, or in hiding. She did not know that a few months later the partition of Bengal would be reversed, with a change to the original boundaries, while the seat of government was removed to Delhi and remained there, in view of what Lady Minto had tactfully described as 'the present unrest'.

As for her friends: Bose had not yet achieved his Research Institute, and his career was uncertain; she could not foresee the knighthood which Britain eventually gave him, nor could she know that like her other close friend, Josephine MacLeod, he would live to an honoured old age. She knew only that she herself would never write his biography, as she had hoped to do.

She did not see the Ramakrishna Order as we see it today. It is now the largest monastic Order in India, with a convent for women also established, and relief work, schools, and hospitals for the needy maintained all over India; but in 1911 all this was only beginning. In England, the Ramakrishna Vedanta Centre in London was established many years later; there was no sign of it then. The work in England had stopped. Centres were certainly growing up in America, as she knew.

The outlook, in spite of these areas of hope, was in general so bleak that the letter she wrote to Josephine MacLeod at that time makes absolutely clear how lightness, detachment and tranquillity were growing in her, at last. The letter had nothing in it of the despair of the frustrated worker, nothing of the bitterness or the intensity of the politician and orator, none of the excited emotion of those hectic years.

> Oh, what sweet memories crowd upon one, for these last thirteen years! How wonderfully full and deep is the wave that overwhelms the soul at twilight! 'Beyond life and death' as Swamiji always insisted. He was never contented to say either word alone. One has need of realizing that, these days – when death is taking so many, so many of those one has known and loved.

'Beyond life and death.' The pendulum had stopped swinging. The evidence is shown in everything that she said, did and wrote at that time.

Three short pieces of writing were found in her papers immediately after her death, written during those last weeks. One, 'The Beloved', refers to God, who is served in serving one's fellow-man, and it expresses the same belief as that parable of the golden bird which the busy and much-involved bird on the lower branches of the tree of life was soon to realize as being his own self. 'Let me ever remember that the thirst for God is the whole meaning of life . . . destroy Thou me utterly, and stand Thou in my stead.'

The second passage, called 'Play', shows in her own attitude all the detached lightness and joy which she noted in her description of Vivekananda on the houseboat and again in the last weeks of his life, when she used the words 'playful' and 'the threshold of an infinite light' to describe him. It is so expressive of detached, amused serenity that it shows clearly what was in her mind as she left Bosepara Lane for the last time; neither pathos nor grim courage.

She had never entirely lost that sense of lightness and play which in recent years had been submerged in the almost aggressive intensity of her fight for Indian independence. Richmond wrote of Vivekananda, 'He had an infinite store of fun. He read the ages in that light.' And it was Richmond who wrote later that his sister, as a girl, 'was eventually able to go for a mile or so on her bicycle without falling off' and so transformed a short cycle ride with her brother to take tea at an old-fashioned public house near Mitcham, into an 'adventure' on the high road leading to an old-time wayside inn. Play was a part of her own knowledge of truth, and of life's purpose, and in this last of her writings she set it out clearly. It is perhaps significant that she did not write it before; she was ready to write it now.

> Play, in this, its spiritual essence, play as it expresses the individual soul, is a conception more than any other characteristic of the Indian people. It is expressed in their poetry, and in their drama, it dominates their humour . . . and above all, it sweetens and enlightens the life of the home . . . This unwillingness to take life seriously is, in the eyes of more serious people, a bar to discipline. But would it not be worth while to enquire whether play has or has not a discipline of its own? . . . It is by no means dependent on selfish ambition. Play must never be taken seriously, as we say, though a man must put into it the utmost of high endeavour. The player must maintain an attitude of light heartedness, of detachment. He must always be ready, in the name of courtesy, to forgo a great advantage . . . Only he who has caught the spirit of play knows how to live.

26

Nivedita and the Boses spent the first few days in Darjeeling resting quietly and doing very little. After the journey from the heat of Calcutta, the first days of a holiday were always spent in rest, before the activity, which to Nivedita was an essential part of any holiday, began. This time, they planned to make a journey on horseback to the Sandak Fu peak; a journey of several days.

On the morning on which they had arranged to leave Darjeeling for the first stage of their journey, Nivedita was taken ill. A doctor diagnosed blood dysentery. Nivedita had seen enough of the diseases of the East to know exactly what lay ahead for her. The disease was incurable at that time, and at that altitude; and she was already worn out.

She made a will in which everything was left to her motherland, and there was no doubt now as to which land that was. She sent a letter home to the family in England, admitting that she was a little ill, but insisting that there was no need for a fuss to be made about it. She talked to the Boses about women's education, about anything that would make the long days a little easier for them, but her strength was ebbing, and they all knew it.

A few days before she left Calcutta, she had translated a Buddhist prayer into English, and it had so expressed what she was feeling that she had even had some copies printed, to give to her friends. Now she asked that it should be read aloud to her. 'Let all things that breathe, without enemies, without obstacles, overcoming sorrow, and attaining cheerfulness, move forward freely, each in his own path . . .'

As the six days passed, from the making of her will, to the end, she several times spoke the words of her favourite Rudra prayer, which Vivekananda had translated for them on the pilgrimage to the Himalayas. 'From the Unreal lead us to the Real! From darkness lead us to light. From death lead us to immortality. Reach us through and through ourselves, and evermore, O Thou Terrible! protect us from ignorance, by thy sweet compassionate face.'

But it is her own words which make it clear to us exactly what was in her mind as she died. The third of the three passages which were found amongst her papers after her death was entitled simply 'Death'.

I thought last night that interfused with all this world of matter, penetrating it through and through, there may be another, call it meditation, or mind, or what one will, and perhaps *that* is what death means. Not to change one's place – for since this is not matter, it can have no place – but to sink deeper and deeper into that condition of being more and more divested of the imagination of body. So that our dead are close to us physically, if it comforts us to think so of them, and yet one with all vastness, one with uttermost freedom and bliss.

And so I thought of the Universal as mingled in this way with the finite and we standing here, on the border-line between the two, commanded to win for ourselves the paradise of both – the Infinite in the Finite. I am thinking, more and more, that death means just a withdrawal into meditation, the sinking of the stone into the well of its own being. There is the beginning before death, in the long hours of quiescence, when the mind hangs suspended in the characteristic thought of its life, in that thought which is the residuum of all its thoughts and acts and experiences. Already in these hours the soul is discarnating, and the new life has commenced.

I wonder if it would be possible so to resolve one whole life into love and blessing, without one single ripple of a contrary impulse, that one might be wrapt away in that last hour and for ever more into one great thought, so that in eternity at least one might be delivered from thought of self, and know oneself only as a brooding presence of peace and benediction for all the need and suffering of the world.

The end came quietly. She had long ago accepted the belief that her body was no more than a boat in which she was sailing, and now she was ready to let it go. She had entered into the deep meditation of death, and only one wish remained; to draw her last breath as the sun rose, as Gopaler-Ma had done, as Hindus hope to do. She loved sunrise, not with sentimentality, but simply as the perfect moment, the moment of holiness.

In the early morning darkness of 13 October, she said, 'The frail boat is sinking, but I shall yet see the sunrise.'

Through the window she saw the first streaks of morning across the sky, and as the sun rose, she died.

With her good friends beside her; without fuss; away from the crowds.

And at peace.

Acknowledgements

I should like to record my gratitude for the encouragement and support I received from the late Swami Ghanananda of the Ramakrishna Order, founder of the London Ramakrishna Vedanta Centre. I also wish to thank other Swamis of the Order for encouragement, cooperation, and interest in the work, especially the Swamis of the London Centre, including their kindness in translating from the Bengali the account of Saralabala Dasi, and for the use of the original letter from Swami Atulananda, as well as extracts from letters of Josephine MacLeod written to her niece Alberta Sturges (Countess of Sandwich) made available to them by Lady Faith Culme-Seymour. My thanks go also to the Pravrajikas administering the Sri Sarada Math and the Nivedita Girls' School.

I also thank: Mr and Mrs R. W. Noble, the son and daughter-in-law of Richmond Noble, and Mrs R. Whitney, the daughter of Richmond Noble, for supplying fresh details of Margaret Noble's girlhood from the late Richmond Noble's memories of her; Professor Sankari Prasad Basu for kindly supplying 'A Brother's Recollections' (of Richmond Noble) from the Reymond Collection, and Mrs Boshishwar Sen, for permission to use extracts from the writings of Sister Christine.

My thanks also to: Dr R. J. Bingle, Assistant Keeper of European Manuscripts in the India Office Library, Foreign and Commonwealth Office, London, for his assistance, and to the India Office for the use of original letters from Margaret Noble to Ernest B. Havell, from the Havell Collection, MSS EUR D736.

Bibliography

*Pravrajika Atmaprana, *Sister Nivedita*: Sister Nivedita Girls' School, Calcutta.

**Sister Nivedita, Complete Works*, vols. i–iv, edited by Pravrajika Atmaprana: Sister Nivedita Girls' School. *The Master As I Saw Him* also published separately, by Udbodhan Office, Calcutta.

Frances Leggett, *Late And Soon*: John Murray.

**Swami Vivekananda, Complete Works*, vols. i–viii (including his letters): Advaita Ashrama.

**Life Of Swami Vivekananda*, by his Eastern and Western disciples: Advaita Ashrama.

*Marie Louise Burke, *Swami Vivekananda. His Second Visit To The West. New Discoveries*: Advaita Ashrama.

**Reminiscences Of Swami Vivekananda*, by Eastern and Western friends: Advaita Ashrama.

**Swami Vivekananda In East And West*, collection of essays by various authors: Ramakrishna Vedanta Centre, London.

Sankari Prasad Basu and Sunil Bihari Ghosh, *Vivekananda In Indian Newspapers*: Dineshchandra Basu, Basu Bhattacharya and Co. Ltd, Calcutta.

*Swami Tapasyananda, *Sri Sarada Devi*, conversations translated by Swami Nikhilananda: Sri Ramakrishna Math, Madras.

*'M' (Mahendranath Gupta), *The Gospel Of Sri Ramakrishna*, translated by Swami Nikhilananda, foreword by Aldous Huxley: Ramakrishna Vedanta Centre, New York.

*Christopher Isherwood, *Ramakrishna And His Disciples*: Methuen.

**Swami Premananda, Teachings And Reminiscences*, edited and translated by Swami Prabhavananda (including letter describing Swami Vivekananda, and his last day): Vedanta Press, California.

J. H. Broomfield, *Élite Conflict In A Plural Society. Twentieth Century Bengal*: University of California Press.

Edward Carpenter, *From Adam's Peak To Elephanta*: George Allen and Unwin Ltd.

(Books marked with an asterisk, obtained through the Ramakrishna Vedanta Centre, London.)

Letters from Sister Nivedita to Alberta Sturges, or to Josephine MacLeod about Alberta, taken from articles by Swami Vidyatmananda published in *Prabuddha Bharata*, January, February and May 1973; the letters quoted are from the collection of the Countess of Sandwich.

Sister Nivedita's letters to G. K. Gokhale, compiled and edited by V. V. Pendse, were published in a centenary memorial journal.

Eric Hammond's account of Sister Nivedita was published in *Prabuddha Bharata*, 1927.

The account by A. J. F. Blair was published in *Prabuddha Bharata*, 1911.

Glossary

ADVAITA VEDANTA Doctrine that the individual soul is ultimately not different from the cosmic soul; non-dual, though sometimes reached through dualism.

ARATI Evening worship, with waving of lights.

ASHRAM(A) Place for community living, associated with religion; sometimes, but not always, for monks.

BRAHMACHARIN A celibate student, serving the guru; a novice.

BRAHMACHARINI Female Brahmacharin.

BRAHMAN The ultimate Reality; the all-pervading principle.

BRAHMIN Priestly caste.

BRAHMO The Brahmo Samaj was a monotheistic society founded by Raja Rammohan Roy.

BUSTEE Mud hut of the very poor.

DHARMA Religious principles, especially as applied to social and family life.

DHOBI Washerman.

GITA The Bhagavad-Gita, or Song of God. Hindu scripture.

GOPAL(A) The god Krishna, as a baby.

GURU The spiritual teacher.

HARIBOL The name of God.

ISHTA(M) Ultimate Brahman worshipped in the form of a chosen deity, incarnation or principle.

JAGADDHATRI Goddess representing the 'supporter-of-the-universe' aspect of God worshipped as Mother.

KRISHNA Incarnation of God, worshipped in Hinduism.

KUNDALINI Spiritual energy believed to be lying latent at the base of the sushumna. (See sushumna.)

LINGA(M) The god Shiva worshipped in a symbol.

MANTRA(M) Formula sacred or appropriate to a deity, chosen ideal or principle, used in continuous concentrated repetition.

MAYA The cosmic illusion which is our common experience, in which One appears as many. Also symbolized as Kali, one aspect of God worshipped as Mother.

NAHABAT Small building near temple, where religious music was played.

OM (AUM) The basic mantra.

RAJAS Activity.

SADHU A monk.
SANNYASIN A monk.
SANNYASINI A nun.
SANTAL Labourer of low caste.
SATCHITANANDA Existence-Knowledge-Bliss.
SHAKTI Universal power (female). Sometimes means a woman.
SHIVA The Dissolver or Destroyer of the Hindu aspects of God (Creator, Preserver, Destroyer). Sometimes the auspicious Great God of Hinduism.
SHLOKA Sanskrit verse of specified length and form.
SUSHUMNA Central channel of the spinal column up which the kundalini energy is believed to rise in meditation.
SWAMI Title of respect added to full name of a monk.
TAMAS Inertia.
TAPASYA Any religious austerity.
UPANISHADS Hindu scriptures; the philosophical parts of the Vedas.
YOGA Path leading to the union of the individual soul with the Ultimate. Yogas mentioned in the book:
Bhakti Yoga: Yoga of love and devotion
Jnana Yoga: Yoga of knowledge and philosophy
Karma Yoga: Yoga of selfless work
Raja Yoga: Yoga of meditation
Hatha Yoga: Yoga of control by bodily postures
YOGI Aspirant who has reached a certain stage in Yoga.
ZENANA Inner apartments for the women of a Hindu household.

Index

Compiled by Patricia Utechin